# CAMBRIDGE
# Primary Computing

### Learner's Book 6
Ceredig Cattanach-Chell, Luke Craig
& Sarah Matthews

# CAMBRIDGE
## UNIVERSITY PRESS

Shaftesbury Road, Cambridge CB2 8EA, United Kingdom

One Liberty Plaza, 20th Floor, New York, NY 10006, USA

477 Williamstown Road, Port Melbourne, VIC 3207, Australia

314–321, 3rd Floor, Plot 3, Splendor Forum, Jasola District Centre, New Delhi – 110025, India

103 Penang Road, #05–06/07, Visioncrest Commercial, Singapore 238467

Cambridge University Press is part of the University of Cambridge.

It furthers the University's mission by disseminating knowledge in the pursuit of education, learning and research at the highest international levels of excellence.

www.cambridge.org
Information on this title: www.cambridge.org/9781009320542

© Cambridge University Press & Assessment 2024

This publication is in copyright. Subject to statutory exception
and to the provisions of relevant collective licensing agreements,
no reproduction of any part may take place without the written
permission of Cambridge University Press.

20 19 18 17 16 15 14 13 12 11 10 9 8 7 6 5

Printed in Poland by Opolgraf

*A catalogue record for this publication is available from the British Library*

ISBN 978-1-009-32054-2 Paperback with Digital Access (1 Year)
ISBN 978-1-009-32055-9 Digital Learner's Book (1 Year)
ISBN 978-1-009-32053-5 eBook

Additional resources for this publication at www.cambridge.org/go

Cambridge University Press has no responsibility for the persistence or accuracy of URLs for external or third-party internet websites referred to in this publication, and does not guarantee that any content on such websites is, or will remain, accurate or appropriate. Information regarding prices, travel timetables, and other factual information given in this work is correct at the time of first printing but Cambridge University Press does not guarantee the accuracy of such information thereafter.

..................................................................................................

NOTICE TO TEACHERS
It is illegal to reproduce any part of this work in material form (including photocopying and electronic storage) except under the following circumstances:
(i) where you are abiding by a licence granted to your school or institution by the Copyright Licensing Agency;
(ii) where no such licence exists, or where you wish to exceed the terms of a licence, and you have gained the written permission of Cambridge University Press;
(iii) where you are allowed to reproduce without permission under the provisions of Chapter 3 of the Copyright, Designs and Patents Act 1988, which covers, for example, the reproduction of short passages within certain types of educational anthology and reproduction for the purposes of setting examination questions.

# Endorsement statement

Endorsement indicates that a resource has passed Cambridge International's rigorous quality-assurance process and is suitable to support the delivery of a Cambridge International curriculum framework. However, endorsed resources are not the only suitable materials available to support teaching and learning, and are not essential to be used to achieve the qualification. Resource lists found on the Cambridge International website will include this resource and other endorsed resources.

Any example answers to questions taken from past question papers, practice questions, accompanying marks and mark schemes included in this resource have been written by the authors and are for guidance only. They do not replicate examination papers. In examinations the way marks are awarded may be different. Any references to assessment and/or assessment preparation are the publisher's interpretation of the Cambridge International curriculum framework requirements. Examiners will not use endorsed resources as a source of material for any assessment set by Cambridge International.

While the publishers have made every attempt to ensure that advice on the qualification and its assessment is accurate, the official curriculum framework, specimen assessment materials and any associated assessment guidance materials produced by the awarding body are the only authoritative source of information and should always be referred to for definitive guidance. Cambridge International recommends that teachers consider using a range of teaching and learning resources based on their own professional judgement of their students' needs.

Cambridge International has not paid for the production of this resource, nor does Cambridge International receive any royalties from its sale. For more information about the endorsement process, please visit www.cambridgeinternational.org/endorsed-resources

Cambridge International copyright material in this publication is reproduced under licence and remains the intellectual property of Cambridge Assessment International Education.

Third-party websites and resources referred to in this publication have not been endorsed by Cambridge Assessment International Education.

# Introduction

Welcome to Stage 6 of Cambridge Primary Computing!

Digital technology has changed the world over the past 50 years. We use technology in so many areas of our life, it is more important than ever that we try to understand how technology works.

In this book you will:

- learn how to use programming constructs such as sub-routines
- create a game for a physical computing device that uses variables
- learn how data is collected and stored on a computer system
- investigate how data is processed
- explore how we can use artificial intelligence.

These computing ideas are not only part of our daily lives, but can be part of certain jobs that people do. People can have an entire career within computing, and learning about computing here may just be the start of your future in computing! Using the computing knowledge and skills that you learn from this book, you'll gain a sense of how people who work in computing may carry out parts of their jobs. For example, programmers often work on projects as part of a team, and work together to test that their programs work. Perhaps you could find a friend at school to work on a project with you.

We have created lots of activities and questions where you can work with a partner or a group. Sharing your ideas with other learners is fun and helps you have exciting conversations about how computers and technology are used.

There is also a project for you to complete at the end of each unit. These will cover the learning in each unit and help you to develop your understanding.

We hope you find learning about computers and technology exciting, and that you will continue to keep learning about computers as you grow older.

*Ceredig Cattanach-Chell, Luke Craig and Sarah Matthews*

# Contents

How to use this book · 6

## 1 Computational thinking and programming
- 1.1 Planning flowcharts · 9
- 1.2 Programming constructs · 19
- 1.3 Sub-routines · 34
- 1.4 Planning programs · 52
- 1.5 Evaluating and testing programs · 67
- 1.6 Using variables with a physical device · 77

## 2 Managing data
- 2.1 Capturing data · 95
- 2.2 Creating a spreadsheet · 119
- 2.3 Creating a database · 135
- 2.4 How is data used? · 149

## 3 Networks and digital communication
- 3.1 Storing and transferring data on a network · 159
- 3.2 Securing data · 174

## 4 Computer systems
- 4.1 Selecting hardware and software · 184
- 4.2 Programming environments · 201
- 4.3 Storing data · 209
- 4.4 Inside a computer · 218
- 4.5 Robots in industry · 224

Glossary · 234
Acknowledgements · 247

> Note for teachers: Throughout the resource there is a symbol to indicate where additional digital only content is provided. This content can be accessed through the Digital Learner's Book on Cambridge GO. It can be launched either from the Media tab or directly from the page. The symbol that denotes additional digital content is: 📲. The source files can also be downloaded from the Source files tab on Cambridge GO. In addition, this tab contains a teacher guidance document which supports the delivery of digital activities and programming tasks in this Learner's Book.

# How to use this book

In this book you will find lots of different features to help your learning.

What you will learn in the topic.

> **We are going to:**
> - understand that we can present algorithms as flowcharts
> - understand the shapes used in a flowchart
> - predict the results of flowcharts.

Important words to learn.

> decision
> flowchart
> input
> output
> prediction

A reminder about what you already know and an activity to start you off.

> **Getting started**
> **What do you already know?**
> - Algorithms follow a sequence (top to bottom, left to right).
> - Algorithms can use inputs and outputs.
> - A conditional (IF THEN ELSE) block causes an algorithm to do either one thing or another.

Fun activities about computing. Sometimes, you will use a computer.

> **Activity 5**
> You will need: a desktop computer, laptop or tablet, simple design software such as Word, PowerPoint or Canva
>
> Use a computer to create a poster that explains what the different shapes in a flowchart mean.
> Use pictures and colour to make it more interesting.

Some activities do not need a computer. These are called unplugged activities. They help you to understand important ideas about computing.

> **Unplugged activity 1**
> You will need: a pen and paper
>
> Write down three statistical investigations where you would collect continuous data.

Sometimes, you will see this question. It will help you to think about your work.

> **How are we doing?**
> Swap your three investigations with a partner.
> Were all three of your partner's suggestions examples that would use continuous data? Give them a mark out of three, one mark for each correct suggestion.
> If they lost any marks, work together to come up with a new suggestion.

# How to use this book

Tasks to help you to practise what you have learnt.

Programming tasks are in Unit 1.

**Programming task 1**

**You will need:** a desktop computer, laptop or tablet, access to Scratch and source file **1.1_space_animation_template**

Marcus had an idea for an animation about space. He drew a flowchart showing what he wanted his program to do. Now Marcus wants to make his animation using Scratch.

Follow Marcus's flowchart to create a Scratch project that follows the same steps. Use source file 1.1_space_animation_template to help you. Some of the blocks have been provided. The blocks need to be put into a sequence.

Start → Spaceship to fly across the screen → Spaceship to land on a planet → Astronaut to appear → Astronaut to say "This is the wrong planet!" → End

Practical tasks are in Unit 2.

**Practical task 1**

**You will need:** your questions from Unplugged activity 5, a desktop computer, laptop or tablet with an internet connection, a Google account

You are now going to create an online form using your questions. Work with your partner. Use your paper plan to help you.
1. Log in to a Google account and go to Google Forms.
2. Under 'Start a new form' press 'Blank'.
3. Create your form. (A template for the first question will appear automatically.)

Look out for this icon. You are going to do an activity at the computer using a source file or website link. This content can be found in the Digital Learner's Book on Cambridge GO. Your teacher will help you to get started.

Questions that help you to practise what you have just learnt. Are you ready to move on?

**Questions**
2. What shape should be at the start and end of a flowchart?
3. When should you use a rectangle in a flowchart?
4. Why would you use a diamond in a flowchart?

Things to remember when you are doing a task.

**Stay safe!**
Some online quizzes have chat features, but you should only speak to people you know and trust online. Tell a trusted adult if you see anything that makes you feel uncomfortable.

Interesting facts connected to the topic.

**Did you know?**
People who work on how a program looks are sometimes called 'front-end developers', while people who work on the programming that users don't see are sometimes called 'back-end developers'.

# How to use this book

Questions to help you think about how you learn.

> What challenges did you and your group have?
> How did you overcome the challenges?
> What new skills did you learn?

What you have learnt in the topic.

**Look what I can do!**
- ☐ I know that we can present algorithms as flowcharts.
- ☐ I know the meaning of different shapes in a flowchart.
- ☐ I can predict the outcome of a flowchart.

At the end of each unit, there is a project for you to carry out, using what you have learnt. You might make something or solve a problem.

**Project**

Create a Scratch quiz

With a partner, you are going to create a quiz in Scratch. Using what you have learnt throughout this unit, complete the following tasks.
- Write a list of success criteria for your program.
- Draw a flowchart algorithm for the program.
- Create a project plan for the program.
- Create a prototype of the program.
- Develop the program.
- Test and evaluate the program.

Here are some ideas for what you could include in your quiz:
- a score variable
- different levels with different backgrounds
- questions that become more difficult as you progress through the different levels
- different reactions when the user gets a question correct or incorrect
- sprite animations
- a timer or countdown for answers.

Questions that cover what you have learnt in the unit. If you can answer these, you are ready to move on to the next unit.

**Check your progress**

1. In a flowchart, what shape are decisions? (Hint: They usually have a 'Yes' and 'No' arrow coming from them.)
2. What three data types did you explore earlier in the unit?
3. In Scratch, which block would you use if you wanted to include a conditional statement in your program?
4. A variable in Scratch contains information that always stays the same. Explain whether you agree or disagree with this statement and give an example.
5. Explain what the green 'join' block does in Scratch.
6. In Scratch, event blocks are used to start a program. For example, 'When green flag clicked' is an event block. Write down as many other event blocks as you can remember.
7. Explain what a sub-routine is and why it can be useful in programming.
8. How might a sub-routine be used in a quiz?
9. What does IPO stand for?
10. Give some examples of inputs and outputs on a micro:bit.

# 1 Computational thinking and programming

## > 1.1 Planning flowcharts

**We are going to:**
- understand that we can present algorithms as flowcharts
- understand the shapes used in a flowchart
- predict the results of flowcharts.

decision
flowchart
input
output
prediction

**Getting started**

**What do you already know?**
- Algorithms follow a sequence (top to bottom, left to right).
- Algorithms can use inputs and outputs.
- A conditional (IF THEN ELSE) block causes an algorithm to do either one thing or another.

# 1 Computational thinking and programming

> **Continued**
>
> **Now try this!**
>
> Work with a partner. Think of something you do every day. Describe the task to your partner as if it was an algorithm that a computer could follow. Include all of the steps in the task, even if they might seem obvious. Try to include a conditional statement in your algorithm.
>
> For example:
>
> IF it is a school day THEN take out my school uniform, ELSE take out my weekend clothes.
>
> IF it is raining THEN . . . ELSE . . .

## Flowcharts

There are many ways to represent algorithms. In Scratch, you use blocks to represent an algorithm. In the Getting started activity, you used speech. You could have also written it down as text.

A **flowchart** is another way to represent an algorithm. A flowchart is a diagram that shows each step of an algorithm.

This is an example of a simple flowchart:

Use your finger to follow the flowchart.

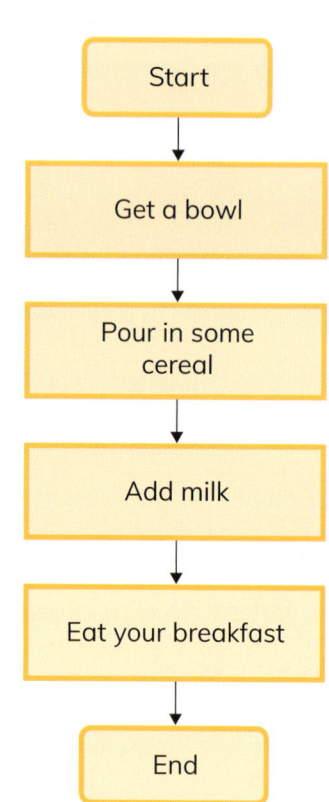

## 1.1 Planning flowcharts

To follow a flowchart, you begin at the start shape at the top and then follow the arrow to the next step in the sequence.

We can use flowcharts to show a process that follows steps in the same order. Engineers use flowcharts to show how to make things, and businesses use flowcharts to explain how to do things.

### Unplugged activity 1

Follow the steps in this flowchart.

1. Which action did you perform first?
2. Which action did you perform last?
3. Which shapes does the flowchart use?

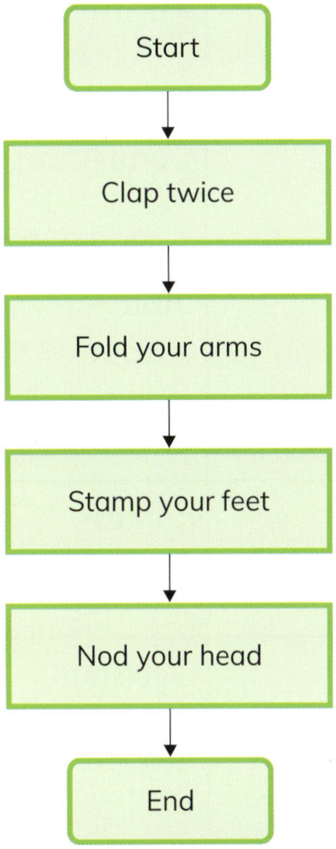

Start → Clap twice → Fold your arms → Stamp your feet → Nod your head → End

**1** Computational thinking and programming

## Flowchart shapes

The shapes we use in a flowchart are important.
They provide more information about what is happening in the algorithm. Look at the table and read the descriptions with a partner.

| Shapes | Name | Description |
| --- | --- | --- |
| (rounded rectangle) | Start or end | This shape appears at the beginning and end of the flowchart. |
| (arrows) | Connectors | These arrows show the order the flowchart should be followed in. |
| (parallelogram) | Input or output | We use this shape when the flowchart needs to get an **input** (information from the user), or when it needs to produce an **output** (give information to the user). |
| (rectangle) | Process | This shape shows actions that will be done. |
| (diamond) | Decision | A **decision** is a choice you make after thinking about the options. We use this shape when we want to decide which path to follow next. A flowchart decision shape asks a question that can only have a 'yes' or 'no' answer. It is very similar to a conditional statement. |

1.1 Planning flowcharts

**Unplugged activity 2**

Look at this flowchart. With a partner, follow the flowchart twice:
- once as if it was a school day
- once as if it was a weekend.

What do you notice?

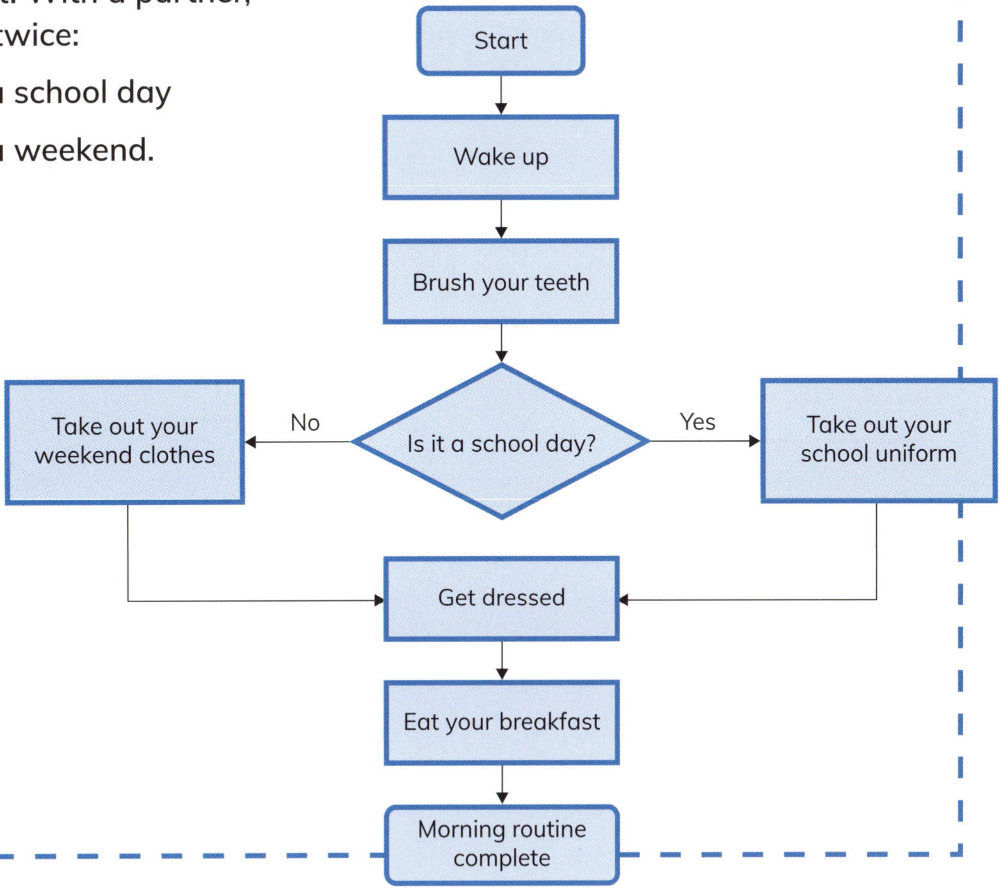

```
Start
  ↓
Wake up
  ↓
Brush your teeth
  ↓
Is it a school day?
  No → Take out your weekend clothes
  Yes → Take out your school uniform
  ↓
Get dressed
  ↓
Eat your breakfast
  ↓
Morning routine complete
```

# Question

1. What is the difference between the cereal flowchart at the start of this topic and the morning routine flowchart in Unplugged activity 2?

# 1 Computational thinking and programming

**Unplugged activity 3**

Look at the flowcharts below. With a partner, take it in turns to follow the flowcharts with your finger.

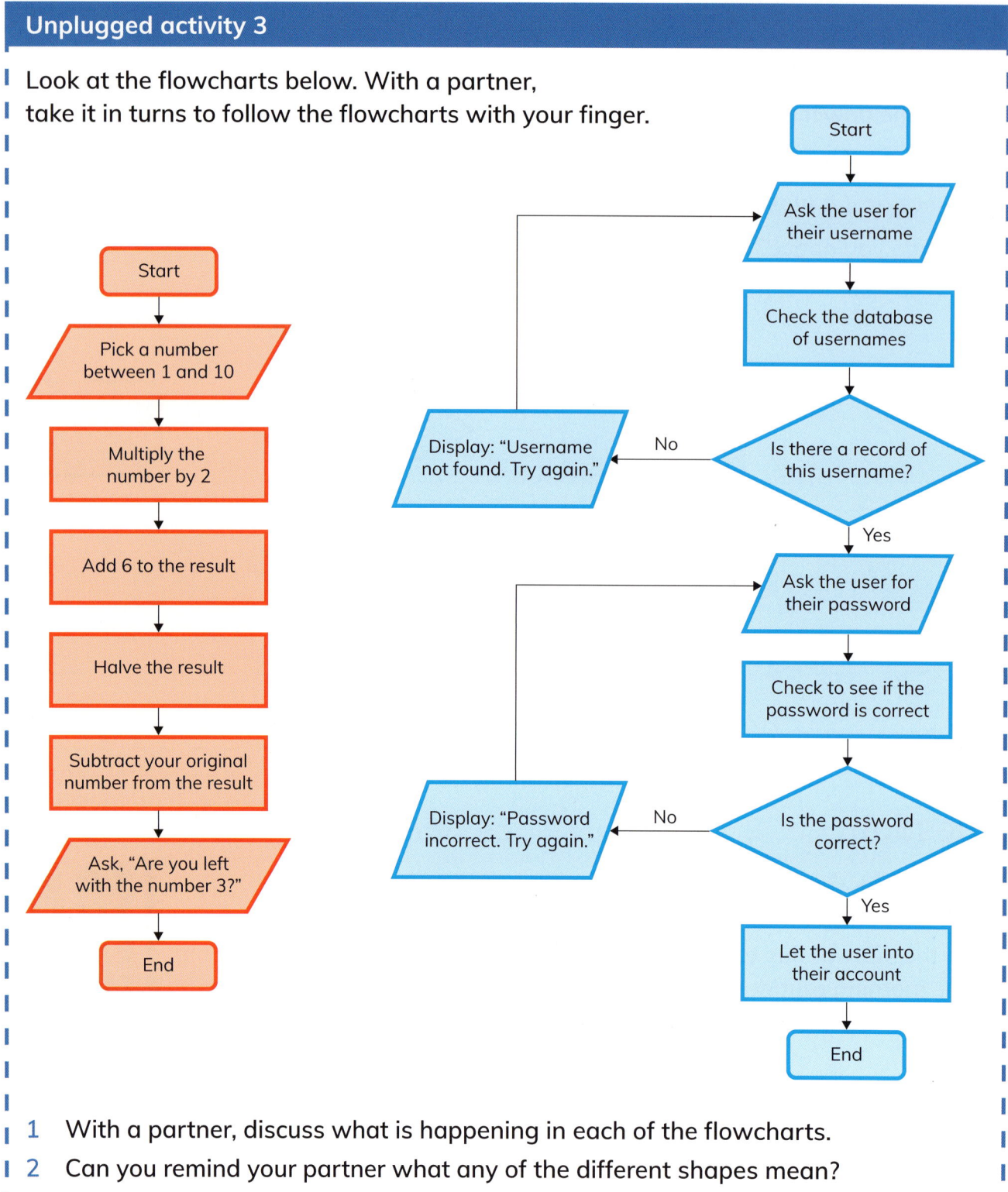

1. With a partner, discuss what is happening in each of the flowcharts.
2. Can you remind your partner what any of the different shapes mean?

## 1.1 Planning flowcharts

### Unplugged activity 4

**You will need:** Worksheet 1.1

Arun draws a flowchart to show how his dad makes tea in the morning, but he isn't sure which shapes he should use.

Look at his flowchart. With a partner, discuss which shape should go with each step.

Use the worksheet to complete the flowchart so it includes the correct shapes and arrows.

Notice that there is a decision in this flowchart. Have a look at the morning routine flowchart to remind yourself how a decision should look. Think carefully about where the arrow from 'No' should point to.

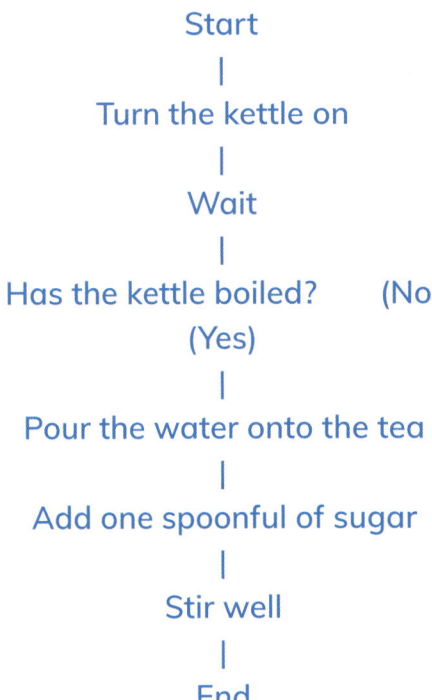

### How are we doing?

Swap your flowcharts with another pair. Have a look at their flowcharts.

- Did they remember to use an oval shape or a rectangle with rounded corners for the beginning and end?
- Did they use a decision shape and draw arrows from the 'Yes' and 'No' labels?
- Are their arrows pointing in the correct directions?

# 1 Computational thinking and programming

## Questions

2. What shape should be at the start and end of a flowchart?
3. When should you use a rectangle in a flowchart?
4. Why would you use a diamond in a flowchart?

### Activity 5

**You will need:** a desktop computer, laptop or tablet, simple design software such as Word, PowerPoint or Canva

Use a computer to create a poster that explains what the different shapes in a flowchart mean.

Use pictures and colour to make it more interesting.

## Following a flowchart

### Programming task 1

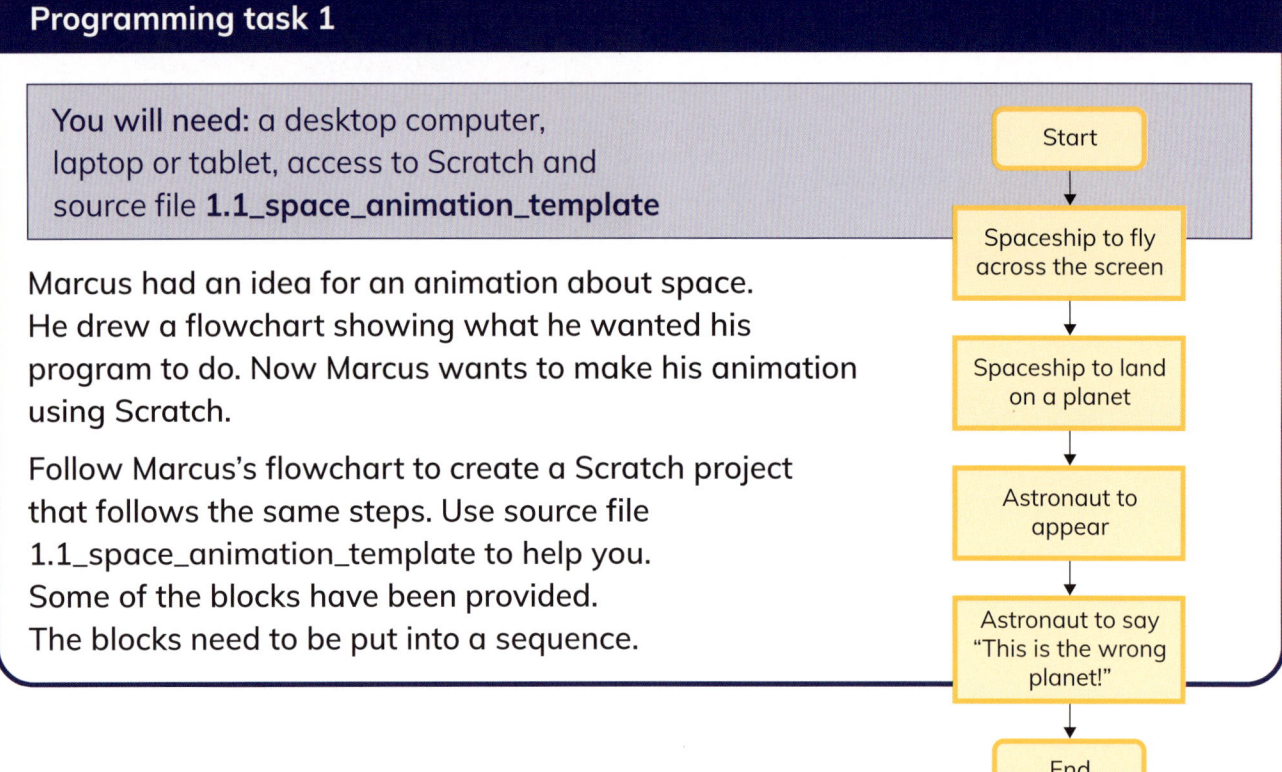

**You will need:** a desktop computer, laptop or tablet, access to Scratch and source file **1.1_space_animation_template**

Marcus had an idea for an animation about space. He drew a flowchart showing what he wanted his program to do. Now Marcus wants to make his animation using Scratch.

Follow Marcus's flowchart to create a Scratch project that follows the same steps. Use source file 1.1_space_animation_template to help you. Some of the blocks have been provided. The blocks need to be put into a sequence.

## 1.1 Planning flowcharts

> **Continued**
>
> **How am I doing?**
>
> Run your code and check whether your program does the following. Give yourself a point if you have successfully completed each step.
>
> - My spaceship flies across the stage.
> - My spaceship looks like it is landing on a planet.
> - An astronaut appears after the spaceship has landed.
> - The astronaut says something.

What do you do to help you remember what the different shapes in a flowchart mean?

## Predicting the outcomes of flowcharts

We can use flowcharts to make predictions. When someone says what they think will happen in the future, they are making a prediction. Imagine a robot that was programmed to play chess using a flowchart. If you understood the flowchart, you would be able to predict where the robot might make its next move!

People use more complex flowcharts and algorithms to predict things in real life, such as who might be more likely to need certain types of healthcare or how the value of gold might go up or down.

To predict the outcome of a flowchart, you need to follow the steps of the flowchart to the end.

# 1 Computational thinking and programming

## Unplugged activity 6

Look at this flowchart to help fix a problem with a computer not working.

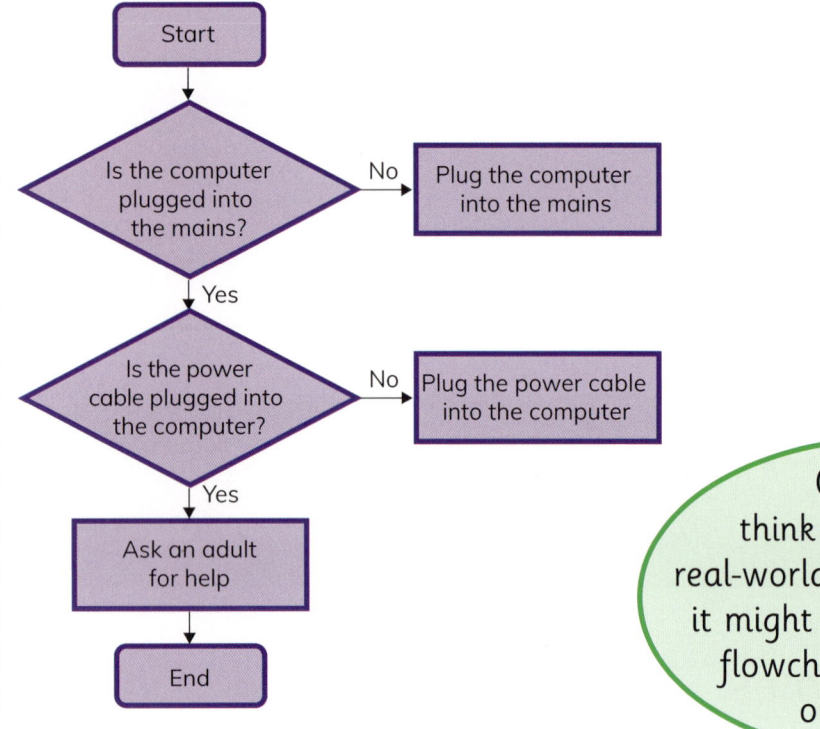

Predict the outcome of the flowchart
if the computer is plugged into the mains
and the power cable is plugged into the computer.

*Can you think of any other real-world examples where it might be useful to use flowcharts to predict outcomes?*

### Look what I can do!

☐ I know that we can present algorithms as flowcharts.
☐ I know the meaning of different shapes in a flowchart.
☐ I can predict the outcome of a flowchart.

# > 1.2 Programming constructs

## We are going to:

- explore programming ideas including sequence, selection and iteration
- use arithmetic operators in our algorithms
- create programs using different data types
- develop a chatbot that uses different data types
- program a talking clock that solves a real-life problem
- create a program with interaction that uses multiple programming ideas.

arithmetic operator    input variable    programming constructs
character              integer           selection
chatbot                interaction       sequence
comparison operator    iteration         string
condition              operator          variable
conditional statement  procedure

## Getting started

### What do you already know?

- How to use 'repeat' loops and conditionals in code.
- How to use mathematical operators for addition and subtraction.
- What variables are and how to use them in programs.
- How to debug errors in code.

# 1 Computational thinking and programming

## Continued

### Now try this!

Look at the Scratch blocks below. How could you arrange them in a sequence to show how to play a simple two-player game like snakes and ladders?

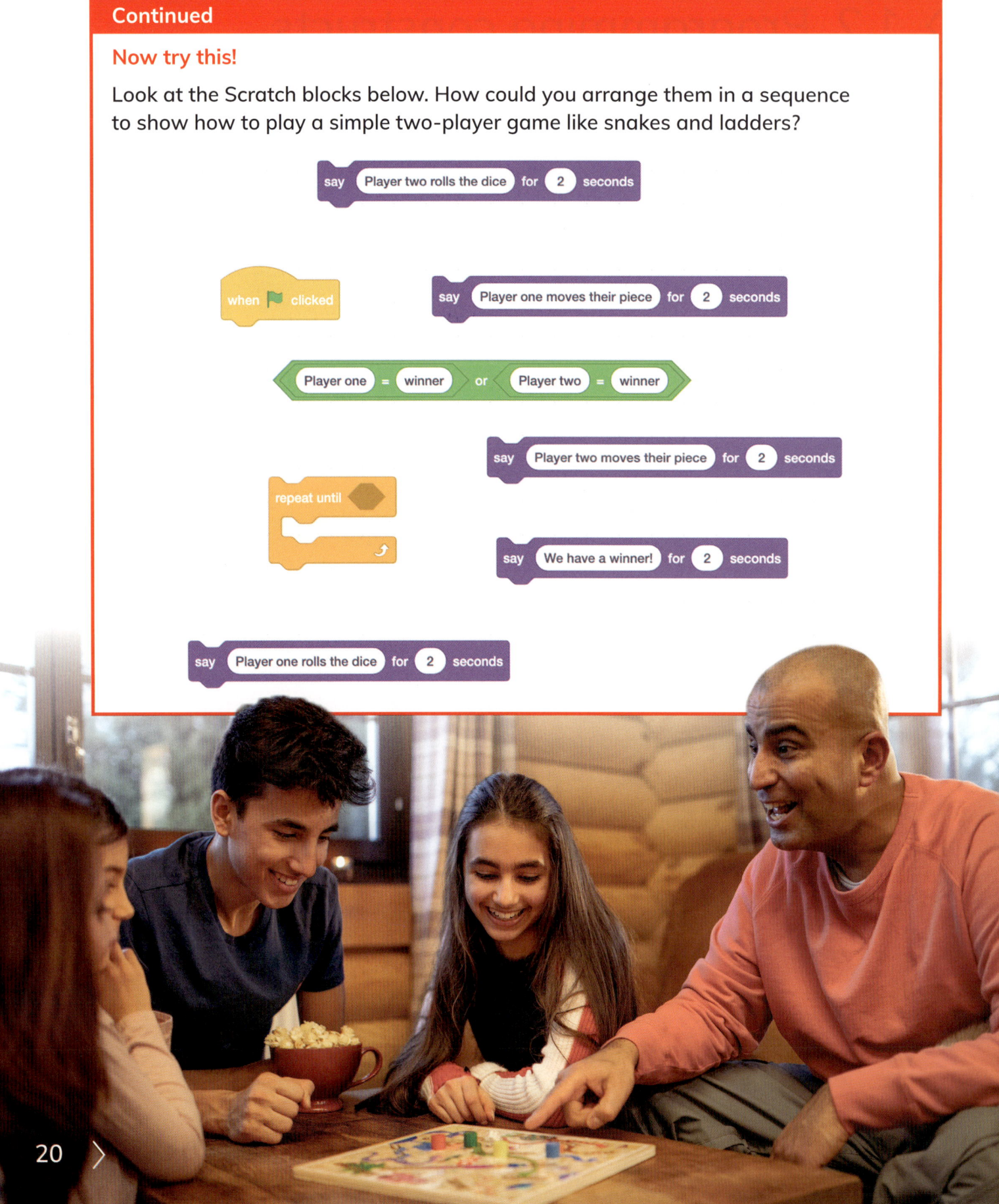

# Programming constructs

We can use lots of different programming ideas, often called programming constructs, to create programs that solve problems. Programming constructs are programming ideas such as sequence, selection and repetition. You learnt about these constructs in the previous chapter. Let's recap some of them now.

Sequence is the order in which instructions run in algorithms and programs. If the instructions are in the wrong order, the algorithm or program may not work in the way you want it to!

Selection means choosing which commands to run. A conditional statement is one way to use selection. A conditional statement is a section of code that tells your program to either run one set of instructions or another set of instructions, depending on whether a condition is true or false. A condition is a situation that tells the computer what to do next.

For example, you could develop a program that asks the user to pick a random number between 1 and 20.

If the user picks a number that is less than 10, the program could say: 'You picked a one-digit number'.

Or else, if the user picks a number that is not less than 10, the program could say: 'You picked a two-digit number'.

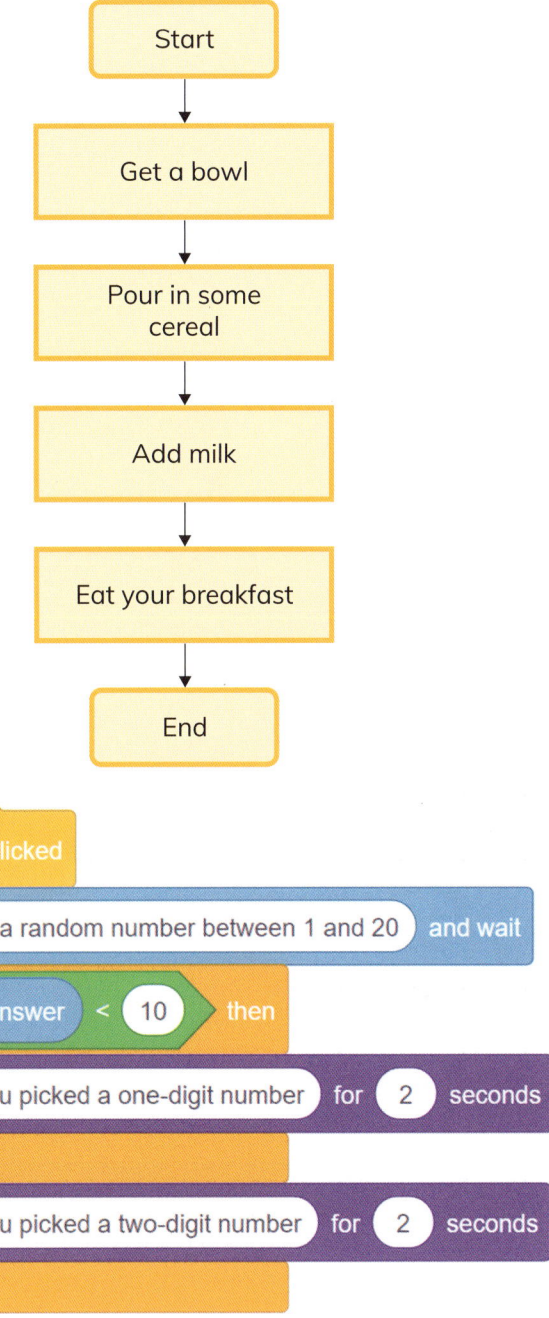

Even though you don't know which number the user will pick, the program can use selection to decide which instruction to follow.

# 1 Computational thinking and programming

**Iteration** means repeating something. When programming in Scratch, we sometimes call iterators 'repeat' blocks or loops.

There are different types of iterators. A 'forever' loop is an iterator that will keep repeating the code forever. A 'repeat [10]' block is an iterator that will repeat the code a set number of times.

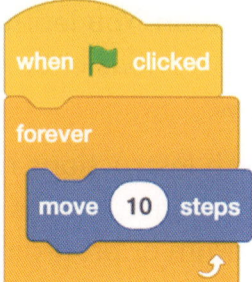

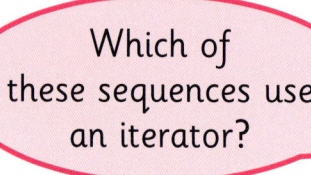

### Activity 1

**You will need:** a desktop computer, laptop or tablet with presentation software

Imagine you are teaching someone about important programming constructs. Work with a partner to create a digital presentation to explain what sequence, selection and iteration are. Try to use examples from your own programming.

## Question

1  Why do you think iterators are useful in programming?

## 1.2 Programming constructs

There are lots of other useful programming constructs that you need to know about, including variables, operators, procedures and interaction.

A variable is a named container (like a box) that stores a piece of data in your program. Even though the data in the variable might be different each time you run your code, your program will still do the same thing with the data in the variable. You might use a variable to keep the score in a game or to store the user's name.

In programming, we use * for the multiply operator instead of x, and / for the divide operator, instead of ÷.

An input variable is a type of variable that asks for information from the user. In Scratch you could use the 'ask' block to create an input variable.

We can use different types of operator in computer programs. An operator is a symbol that tells the program to do a certain action with the information surrounding the operator, such as comparing, adding, or working out if a statement is true or false.

We can use arithmetic operators in computer programs that involve numbers. Arithmetic is another word for mathematics. Arithmetic operators are used to do calculations. The main arithmetic operators are plus, minus, multiply and divide. In Scratch, the blocks look like the example on the right.

### Unplugged activity 2

**You will need:** a pen and paper

With a partner, write out an algorithm for a simple program in Scratch that uses arithmetic operators. For example:

1. When the green flag is clicked
2. Say 'What is 5 times 4?' for 5 seconds
3. Say 'The answer is ' [5 * 4] for 5 seconds

# 1 Computational thinking and programming

We can also use **comparison operators** in programs that involve numbers. There are three comparison operators in Scratch: greater than, less than and equal to. They compare the first number with the second number and output either true or false. Look at an example on the right.

A **procedure** is a small section of code that we can use multiple times in a program. Using procedures can save time for developers so they don't need to keep writing the same set of commands.

**Interaction** is when one part of a program changes or affects another part. For example, in Scratch you might have two sprites and if one of them touches the other, the first one might disappear or play a sound.

# Data types

Computers store data in an organised way to make it easy to find information quickly. One of the ways that computer programs organise information is by categorising data into different types. We are going to look at three data types: integer, character and string.

## Integer

An **integer** is a whole number. For example, 3 is an integer, but 3.14 or three are not integers. Programs can perform mathematical operations with data items if they are integers.

## Character

A **character** is any individual letter, symbol or number. A is a character and so is ! and 4. A computer keyboard is filled with characters!

You use characters to create passwords. Often you need to include a mixture of letters, symbols and numbers to make sure that it is a strong password.

1.2 Programming constructs

## String

If you combine characters, it creates data with another data type called a string. Strings can also include spaces and are often used for written messages.

An example of a Scratch block that requires a string is the 'say' block:

This is a string made up of six characters. Can you think of any other Scratch blocks that use integers or strings?

### Unplugged activity 3

The Scratch blocks below all require an input of certain data types.

For each block, discuss with your partner which data type the block uses.

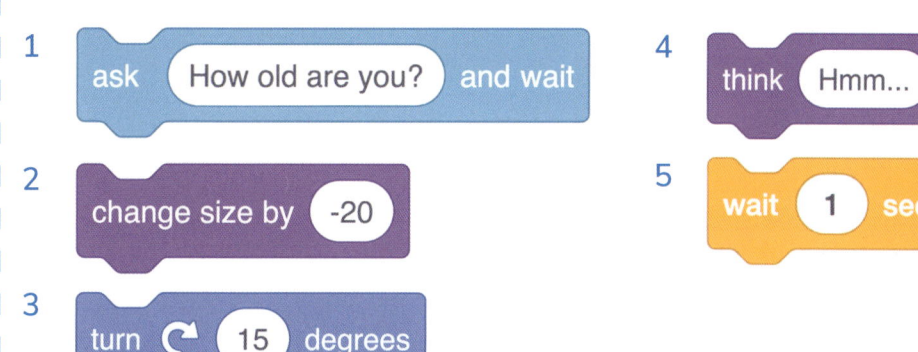

In Scratch, if you enter a string where only the integer data type is accepted, Scratch will automatically convert the string to 0.

Yes. When I tried to do 'three' + 'five' it thought the answer was 0 because you can't add two strings together.

# 1 Computational thinking and programming

You are going to create a chatbot program that requires different data types.

A **chatbot** is a program that has been designed to speak and respond to a user in a human way. Some chatbots listen to your voice and speak aloud, but other chatbots respond online with text. They can sometimes answer questions and provide helpful information.

## Programming task 1

You will need: a desktop computer, laptop or tablet, access to Scratch and source file **1.2_chatbot_example**

### Part A

Look at the code for a chatbot. Work with a partner to discuss what you think this code will do. Explain each block in the sequence.

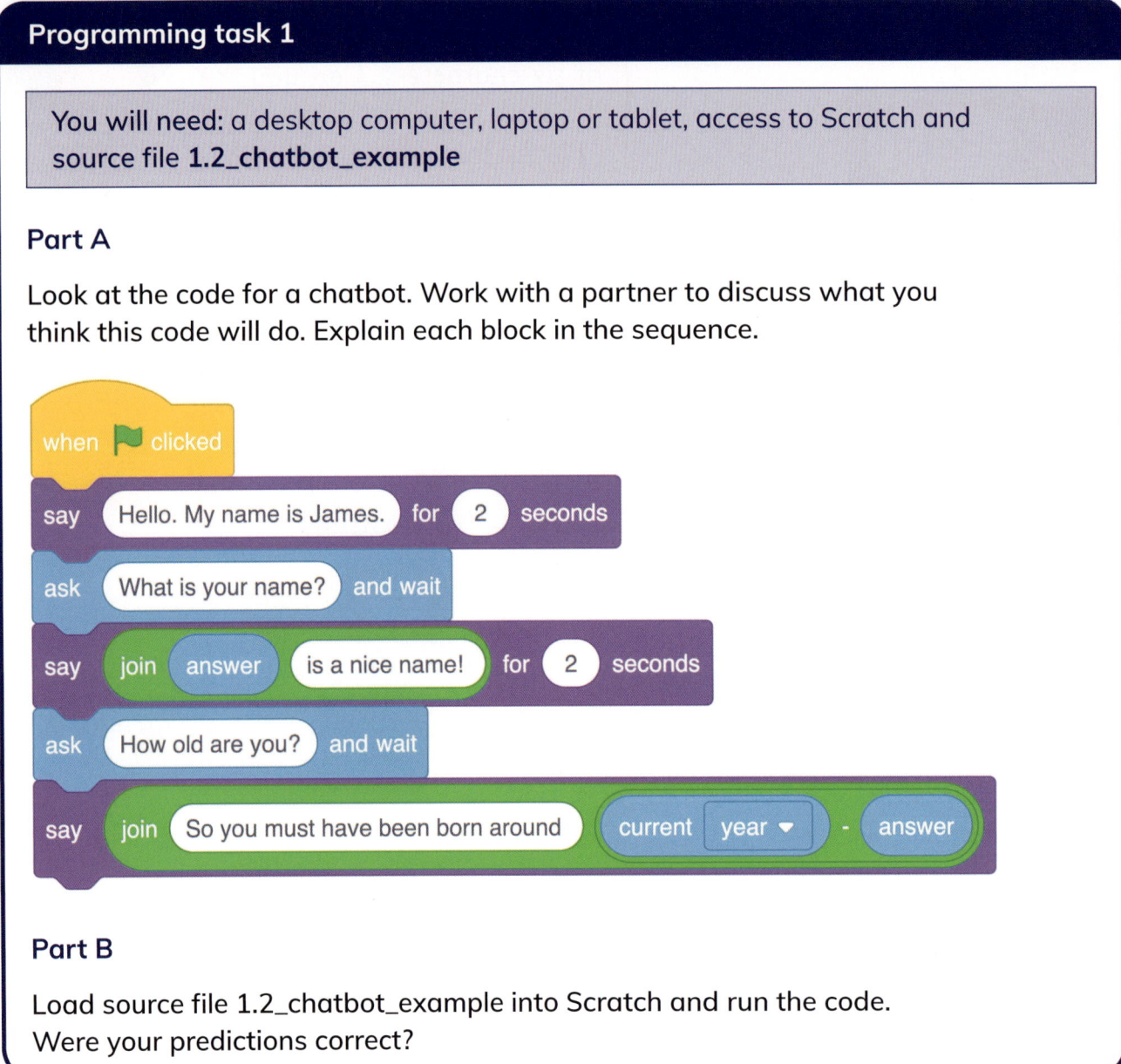

### Part B

Load source file 1.2_chatbot_example into Scratch and run the code. Were your predictions correct?

26

## 1.2 Programming constructs

> **Continued**
>
> ### Part C
>
> Add comments to the code explaining the role of the different blocks.
> One of these blocks asks for a string input and the other requires an integer.
>
> 1. What happens if you type a string as a response for the integer question?
> 2. What happens if you type an integer as a response for the string question?
> 3. There is an arithmetic operator block in this code. Did you spot it?
>    Add a comment to this block explaining how this works.
>
> ### Part D
>
> Change some of the blocks to make the program different.
> Here are some ideas for things to try:
>
> - Change the cat's name.
> - Add another greeting message before it asks a question.
> - Make the cat respond saying they know someone with the user's name.
> - Change the arithmetic operator so that it tells the user how old they will be next year.
>
> ### Part E
>
> Create your own version of a chatbot that uses the 'ask' block to get data input from the user. In one of your questions, ask the user for an integer so that you can perform a maths calculation in your response.
>
> You could program your chatbot to:
>
> - ask about the user's favourite food and respond by saying you like to eat that as well
> - ask for the year the user was born and work out how old they are
> - ask them to think of a number between 1 and 10 and then respond by saying you know what that number squared is, then tell them the answer.

> **Stay safe!**
>
> Although chatbots can be really useful, it is important to remember that they are only programs following an algorithm so their answers might not be very reliable. Also, some hackers design chatbots to get your personal information. Make sure you trust the website or app before responding to a chatbot.

## 1 Computational thinking and programming

# Solving a problem using different programming ideas

Computer programs are often designed to solve problems.

You are going to develop programs that solve real-life problems.

The programs you create will use:

- conditional statements
- iteration
- variables
- arithmetic and comparison operators
- procedures
- interaction.

## Question

2   What does it mean when we use interaction in a program?

**Programming task 2**

> You will need: a desktop computer, laptop or tablet, access to Scratch and source file **1.3_predict_activity**

### Part A

Work in a group of three. Look at this program. Discuss what you predict will happen when the code runs. Use the key words 'variable', 'iterator' and 'comparison operator'. Look at the Glossary if you can't remember what these words mean.

### Part B

Open source file 1.3_predict_activity and run the code.

28

## 1.2 Programming constructs

### Continued

1. Did the program do what you predicted?
2. Did it count all the way to 20 or did it stop on a different number? Why do you think this happened?
3. How could you make it count faster or slower?
4. Which data type did this program require?

### Part C

Investigate what the 'join' operator does when you add it to the code.

Add the 'join' operator to the algorithm inside the 'say' block instead of the *number* variable. Try some of the combinations below and click them to see the output.

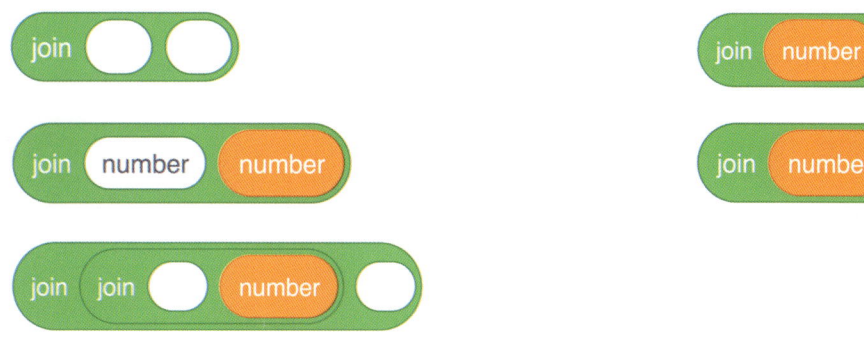

### Part D

Modify the algorithm so that it becomes a times table counter. Instead of counting to 20, it should count up in 5s or any number you choose.

Hint: Most of the algorithm can remain the same but you will need to use the multiplication operator.

### How am I doing?

Discuss with your partner how confident you feel, from 1 to 5, about each of the statements below. 1 means you are not sure and 5 means you are very confident.

- I understand what an iterator does.
- I can explain why iteration is useful.

# 1 Computational thinking and programming

Scratch allows you to convert written text into spoken language. We can use the 'Text to Speech' extension to do this. You can find the 'Add Extension' button at the bottom of the Scratch blocks palette. It looks like this:

## Programming task 3

> You will need: a desktop computer, laptop or tablet, access to Scratch and source file **1.4_talking_clock**

Zara's friend is blind. She can't read the time on a standard clock so Zara wants to create a program that will speak the time aloud for her. She has started to pull together the blocks that she thinks she will need in Scratch. Can you help her to complete her project?

Open source file 1.4_talking_clock and use the 'current [time]' blocks, 'join' operators and the 'Text to Speech' extension to create a program that provides a solution for this problem.

*Think about how you will use the 'Text to Speech' extension!*

### How are we doing?

Swap your program with a partner and evaluate whether the program solves the problem for Zara's friend. Look at the criteria below. Give your partner's program a score from 1 to 3 for each of the following (where 1 means 'no', 2 means 'nearly' and 3 means 'yes').

Does your talking clock:

- say the time out loud?
- say the correct number of minutes?
- say the correct number of hours?

Discuss what could be done to make your program even better.

## 1.2 Programming constructs

### Programming task 4

**You will need:** a desktop computer, laptop or tablet, access to Scratch and source file **1.5_Zara_talking_clock**

Developers often create programs that work and then try to think of ways to improve them.

Open source file 1.5_Zara_talking_clock and look at Zara's program. Although Zara's program works, she has some ideas about how to make it even better. It uses a 24-hour clock. If you run the program in the afternoon, it might say, 'The time is 14:26'. She wants it to use a 12-hour clock so that it will say '2:26' instead.

Help Zara solve this problem and improve her code. (Hint: You will have to use a conditional block that checks to see if the current time is before or after midday.) You might have your own ideas about things to improve, too. You could also see if you can change the code so it says that the time is a certain number of minutes past the hour, or a certain number of minutes to the hour.

## Bugs!

Did you notice any bugs in your code? Remember: debugging means finding and fixing any errors in an algorithm or program.

For example, in the code below, if it was 1 minute past 10, this program would say 'One minutes past ten' How would you fix this?

```
when [space] key pressed
if <(current hour) > 12> then
    speak (join (join "The time is" (current minute)) (join "minutes past" ((current hour) - 12)))
else
    speak (join (join "The time is" (current minute)) (join "minutes past" (current hour)))
```

**1** Computational thinking and programming

Errors are very common in computing, even for experienced programmers. How do you feel when you realise you have made an error in your code? What helps you to fix it?

### Programming task 5

**You will need:** a desktop computer, laptop or tablet, access to Scratch and source file **1.6_interacting_sprites**

**Part A**

Open source file 1.6_interacting_sprites. Click the green flag and follow the instructions.

Discuss with a partner how the different sprites interact with each other.

Explain which other programming constructs are used in this program.

**Part B**

Add another number sprite. When that sprite is clicked it should cause Devin to say the times table for that number.

Sequence, selection, iteration, variables, sprite interaction, arithmetic operators, procedures . . . You have learnt so many programming constructs! Don't worry – you don't need to use them all in every program. Think of them like tools that you can use to help you when programming!

32

## 1.2 Programming constructs

**Look what I can do!**

- ☐ I can explain programming ideas including sequence, selection and iteration.
- ☐ I can use arithmetic operators in my algorithms.
- ☐ I can create programs that use character, integer and string data types.
- ☐ I can develop a chatbot that asks questions and uses the given answers.
- ☐ I can create a talking clock that solves a real problem.
- ☐ I can create programs with interaction that use multiple programming ideas.

# 1 Computational thinking and programming

## > 1.3 Sub-routines

**We are going to:**
- learn that a sub-routine can be used multiple times in an algorithm
- understand how a sub-routine can be used across different algorithms
- understand how to create algorithms with more than one variable
- understand how variables can be used in different algorithms
- develop a quiz program that uses sub-routines and variables
- develop a program where two sprites interrelate.

broadcast    initialisation
call         interrelate
define       sub-routine

**Getting started**

**What do you already know?**
- What sub-routines are.
- How conditional statements (IF THEN ELSE) can be used in an algorithm.
- How to use a variable to keep a score and how to add or remove points.
- The 'ask' block can store a response in the answer variable.

1.3 Sub-routines

> **Continued**
>
> **Now try this!**
>
> Look at the code below, which is used to control a dinosaur sprite. With a partner, predict what the program will do and explain how the Score variable will work.
>
>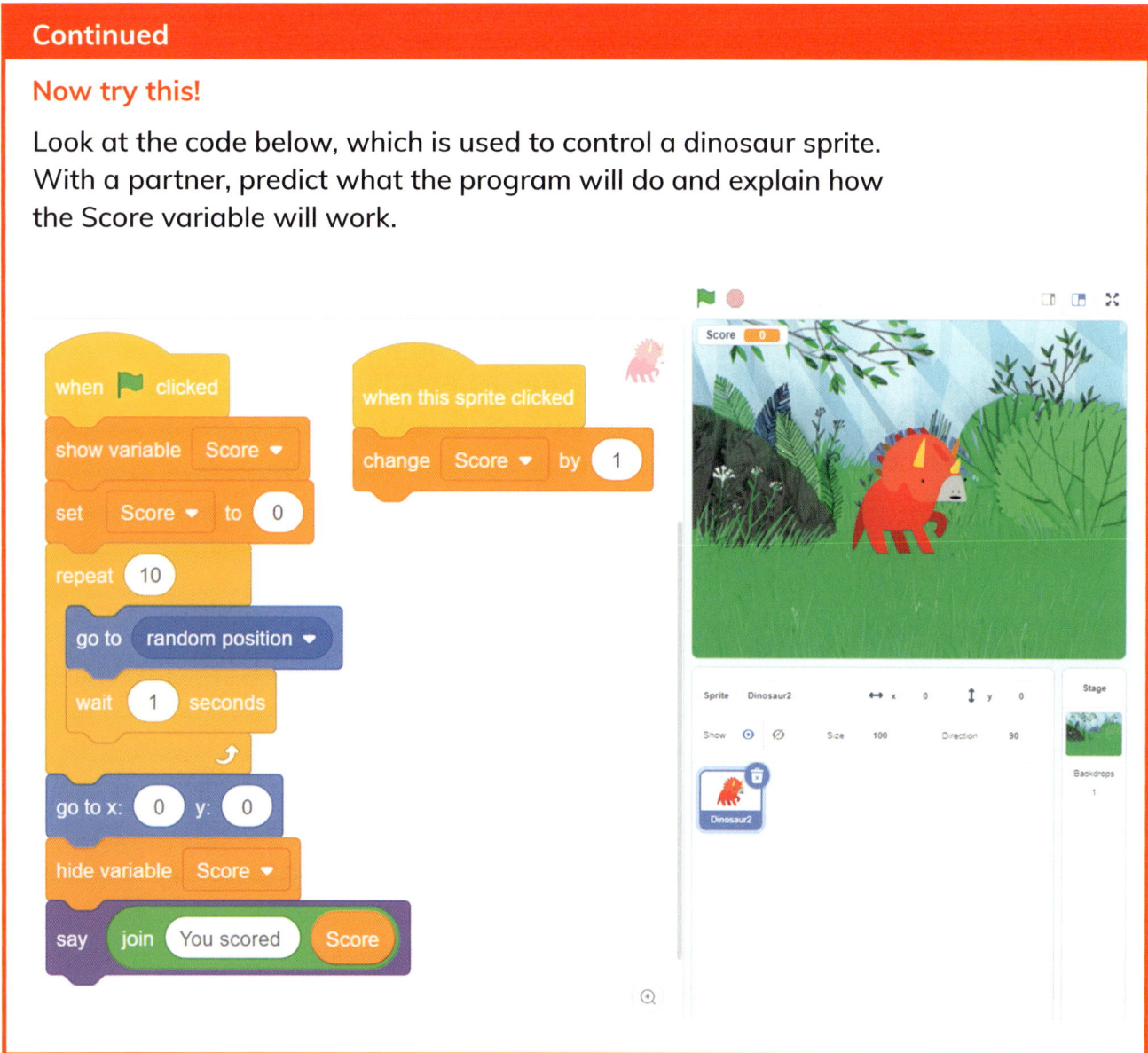

# Using sub-routines

A sub-routine is a section of code that is separate from the main code and performs a specific task. This section of code is often used multiple times in an algorithm. Programmers use sub-routines to make their code easier to understand and to reduce repetition.

When we write a sub-routine for an algorithm, we have to define it. To define a sub-routine means to give the sub-routine a name and write all the instructions that need to be included in the sub-routine.

**1** Computational thinking and programming

When we want to use a sub-routine, we can *call* it. You might call someone's name in the playground and they will respond. Calling a sub-routine works in the same way: when you call, there is a response. In programs, a sub-routine can be called more than once, and different algorithms in the program can call the same sub-routine.

## Using sub-routines within the same algorithm

Imagine you are a gymnast preparing a routine for a performance. You have a list of instructions to follow. The instructions contain a mixture of moves that you already know how to do, such as a forward roll and a handstand. For example:

| Handstand | | Forward roll | |
|---|---|---|---|
| 1 | Put your hands in the air | 1 | Crouch on the floor |
| 2 | Fall forwards | 2 | Put your head to the floor |
| 3 | Stand upside down | 3 | Roll over |
| 4 | Put your feet back on the floor | | |

If the instructions for your routine included all of the steps for each move, the instructions would be very long, especially if you were repeating the same moves multiple times.

You could use sub-routines for each of these moves to help reduce repetition. Each sub-routine could be used multiple times in the routine.

## 1.3 Sub-routines

**Unplugged activity 1**

**You will need:** a pen and paper

Look at the algorithm below for a gymnastics routine.
Identify where sub-routines could be used to remove repetition
and make the routine easier to understand. Write down the new algorithm.

1. Put your hands in the air
2. Fall forwards
3. Stand upside down
4. Put your feet back on the floor
5. Step to the right
6. Step to the left
7. Crouch on the floor
8. Put your head to the floor
9. Roll over
10. Do a star jump
11. Crouch on the floor
12. Put your head to the floor
13. Roll over
14. Put your hands in the air
15. Fall forwards
16. Stand upside down
17. Put your feet back on the floor

# 1 Computational thinking and programming

## Questions

1. How many times is each sub-routine called in your new algorithm for Unplugged activity 1?
2. How would sub-routines help if you needed to give instructions for a gymnastics routine with 5 different moves that were called multiple times each?

Did you see how using sub-routines helps to reduce the length of the instructions?

## Using sub-routines in different algorithms

We can also use the same sub-routine in two (or more) different algorithms. Imagine you want to create two new gymnastics routines for a competition. You can use the same sub-routine in both of these routines. For example:

DEFINE handstand
1   Put your hands in the air
2   Fall forwards
3   Stand upside down
4   Put your feet back on the floor

DEFINE forward roll
1   Crouch on the floor
2   Put your head to the floor
3   Roll over

Routine 1
1   CALL forward roll
2   CALL forward roll
3   CALL handstand
4   Turn around
5   Do a star jump

Routine 2
1   Do a star jump
2   CALL handstand
3   Clap your hands
4   CALL forward roll
5   CALL handstand
6   CALL forward roll
7   Turn around

1.3 Sub-routines

**Unplugged activity 2**

You will need: a pen and paper

Write algorithms for two different gymnastics routines that both use the sub-routines for a handstand and a forward roll.

You can create more sub-routines for other gymnastics moves if you like!

# Using variables in algorithms

You have already started to use variables in your programs.
Remember: a variable stores data that can change.
This makes it a very useful programming construct.

# Using more than one variable in an algorithm

Sometimes, we need to use more than one variable in an algorithm or program. This allows us to make our programs more complex.

For example, in a quiz game, we might want:

- a variable for the score, so we can keep track of how many points a player has scored
- a variable for 'lives', to limit the number of times a player can answer a question incorrectly.

# 1 Computational thinking and programming

## Questions

Look at this algorithm that uses two variables:

| | |
|---|---|
| 1 | When green flag clicked |
| 2 | Set Score to 0 |
| 3 | Set Lives to 3 |
| 4 | Say 'Welcome to this quiz!' for 2 seconds |
| 5 | Ask 'What is 3 + 4?' and wait |
| 6 | IF answer = 7 |
| 7 |     THEN change Score by 1 |
| 8 |     ELSE change Lives by -1 |

3. What are the names of the two variables the programmer has created?
4. What data does each variable store at the beginning?
5. What would happen to the variables if the player entered 5 as their answer?
6. What would happen to the variables if the player entered 7 as their answer?
7. How could you change the program so that you started with 5 lives?
8. How could you change the program so that the player would receive 2 points for the correct answer?

## Using the same variable in different algorithms

We can also use the same variable in two different algorithms.

For example, in Scratch, the 'ask' block could be used to store a response from the user in the *answer* variable. Two different sprites could then use the information stored in the *answer* variable in their own separate algorithms.

## 1.3 Sub-routines

**Unplugged activity 3**

Look at the code below. There are two separate sprites and they both use the *answer* variable in their algorithms.

Discuss with a partner what both the sprites will say if the user entered the answer 'basketball'.

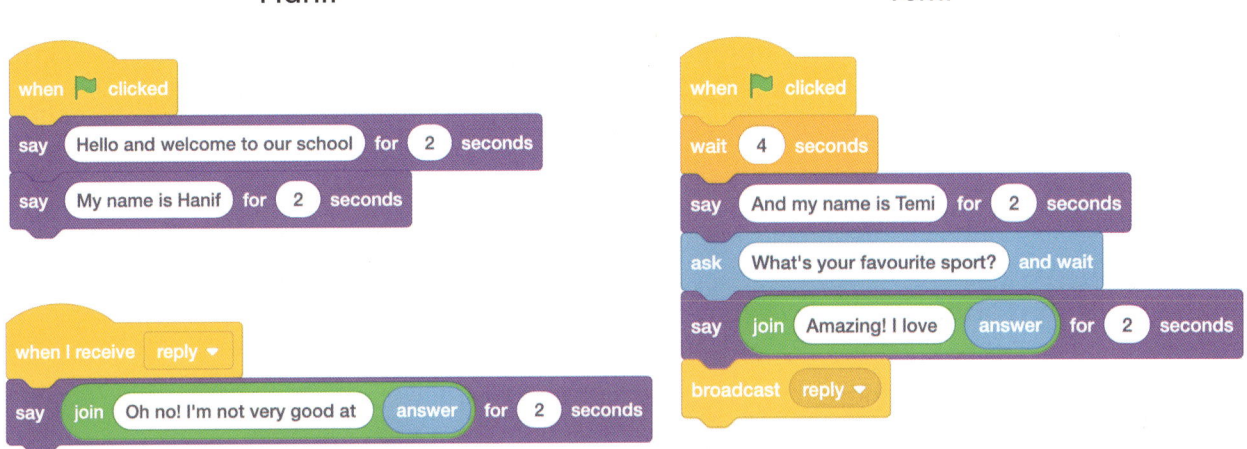

With your partner, think of another question this program could ask the user. Discuss how both of these sprites could use the *answer* variable in their algorithms.

# Developing programs with sub-routines

We can use block-based programming languages to develop programs with sub-routines. Block-based programming languages allow users to drag and drop code blocks to create programs. Scratch is an example of a block-based programming language. You will learn more about the difference between block-based and text-based programming languages in Unit 4.

We can create sub-routines in Scratch using the 'broadcast' and 'receive' blocks. To broadcast means to send a message out into the world for people to receive.

41

**1** Computational thinking and programming

In real life, messages are sent around the world and even into space using broadcast masts like the one in the photo on the previous page.

In Scratch, using a 'broadcast' block is a bit like sending a signal or message to all the other sprites and scripts in the project.

### Programming task 1

**You will need:** a desktop computer, laptop or tablet, access to Scratch and source file **1.7_car_game_subroutine**

Look at the code for this car game. With your partner, go through each of the blocks in the algorithm and explain what they do. There is a sub-routine used somewhere in the code. See if you can find it and explain what it does.

Open source file 1.7_car_game_subroutine in Scratch. Run the code and see if your predictions were correct.

How many times did the sub-routine run?

Add a comment to the sub-routine code explaining how it works.

> This program uses **initialisation**. Initialisation means getting everything ready for the start of the game. The 'go to x: (-100) y: [110]' block and the 'point in direction [90]' block at the start of the main code reset the car back to the same position each time the green flag is clicked.

# 1.3 Sub-routines

Sub-routines can be very useful for developers when they are creating programs that might repeat sets of instructions.
In the program on the previous page, the developers could make it a two-player game and add a second car sprite for another player. If this car goes off track, they could call the same 'Off course!' sub-routine instead of having to recreate the algorithm.

> **Did you know?**
>
> The sub-routine in Programming task 1 was created using the 'broadcast' block. You can also create a sub-routine in Scratch using 'Make a Block'. It is very similar to the 'broadcast' block but you can use it in more complex ways.

## Question

9  Can you think of other times when a sub-routine might be useful in real life?

# Using variables and sub-routines to create a quiz

Have you ever done an online quiz? When you get a question correct, what might happen? What might happen if you get a question wrong?

Online quizzes often use conditional logic in their algorithms. For example: IF the answer is correct, THEN give the player a point, ELSE say 'Game over'.

Quizzes require input from the player to get their answer. In Scratch, we can do this using the 'ask' block, which asks the player a question and opens a typing box. The player can then enter their answer, which is stored in the 'answer' variable.

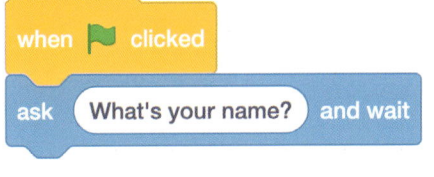

If the player gets an answer correct, there might be a few possible actions that happen in the code, and these possible actions might be the same for all the other questions. This provides a good opportunity to use sub-routines.

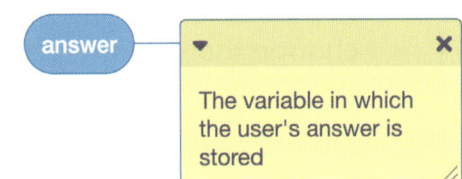

**1** Computational thinking and programming

# Creating a spelling quiz

Do you have spelling quizzes at school?

We can create a similar quiz in Scratch, where we tell the user which word they need to spell. However, we can't display the word as written text because this would give the user the answer!

### Stay safe!

Some online quizzes have chat features, but you should only speak to people you know and trust online. Tell a trusted adult if you see anything that makes you feel uncomfortable.

## Activity 4

You will need: a desktop computer, laptop or tablet, access to Scratch

Click the 'Add Extension' button in the bottom left corner of the Scratch screen. Select the 'Text to Speech' extension, which looks like this:

A new set of blocks will appear in the blocks palette. They look like this:

**Text to Speech**

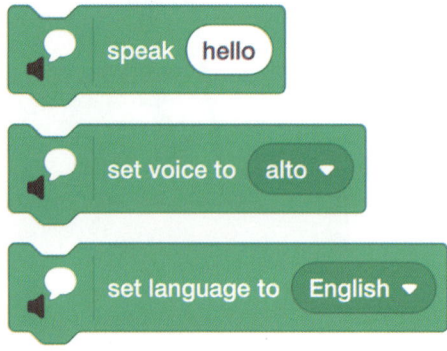

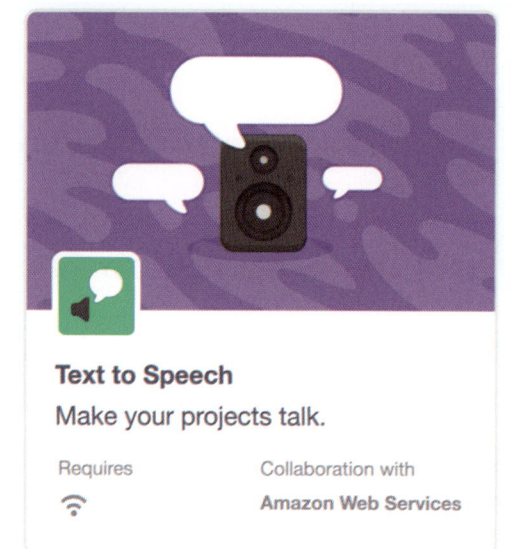

**Text to Speech**
Make your projects talk.

Requires / Collaboration with Amazon Web Services

Try these blocks out and investigate what they do.

Can you:
- make a block speak your name?
- make a block speak a sentence?
- change the way the voice sounds?
- make a program that speaks a sentence in a different accent?

## 1.3 Sub-routines

Before you program the spelling quiz, you need to create a plan.

### Unplugged activity 5

As a class, discuss what features might be included in a good online quiz. What might happen if the player gets an answer correct or incorrect? How might you achieve this using Scratch blocks?

With a partner, use the criteria below to write an algorithm for your Scratch quiz on paper.

Things to include:

- at least two variables (Will you have a score? Will your program have lives?)
- sub-routines to reduce repetition.

If a user gets an answer correct, the program should:

- play the sound 'Tada'
- give them a point
- say 'Correct!'
- change the backdrop to 'Party'.

If the user gets an answer wrong, the program should:

- play the 'Clang' sound
- deduct one life
- say 'Not quite . . .'
- change the backdrop to 'red' (you might need to create this backdrop).

45

**1** Computational thinking and programming

## Programming task 2

**You will need:** a desktop computer, laptop or tablet, access to Scratch, source file **1.8_spelling_quiz_incomplete** and your algorithm from Unplugged activity 5

Open source file 1.8_spelling_quiz_incomplete and sequence the blocks to create a program that asks the user to spell the word 'variable'.

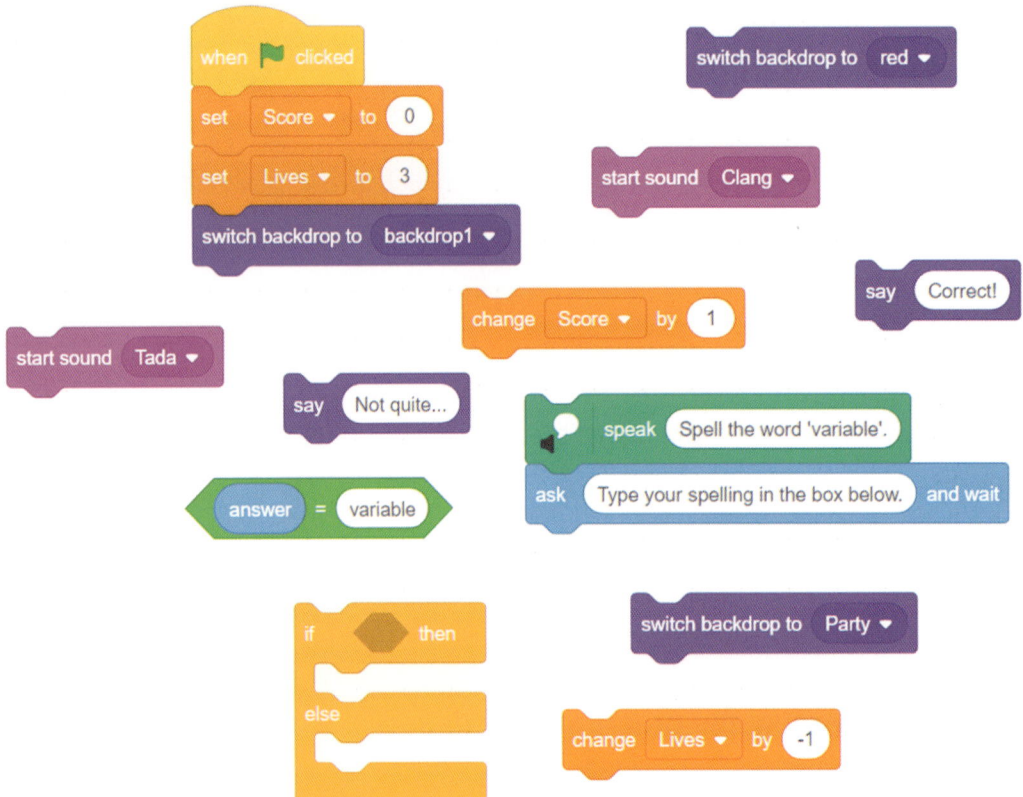

Answer the questions:

1. Explain how you use both variables in this program.
2. What would happen if the user spelt the word using a capital letter? Using the Scratch project, investigate this and think about what it might mean for your quiz.
3. How could you modify the program to ask for a different spelling?
4. How could a sub-routine be used in this program?

## 1.3 Sub-routines

**Unplugged activity 6**

Look at the code below. Work with a partner to trace the code starting at the green flag block. Explain what the code does.

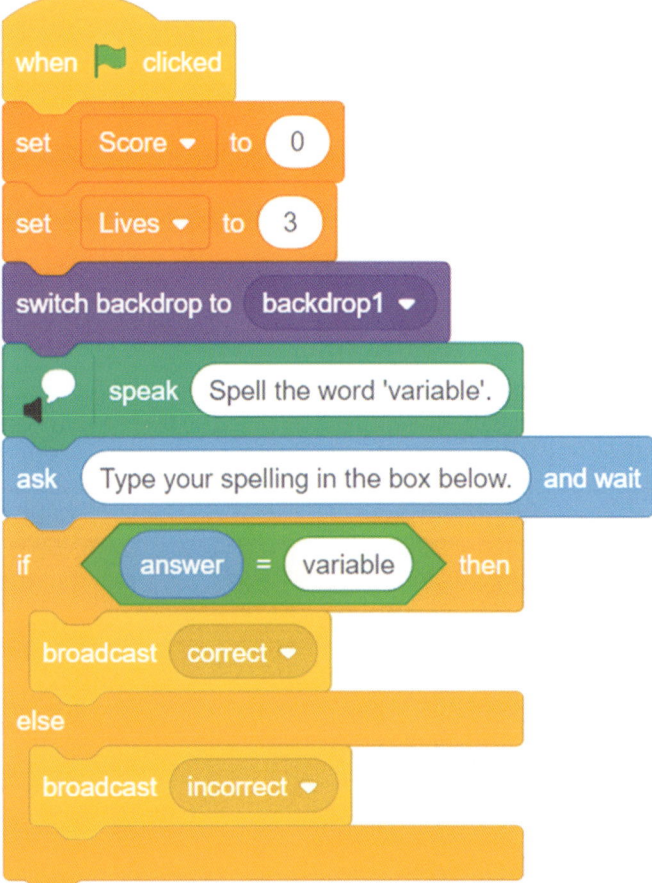
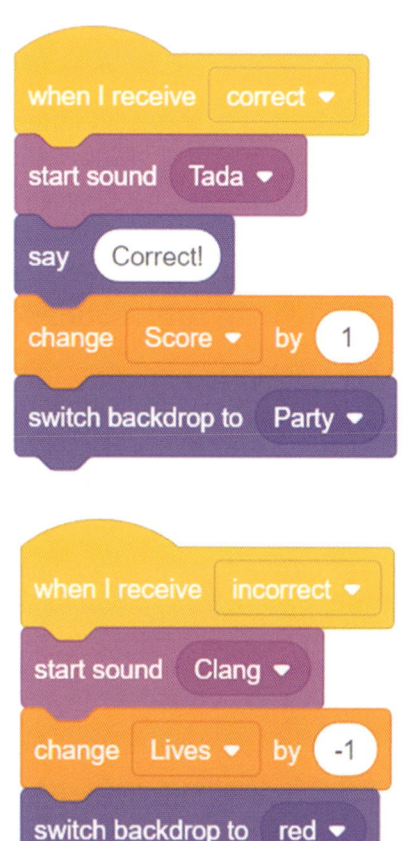

With your partner, discuss why using sub-routines in the quiz might be more useful than not using them, and then share your ideas with the rest of the class.

> As you create more complex programs, using sub-routines will make it much easier to test and find errors in your code. It is a very good skill to learn!

# 1 Computational thinking and programming

## Programming task 3

**You will need:** a desktop computer, laptop or tablet, access to Scratch, source file **1.9_spelling_quiz_no_subroutines** and source file **1.10_spelling_quiz_subroutines**

You are going to extend the spelling test program to ask for two more spellings.

Work in a pair. One of you should use source file 1.9 (the spelling quiz without sub-routines), while the other should use source file 1.10 (the spelling quiz with sub-routines).

Add two new spelling questions to the program. Ask for the spellings of the words 'subroutine' and 'conditional'.

What do you notice when comparing your programs?

## Programming task 4

**You will need:** a desktop computer, laptop or tablet, access to Scratch, your Scratch programs from Programming task 4 or source file **1.11_spelling_quiz_no_subroutines_solution** and source file **1.12_spelling_quiz_subroutines_solution**

When developing code, programmers may decide to adapt their code to improve its function. You are going to make the quiz do something slightly different when an answer is correct.

You are going to make changes to both versions of the code: the Programming task 4 solution that does not use sub-routines and the solution that uses sub-routines. Make the following changes:

- Instead of saying 'Correct!', change the message to: 'Well done! You get a point.'
- Change the sound from 'Tada' to 'Cheer'.

Once you have made these changes, discuss with a partner how you did it. Was it easier to make the changes to the solution without sub-routines, or the solution with sub-routines? Why?

1.3 Sub-routines

> **Continued**
>
> **How am I doing?**
>
> For each of the following statements, give yourself a 1 if you don't agree, a 2 if you partially agree and a 3 if you fully agree.
>
> - I added more questions to the spelling program using conditionals (IF THEN ELSE).
> - I used the 'broadcast' block to call the relevant sub-routines if the user was correct or incorrect.
> - I understand the benefits of using sub-routines in a program.

Think about when you have learnt a new way of doing a task, that was hard at first, but made the task easier in the end. What did you do to adapt to the new way?

# Developing programs where multiple algorithms interrelate

When learning about object interaction, you learnt how to create algorithms where two objects interrelate.

Remember, objects that interrelate are connected so that each object has an effect on, or depends on, the other.

In Scratch, multiple algorithms for sprites can interrelate through sub-routines. In the following program, there are two sprites that interrelate.

# 1 Computational thinking and programming

The dancing man sprite (in the centre of the stage) has a variety of sub-routines for different dance moves. What do you think would happen if you clicked one of these sub-routines?

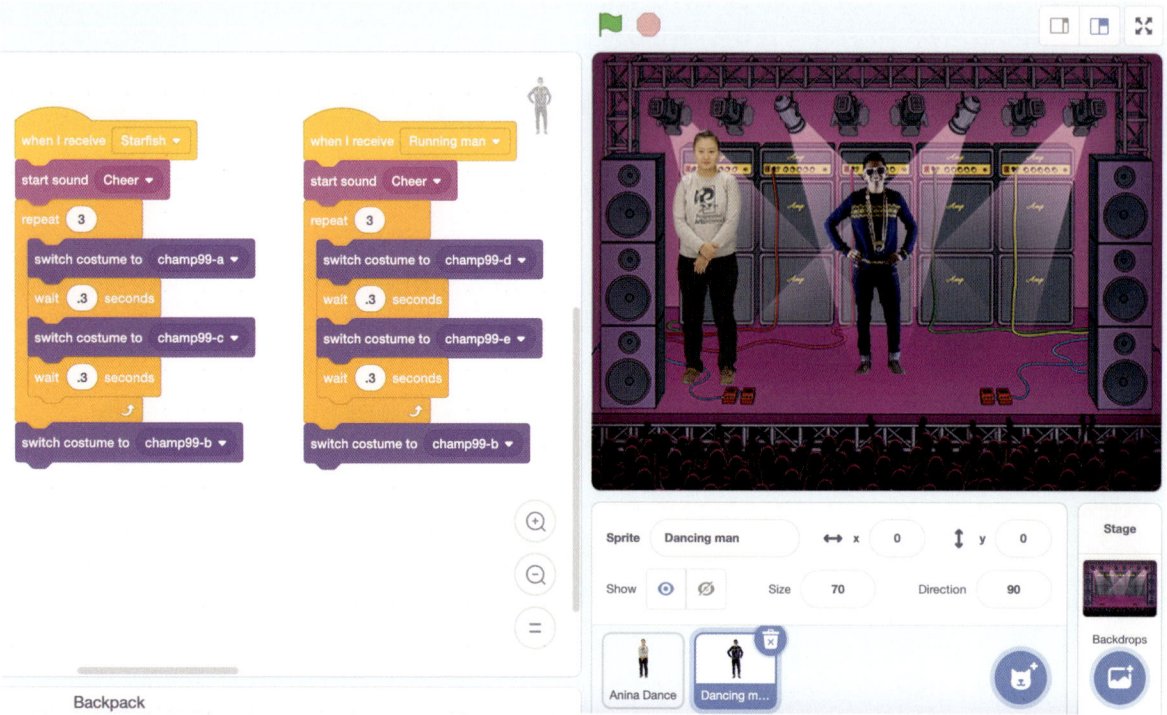

The sprite, Anina (on the left of the stage) uses the 'broadcast' block to call some of these sub-routines which causes the man to dance.

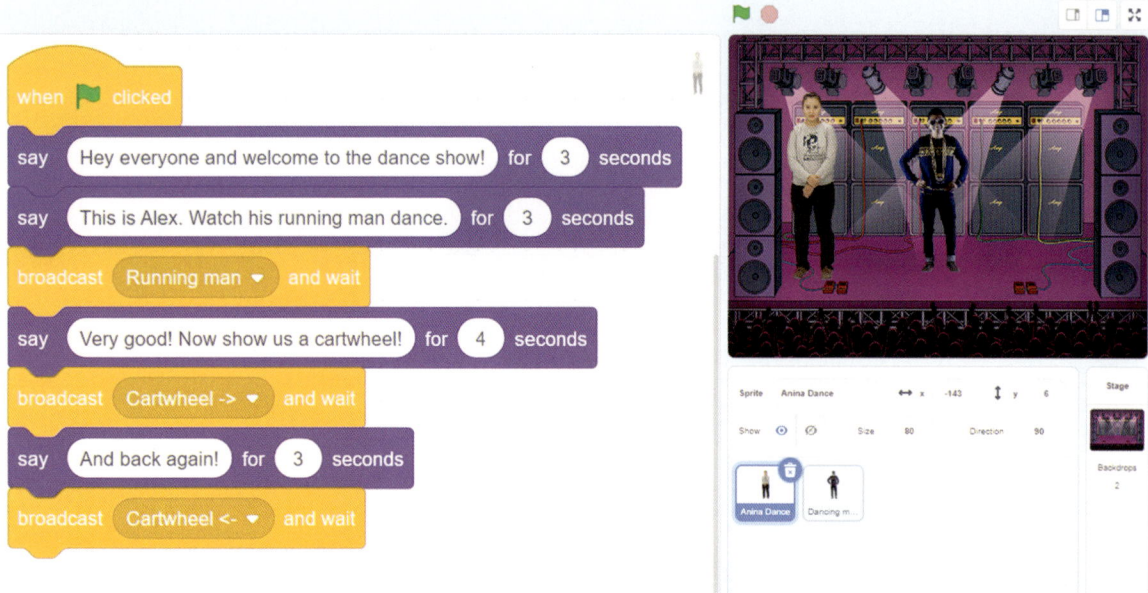

## 1.3 Sub-routines

### Programming task 5

**You will need:** a desktop computer, laptop or tablet, access to Scratch and source file **1.13_dancing_program**

Open source file 1.13_dancing_program.

1. Click on the dancing man sprite and click on the sub-routines.
2. Click the green flag to see what the program does.
3. Modify the female host's algorithm to make the man complete a different combination of his dance moves.
4. Create a new sub-routine for the dancing man and call it from the female host's algorithm.

### Look what I can do!

- ☐ I know that a sub-routine can be used multiple times in an algorithm.
- ☐ I understand how a sub-routine can be used across different algorithms.
- ☐ I understand how to create algorithms with more than one variable.
- ☐ I understand how variables can be used in different algorithms.
- ☐ I can develop a quiz program that uses sub-routines and variables.
- ☐ I can develop a program where two sprites interrelate.

# 1 Computational thinking and programming

## > 1.4 Planning programs

**We are going to:**

- understand how a clear plan can improve a program
- describe how prototypes are useful when designing programs
- create a plan for a programming project
- develop an interface for a program
- use a plan to develop a rock, paper, scissors game in Scratch.

---

decomposition   prototype
interface       prompt
prioritising    random

---

### Getting started

**What do you already know?**

- Variables are used to store data in a program.
- The value stored in a variable can change while a program runs.
- The 'ask' block in Scratch prompts the user for an answer and stores it in the 'answer' variable.
- The 'random' block in Scratch can generate a random number.

> **Continued**
>
> **Now try this!**
>
> Think about a time when you created a program in Scratch. Did you plan what you wanted the program to do before you started programming? How did you do this? Did the plan help you to create your program? Why?
>
> Share your ideas with the rest of the class.

## Planning programs

When programmers work on a new program, they need to plan their work and the project in advance. The program is more likely to be a success if they spend time planning what the program will do and how it might look for the user.

Decomposition is the process of taking a complex problem and breaking it down into smaller parts. These parts can be worked on one by one. Programmers often use decomposition when they write project plans for complicated programs.

A project plan might include a list of these smaller decomposed parts that the program will need to do. It might include sketches and annotations (labels or notes) and it might be handwritten or typed. Different people like to plan their projects in different ways.

In this topic, you are going to create a project plan and an interface prototype for a Scratch game of rock, paper, scissors. You will then follow your project plan to create the game.

# 1 Computational thinking and programming

> **Unplugged activity 1**
>
> **You will need:** a pen and paper
>
> Create a project plan for a Scratch game of rock, paper, scissors for a user to play against the computer.
>
> Use the questions below to help you. On your own, think about each question and what the solution might be. Try to think of as many solutions as you can for each question and write them down.
>
> - How will the game begin?
> - How will the user input their choice of rock, paper or scissors?
> - How will the computer make its choice?
> - How will the program know who has won?
> - How will the sprites react?
> - Will there be a scoring system?
> - How long will the game last?
>
> Now discuss your ideas with your partner. Did you have any similar solutions? Were any of your ideas very different?

*Maybe the game could begin with a welcome message. The sprite could do a cartwheel, and maybe it could ask for the user's name and say hello to them . . .*

## The game interface

It is important when planning a program that you consider what it will look like for the user as well as how the programming will work. The interface is what the user will see on the screen when they use a program. In Scratch, the user may not always see all the code, but they will see how the sprites look, when the backdrops change and any messages that appear.

The interface of a program is really important because it tells or shows the user what they need to do.

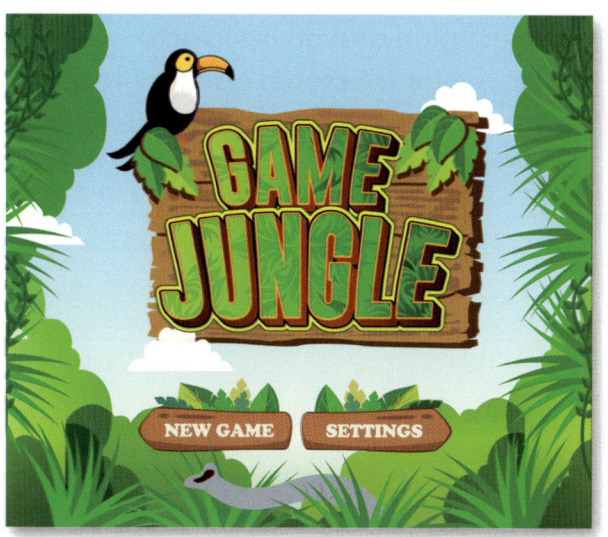

## 1.4 Planning programs

Think about some of your favourite online games. What do you see on the screen when you start the game? Different games might have different controls. At the start of a game there is often a screen with instructions on how to play. Some games use the arrow keys to control a sprite. Other games might use the mouse.

A prompt is a message on the screen that shows a program is waiting for input. Sometimes the interface might prompt you for information, such as your name, which character you want to play as, or to find out whether you are ready to begin. These are important features of the game's interface.

Programmers often use design programs to design an interface for a program, but sometimes they start by sketching their ideas out on paper.

> **Did you know?**
>
> People who work on how a program looks are sometimes called 'front-end developers', while people who work on the programming that users don't see are sometimes called 'back-end developers'.

### Unplugged activity 2

**You will need:** paper and colouring pens or pencils

Design an interface for your rock, paper, scissors game.

Your game's interface will look different at different times. Choose a certain time in your game and draw a sketch of what the interface might look like for your user. Add annotations to your sketch to include more information.

At some times in your game, you might need to add a prompt which will ask the user for information, such as when they need to choose rock, paper or scissors. Annotate your drawings with any prompts you might include.

# 1 Computational thinking and programming

## Continued

Repeat this process for other times or situations in your game. For example:

- the beginning of the game
- when the user has to choose either rock, paper or scissors
- when the user wins a round
- when the user loses a round
- when the game is over.

### How am I doing?

Share your ideas with the rest of the class and compare each other's sketches.

Which ideas did you see on someone else's plan that you might use in your program?

Did you have any ideas that other people wanted to use?

> Developers share programming ideas all the time and it helps them improve.

## Prototypes

When developers create new programs, they often spend time planning what they want the program to do and then create a *prototype* of the program. A prototype is a basic version of something that users can test. The users provide feedback about how the program could be improved. The developers might make changes to the program based on the feedback.

Programmers use prototypes all the time: when designing apps, when creating websites and even when building robots. It is a bit like writing a story: first you might plan what will happen, then you might write a first draft (the prototype) and get feedback from your friends or teachers, and then you might make changes based on the feedback. Even popular games consoles, like the Nintendo DS,

## 1.4 Planning programs

started as a prototype before the final product was released in 2004.

Here are some of the benefits of creating a prototype:

- Allows programmers to see their ideas working in a simple way.
- Helps programmers to think about what else they could add to their program.
- Easier to fix mistakes at the prototype stage.
- Means other people can see how the program might look and add their ideas.
- Allows users to provide feedback at an early stage while it is easy to make changes.

## Questions

1. What activities do you do at school that work best when they have been well planned?
2. What about outside of school?

> **Activity 3**
>
> **You will need:** your interface design from Unplugged activity 2, a desktop computer or laptop, access to Scratch
>
> Use your design from Unplugged activity 2 to create a prototype of the interface for your rock, paper, scissors game.
>
> Your prototype could include:
>
> - a screen design – think about creating a simple graphic
> - a message to welcome the user and explain the rules of the game
> - an 'ask' block to store the user's name in the answer variable.
>
> Your prototype must include:
>
> - a prompt to ask your user if they want to choose rock, paper or scissors.
>
> Remember: you do not need to create the full rock, paper, scissors game!

# Using project plans to develop programs

Once developers have created a project plan and planned and designed the interface of a program, they can start thinking about programming the different parts.

As part of planning, programmers may introduce features such as randomness. This is important in programming, especially with online games. Random means that you can't predict what the outcome will be. In a racing game like Super Mario Kart, you might get a random bonus after driving through a mystery box.

## Prioritising

Once a programmer has created a project plan, they need to decide which part to program first. This is called prioritising. It usually makes sense to prioritise the more complex parts of the problem and work on them first.

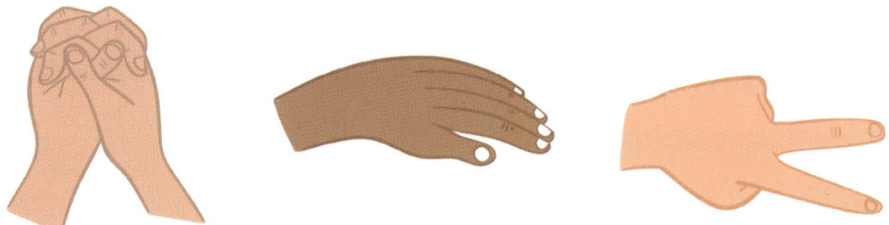

Sofia has created a project plan for the game of rock, paper, scissors. There are two complex parts:

- Program the computer to make a random choice (one that cannot be predicted) of rock, paper or scissors and store that choice.
- Get the program to work out who has won a round – the user or the computer.

Once these parts have been programmed and are working, then other details can become the focus, such as the appearance of sprites and the content of messages.

Which part should I program first?

1.4 Planning programs

# Question

3   Think about games you play online. How is randomness used in the game?

### Activity 4

> You will need: a desktop computer, laptop or tablet, access to Scratch and source file **1.14_Scratch_random_game**

Marcus wants to create a program that randomly says either 'true' or 'false' after his friends have made a statement. He has planned how it should look and he knows that there is a random block in Scratch.
At the moment the program only randomly says 1 or 2 instead of 'true' or 'false'.

Work with a partner. Open source file 1.14 and change the code so that the program says the words 'true' or 'false' randomly.

Share your solution with the rest of the class.

Discuss the different methods people used to add randomness to a program. Which solutions were the most effective? Why?

Try using a conditional block to check if the random number inside the variable is 1 or 2, and then change the variable to be the word 'true' or 'false' instead of 1 or 2.

**1** Computational thinking and programming

### Programming task 1

You will need: a desktop computer, laptop or tablet, access to Scratch, source file **1.15_rock_paper_scissors_game**, a pen and paper

You now need to program this part of Sofia's project plan:

- Program the computer to make a random choice of rock, paper or scissors and then store that choice.

**Part A**

Sofia has tried to create a program that will choose either rock, paper or scissors. With a partner, predict what her code will do and discuss why her code may not work as she expects.

60

1.4 Planning programs

### Continued

Open source file 1.15_rock_paper_scissors_game. Run the code to test whether your predictions were correct.

Now, run the code 10 times and note down the computer's choice each time.

Did you see any blank results? Discuss with your partner why there might be blank results.

#### Part B

Sofia's code contains three conditional IF statements. When the code is run, it picks a new random number each time.

With a partner, modify Sofia's code to see if you can fix this bug.

You want the program to choose the random number once and then store that number somehow . . .

#### How are we doing?

Swap your program with another pair. Test it to see if the program randomly says 'rock', 'paper' or 'scissors'. Test it at least 10 times to check.

Feed back to the other pair.

# Choice combinations

In Programming task 1, you followed Sofia's project plan to program the computer's random choice.

You now need to look at the next parts of Sofia's project plan:

- Allow the user to input their choice of rock, paper or scissors and store that choice.
- Get the program to work out who has won a round – the user or the computer.

There are many possible combinations of the user's choice and the computer's choice. As part of the development process, it is important to think carefully about how your program will decide who has won a round. To do this, you need to consider all possible combinations of answers.

# 1 Computational thinking and programming

## Unplugged activity 5

**You will need:** a pen and paper

For each round of the rock, paper, scissors game, there will be a user choice, a computer choice and then a result (who has won the round, or if it was a draw).

Copy the table below to help you write down all the combinations that you can think of, and the results.

*Is there a way you can do this to make sure that you have thought of all the possibilities?*

| User choice | Computer choice | Result |
|---|---|---|
| Rock | Paper | Computer wins |
| Rock | | |
| | | |

## Turning combinations into conditionals

In the previous activity you helped Sofia to find all the possible choices for her game. One efficient method to find all the possibilities is to first find all the combinations for when the user chooses rock. There are three possibilities because the computer could also choose rock, or paper or scissors. Then if the user chooses paper, there are three more possibilities for the computer's choice. There are three more combinations for if the user chooses scissors. This means there are nine possible combinations in total.

To turn this into code that a program can understand, you can use conditionals (IF, THEN). As there are nine possible combinations, you can use nine conditional statements that will check the choices that the computer and the user have made and then announce the result.

For example:

1    IF the user selects rock THEN
2        IF the computer selects rock THEN
3            the result is a draw
4        IF the computer selects paper THEN
5            the result is the computer wins . . .

### Activity 6

You will need: a desktop computer, laptop or tablet and source file 1.16_conditional_algorithm_template

Write an algorithm in words using conditionals, to show all the possible combinations of user and computer choices.

Use source file 1.16_conditional_algorithm_template to help you.

## User's choice

So far you have created the part of your program that gets the computer to make a random choice of rock, paper or scissors. The next step is to create the part of your program that allows the user to make their choice and then works out who has won.

The user needs to input their choice of rock, paper or scissors. One way to do this is using the 'ask' block. This will store the user's response in the 'answer' and then the program can compare this with the computer's choice.

# 1 Computational thinking and programming

## Activity 7

> **You will need:** a desktop computer, laptop or tablet, access to Scratch and source file **1.17_Sofia_rock_paper_scissors**

Sofia has started to create the rock, paper, scissors program but it is incomplete. She is trying to complete this part of her project plan:

- *Allow the user to input their choice of rock, paper or scissors and store that choice.*

Open source file 1.17_Sofia_rock_paper_scissors. You can see that Sofia has decided to use two sub-routines that are called from the main code on the left.

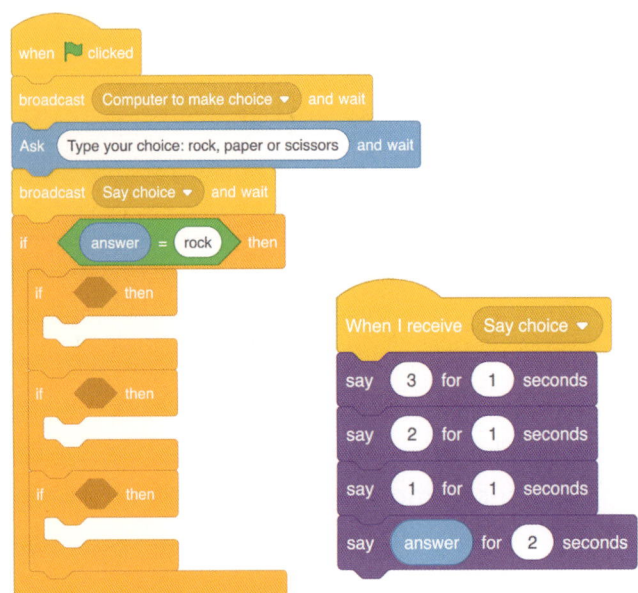
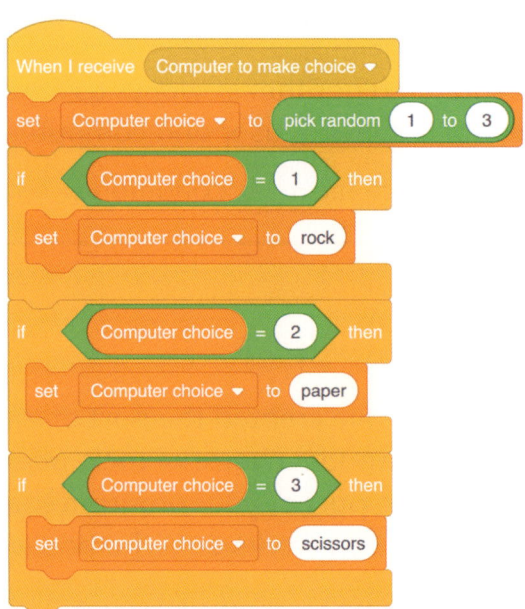

Work with a partner and discuss what the code does.
Then label the sub-routines with what they do, using comments.

1.4 Planning programs

So far, the program generates a random choice for the computer, it asks the user for their choice and then it counts down from 3 and displays both choices at once. But that is all it does. It doesn't yet know which player has won the round or whether it's a draw.

> **Programming task 2**
>
>
>
> **You will need:** a desktop computer, laptop or tablet, access to Scratch, source file **1.17_Sofia_rock_paper_scissors**, your completed table from Unplugged activity 5
>
> ### Part A
>
> You now need to complete this part of Sofia's project plan:
>
> - Get the program to work out who has won a round: the user or the computer.
>
> Use your table from Unplugged activity 5 to help you. Modify Sofia's program so that it can decide who has won the round and then announce the result.
>
> Focus on getting the program to work *only* when the user selects 'rock' first.
>
> Test your program:
>
> - What happens when you enter the choice 'rock'?
> - What happens if you enter something else as your choice?
>
> ### Part B
>
> Now your program can work out the result if the user enters rock, but not if they enter anything else. Continue modifying your code so that it will work if the user selects 'paper' or 'scissors'.
>
>
>
> You could use the 'Duplicate' feature to save you having to put together lots of the same blocks. Try right-clicking a section of code and selecting 'Duplicate'.

# 1 Computational thinking and programming

## Programming task 3

**You will need:** a desktop computer, laptop or tablet, access to Scratch, your project plan from Unplugged activity 1 and your interface prototype from Activity 3

Now you have all the programming parts ready for your game of rock, paper, scissors. Use your project plan and interface prototype to start to develop your game.

Are there any extra features you might add to your game? If you decide to make changes to your plan, that's OK. Programmers do this all the time.

### How am I doing?

Swap your program with a partner. Run your partner's program and then compare your programs.

- How are your programs similar?
- How are they different?
- Explain to your partner how the project plan helped you to develop your program.
- Tell your partner what you would do differently if you were to start again from the beginning.

---

Some programmers like to write really detailed plans that they stick to when programming. Others like to write less detailed plans and come up with new ideas while they program. Discuss with your partner how you prefer to plan when programming and why.

---

### Look what I can do!

- [ ] I understand how a clear plan can improve a program.
- [ ] I can describe the role of prototypes when designing a program.
- [ ] I can create a plan for a programming project.
- [ ] I can develop an interface for a program.
- [ ] I can use my plan to develop a rock, paper, scissors game in Scratch.

# > 1.5 Evaluating and testing programs

**We are going to:**
- think of criteria for a program and use them to evaluate a program
- test a program using a range of data.

evaluation    systematic
success criteria    user experience

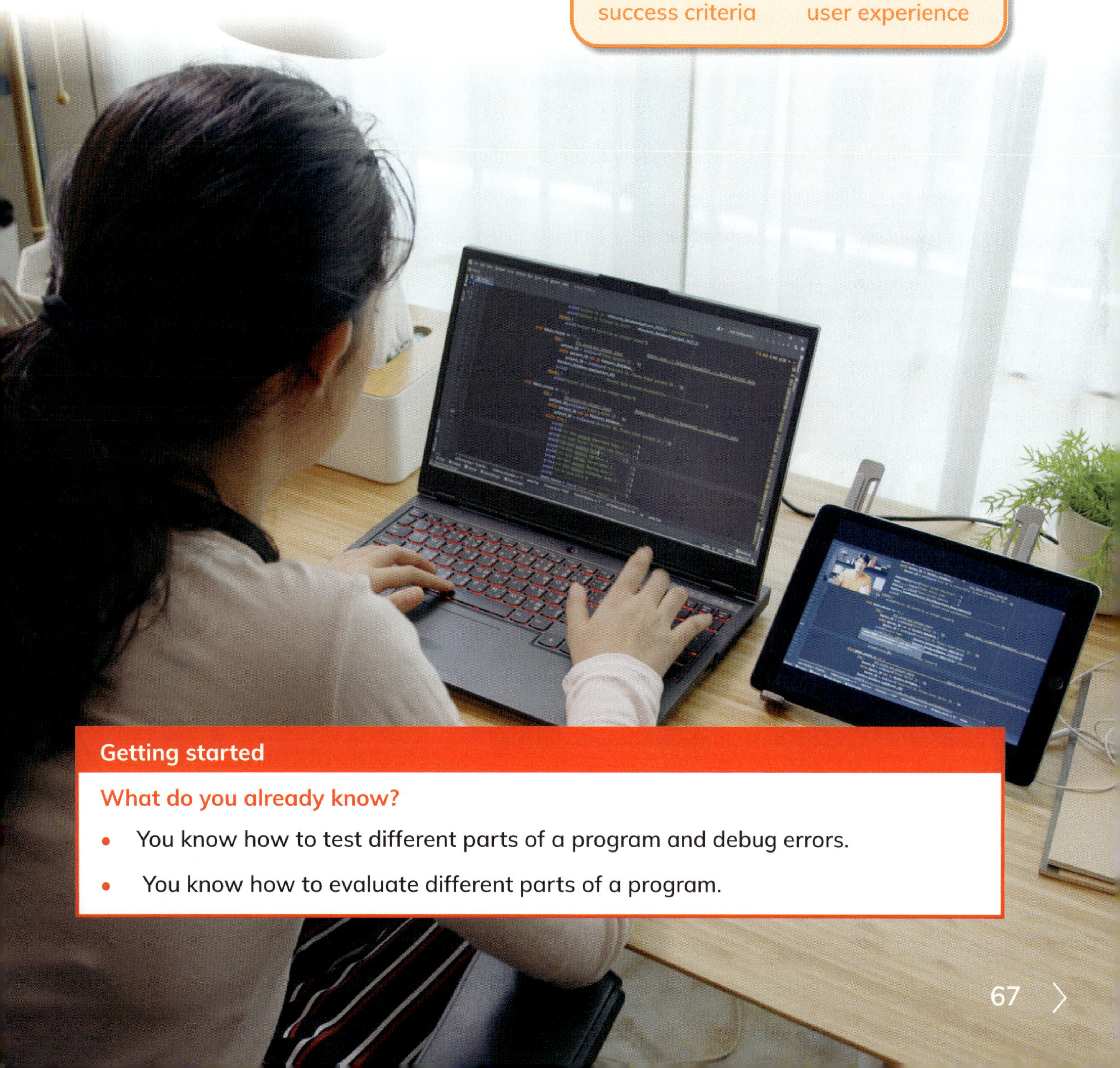

**Getting started**

**What do you already know?**
- You know how to test different parts of a program and debug errors.
- You know how to evaluate different parts of a program.

67

1 Computational thinking and programming

> **Continued**
>
> **Now try this!**
>
> Sofia is trying to reduce how much paper and ink she uses. She decides to send Marcus an online birthday card that she created using Scratch.
>
> Have a look at the code for her project.
>
> ```
> when [flag] clicked
> switch backdrop to Happy birthday
> show
> start sound Cheer
> play sound Birthday until done
> switch backdrop to From Sofia
> say I hope you have a great day! for 1 seconds
> hide
> switch backdrop to Message for Marcus...
> ```
>
> ```
> when [flag] clicked
> forever
>   next costume
>   wait .2 seconds
> ```
>
> With a partner, evaluate Sofia's program. Think about which parts you like and which parts could be improved. Share your ideas with the rest of the class.

# Evaluation

**Evaluation** means thinking about what we like or dislike about something and how it can be improved.

Evaluation is an important skill in life and something that often takes place in your classroom or in activities outside of school, such as hobbies. You might create a work of art and then evaluate what you did well and what you could have done better.

Evaluation is one of the ways we keep learning and keep improving.

Think of a time when you evaluated something that you created. How did it help?

## 1.5 Evaluating and testing programs

> **Programming task 1**
>
> **You will need:** a desktop computer, laptop or tablet, access to Scratch and source file **1.18_Marcus_polar_bear**
>
> Open source file 1.18_Marcus_polar_bear and run Marcus's animation. Work with a partner to discuss what you like about the program and how it could be improved.
>
> Modify the project with your partner to make the improvements you have suggested.

# Success criteria

To make evaluations more effective, we need success criteria. Success criteria can be used to tell us what a program should do in order to be successful. Different programs have different success criteria. Having a defined set of success criteria can help to focus our evaluations and make it easier to see what we could do to improve a project.

> **Unplugged activity 1**
>
> Marcus asked both Arun and Sofia to evaluate the polar bear animation. The animation should tell a story that makes sense. Arun did not receive any success criteria but Sofia received the following criteria:
>
> - The sizes of the sprites should be appropriate.
> - The text should appear for long enough for a user to read.
> - The animation should make sense.
> - The program should use 'repeat' loops.
>
> With a partner, have a look at the two evaluations below. Discuss which evaluation you think is more effective and why.

I really liked Marcus's animation. I liked that the polar bear did a backflip, but it was a bit small.

The size of the sprites could be improved by making the polar bear bigger and the llama smaller. The text didn't appear on the screen for long enough — perhaps it could have been there for three or four seconds instead of one. I liked how it used a repeat loop to do a backflip.

**1** Computational thinking and programming

## Defining success criteria

When defining criteria for a successful project, you should think about what the project needs to do.

In Programming task 1, the polar bear animation was supposed to tell a story that made sense. It needed characters to tell the story using text in speech bubbles.

Your teachers may define criteria for your work. For example, in an art project, recreate a piece of art in the style of an established artist. In a science experiment, you might be successful if you explain how it was a fair test.

In the next activity, you are going to work together to define criteria for a successful rock, paper, scissors game.

## User experience

Whenever you use a computer program, whether you are playing an online game or typing in a document, everything you see and hear in the program is part of the *user experience*. This is the experience you have (how you feel) as a user of that program. It does not include the actual programming code because users almost never see the code.

Programmers think very carefully about user experience. In a word-processing program like Word or Google Docs, developers have thought carefully about where the menus will go, how the page will look and which buttons should be on display.

> **Did you know?**
>
> The user experience of computer programs (sometimes shortened to UX) has changed a lot over time. If you have ever played old games or seen videos of old software, you will know how much user experience has improved.

## Questions

1. Have you used any programs where the user experience was really good? What were they?
2. Have you used any programs where the user experience was really bad? What were they?
3. What was it about these programs that made it a good or bad user experience?

**Unplugged activity 2**

> You will need: a pen and paper

In the previous topic, you created a rock, paper, scissors game in Scratch.

Look back to Topic 1.4 and read the description of what the game needs to do. Define criteria you could use to evaluate the user experience of these games. What would a successful game include?

Discuss your ideas in small groups of four and decide on a set of success criteria that you can use to evaluate your games. Write your group ideas down and then share them with the rest of the class. Decide as a class what the success criteria should be.

**How are we doing?**

Swap your rock, paper, scissors game with a partner and use the criteria you decided on as a class to evaluate each other's games. Tell your partner what they have done well and how they could improve the user experience of their game.

Listen to your partner's evaluation of your game. If you agree with them, make the changes to your project. You could even add a note in the Scratch project page to say this is now version 2, 3 or 4.

**1** Computational thinking and programming

## Improving the code

You may have noticed that sometimes an update becomes available for you to install on your device. In order to keep your device running well, you need to install the latest software update.

The reason you sometimes need to update digital devices and software is because there are teams of developers constantly trying to improve the code for the programs you use. Developers may need to run an update to fix errors in the code, or they may think of ways to improve the user experience. They do this by creating updates to the programs, which you need to accept and apply before you can see the improvements.

> **Stay safe!**
>
> It is always a good idea to install software updates because they often contain security improvements that can keep your device safe and secure.

> Don't feel bad if a classmate finds things to improve in your programs. The biggest tech companies in the world find ways to improve their programs too!

## Testing programs

When a software developer wants to release a new program, they will test that program before they let members of the public use it.

However, even after a program has been released, the developers might still find errors or improvements to make. This is why you sometimes get software updates.

## 1.5 Evaluating and testing programs

> **Did you know?**
>
> Sometimes programs are released that haven't been properly tested. One famous online game was released before it was ready and it contained lots of bugs in the code. Users from around the world complained and it got such bad reviews that the game company had to give everyone their money back. The company lost millions of dollars.

Just as developers test their programs before releasing them to the general public, you should thoroughly test your rock, paper, scissors game before sharing it on Scratch. If it works successfully every time, then you can be more confident that there are no bugs in your code. If you do find any bugs, then you can go back to your code and correct the errors.

### Programming task 2

> **You will need:** a desktop computer, laptop or tablet, access to Scratch and your rock, paper, scissors game from Topic 1.4 or source file **1.19_rock_paper_scissors_game**

You now need to test the program using a range of data.

1. What would happen if the user entered something you didn't expect, for example 'bananas'? Test your program to see what happens.
2. Now you are going to try other data types. Try entering a number and write down what happens. Then enter a single letter and note down what happens.
3. How *should* your program react if the user enters unexpected data? Discuss this question with a partner and share your solutions with the class.

**1** Computational thinking and programming

## Systematic testing

**Systematic** testing means thinking carefully about the way you will test something instead of just testing it randomly. Imagine that your friend had developed a calculator app in Scratch and wanted you to test it for them. One way to test it systematically would be to start by inputting some addition calculations and checking that the answers were accurate. Next you might test subtraction, then multiplication and then division. If all of the answers were accurate, you could be more confident that the app was working correctly because there was a system to your testing.

Another important thing to consider when testing a program is the number of times you run the code. The more times you run your program successfully, the more confident you can be that it will always show the correct result. How many times do you think it would be reasonable to test your code?

I will test my code 15 times and if it is correct every time, I can be very confident that my program has no bugs.

I like your systematic thinking!

Good idea, Marcus. I am going to test my program five times for rock, five for paper and five for scissors.

1.5 Evaluating and testing programs

**Programming task 3**

You will need: a pen and paper, a desktop computer, laptop or tablet, access to Scratch and source file **1.20_Marcus_rock_paper_scissors**

Marcus has created a rock, paper, scissors game.

Open source file 1.20_Marcus_rock_paper_scissors. Work in pairs to test Marcus's program 15 times. Copy the table below to help you record the results.

For the first five tests:

- input the data 'rock'
- record the computer's choice
- record whether the program announces the result correctly.

Repeat this five times with 'paper', and finally repeat it five times using 'scissors'.

| Attempt | User choice | Computer choice | Who should win? | Who did win? | Was the program correct? |
|---|---|---|---|---|---|
| 1 | | | | | |
| 2 | | | | | |

Maybe one of you can input the choice while the other can record the outcomes in the table?

Make sure you spell the choices correctly!

What did you notice when you typed 'paper' into Marcus's game? How might you correct Marcus's code?

If you created your own game in Topic 1.4, test your code using the same table to check that your program works correctly.

**1** Computational thinking and programming

The best programmers get excited when they find a 'bug' in their code because it means they know it is there, so they can solve the problem and improve their program.

Next time you find a mistake in your code (which happens to everyone), see if you can feel positive about it!

## Questions

4  How did you test the program in a systematic way?
5  If you found any bugs, how did you fix them?
6  Would you rather find no bugs in code or lots of bugs? Why? Discuss your answers with the rest of your class.

What would you need to consider when testing future programs in this way?

How could systematic thinking be used in other areas of your life?

**Look what I can do!**

☐  I can define and use criteria to evaluate a program.

☐  I can test a program using a range of data.

# > 1.6 Using variables with a physical device

## We are going to:

- develop a game for the BBC micro:bit that uses inputs and variables
- develop a game for the micro:bit that generates an output.

function
input
input–process–output (IPO) model
output

physical programming device
portable game console
process

## Getting started

### What do you already know?

- You know how to use the MakeCode interface to program a micro:bit.
- You know how to use a condition to check if a micro:bit has received an input.
- You know how to describe the input–process–output model.
- You know how to create programs that produce an output from a micro:bit when you use micro:bit inputs.

# 1 Computational thinking and programming

## Continued

### Now try this!

Play a game of 'higher or lower'. Your teacher will call out a random number between 1 and 9. Decide whether the next random number will be higher or lower.

If you think the next number will be higher, go to one side of the room. If you think the next number will be lower, go to the other side of the room.

If your guess is correct, you stay in the game and play again. If your guess is incorrect, go back to your seat.

The game continues until there is a winner!

Did you have a strategy for choosing your numbers?

I have a strategy that I use for 'higher or lower'. If the number is above 5 I predict that the next number will be lower. If it is below 5 I predict the next number will be higher.

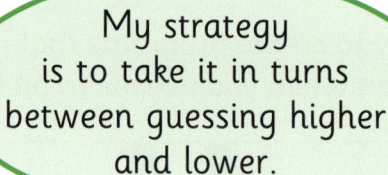

My strategy is to take it in turns between guessing higher and lower.

1.6 Using variables with a physical device

# Computing devices

Computers need an input device so that they can receive information. An input device allows a user to provide input (tell the computer what they want it to do). The input device could be:

- a keyboard or a mouse for a laptop computer

- a button or touchscreen for a smart watch

- a microphone for a voice-controlled computer.

When the computer has received an input, it processes the data according to its programming. To process means to carry out calculations and instructions. The computer then provides an output back to the user. An output is information that the program gives to the user. The output could be information displayed on a screen or it could be music that plays through a speaker.

For example, you might press some buttons on a calculator (input), then the calculator will work out the answer (process) and then it will display the answer on its screen (output). All of this happens very quickly.

**1** Computational thinking and programming

This is an example of the input–process–output (IPO) model. The IPO model is a way of describing how a program or system operates: it takes in data, works on it, then gives out data.

## Computer games

Personal computers have been around since the 1970s. This photo shows one example of what computers used to look like.

Soon after electronic computers were invented, people started using them to program simple games.

As computers became more complicated, so did computer games. You may have heard of classic computer games such as PacMan, Space Invaders and Frogger.

> **Did you know?**
>
> The first ever machine that could be considered a computer was designed in 1837 by an English mathematician called Charles Babbage. He called his machine the Analytical Engine. Ada Lovelace, daughter of the poet Lord Byron, was one of the first people to 'program' this 'computer' and therefore she was one of the first ever computer programmers.

All of these games had to be quite simple. They looked very two-dimensional (2D) and they didn't use many colours, unlike many of the more advanced computer games you might play today. This is because the computers at that time were not as powerful as they are now.

## 1.6 Using variables with a physical device

As technology improved, computer scientists developed the portable game console – a small, handheld computer that didn't need to be plugged in like other computers did. This meant that for the first time, people could take their game consoles wherever they liked and play games outside their home.

Portable game consoles normally used buttons as their input devices and had a small screen to display the output to the user.

## Physical programming devices

A physical programming device is a computing device that you can program.

The micro:bit is an example of a physical programming device. It is a small, programmable device that has a variety of inputs (such as buttons) and outputs (such as the LED display). You can write code on your computer using the MakeCode interface and then download the program to your micro:bit.

**1** Computational thinking and programming

Just as computer programmers develop computer games for consoles, you are going to create code for a game that you will download to a micro:bit. It will use buttons as its input devices and the screen as its output device. Once your game is downloaded onto the micro:bit you can take your game out into the playground, like your very own portable game console!

Think of a game you have played before. Whole teams of developers would have planned exactly how that game should start, which buttons you should press and other details about how the game looks. They would have spent months developing, testing and updating the code before the game was ready for users to play.

In this topic, you are going to work like a game developer to plan and program a micro:bit version of the game 'higher or lower'.

> ### Unplugged activity 1
>
> - Think about when you have used a micro:bit in the past.
> - Discuss with a partner how you might program a micro:bit to play the game 'higher or lower'. How might the user find out the first number? How might they tell the device they think the next number will be higher or lower?
> - Share your ideas with the rest of the class.

### Stay safe!

When you use a physical computing device like the micro:bit, some of the electrical components are on the outside of the device. It is best to handle the device by its edges when the power is running.

Since the micro:bit is a small and simple computer, it uses the input–process–output (IPO) model.

The micro:bit has a variety of input devices, including buttons, a microphone and other sensors. (Older versions of a micro:bit may have different input or output devices.) This means your user could input data (tell the device what to do) by shaking it, pressing a button or tilting it.

## 1.6 Using variables with a physical device

The program that you create in MakeCode and then download to the micro:bit allows the device to process the input. For the game of 'higher or lower', the process will involve working out if the number is higher or lower and what to do if the user is correct or incorrect.

The micro:bit has a variety of output devices, including a tiny speaker and a screen made up of LEDs. If the user guesses correctly, you could program the speaker to play a sound or you could use the screen to display a simple message.

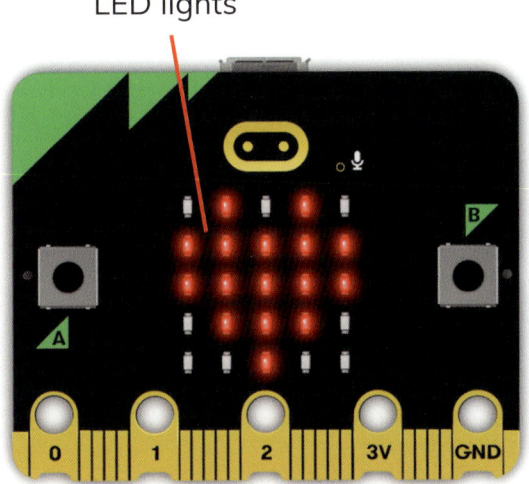

Front of micro:bit

Back of micro:bit

### Programming task 1

**You will need:** a desktop computer, laptop or tablet, access to Scratch and source file **1.21_higher_or_lower**

#### Part A

Marcus and Sofia have worked together to develop a 'higher or lower' game using Scratch. In their game, the user inputs their choice of higher or lower by clicking on the higher or lower sprite. They use sub-routines: one for 'Correct guess' and one for 'Incorrect guess'. With a partner, look at their code and predict what will happen when this code runs.

**1** Computational thinking and programming

### Continued

```
when I receive [Incorrect guess ▼]
stop all sounds
switch costume to [dinosaur4-d ▼]
play sound [Clown Honk ▼] until done
say (join [The next number was] (Next random number)) for (3) seconds
switch costume to [dinosaur4-c ▼]
say (join [Game over! You scored] (Correct guesses in a row)) for (4) seconds
stop [all ▼]
```

### Part B

Open source file 1.21_higher_or_lower and take it in turns with a partner to play this version of 'higher or lower'.
Were your predictions correct?

### Part C

Look at the code. Choose one block of code and discuss what it does with your partner.

Look through all of the other blocks of code in the program. Remember to click on all the sprites and the backdrop too.

Add comments to each of the blocks of code describing what they do. Include as much information as possible.

With the rest of your class, discuss any of the blocks that you weren't sure about, or that you found difficult to describe.

*Who will get the most correct guesses in a row?*

1.6 Using variables with a physical device

# Adapting the game for micro:bit

The game in Programming task 1 was developed for Scratch but you are going to develop your game for the micro:bit.

## Unplugged activity 2

**You will need:** a pen and paper

Discuss with your partner which parts of the Scratch game might be similar in your micro:bit game and which parts might be different.

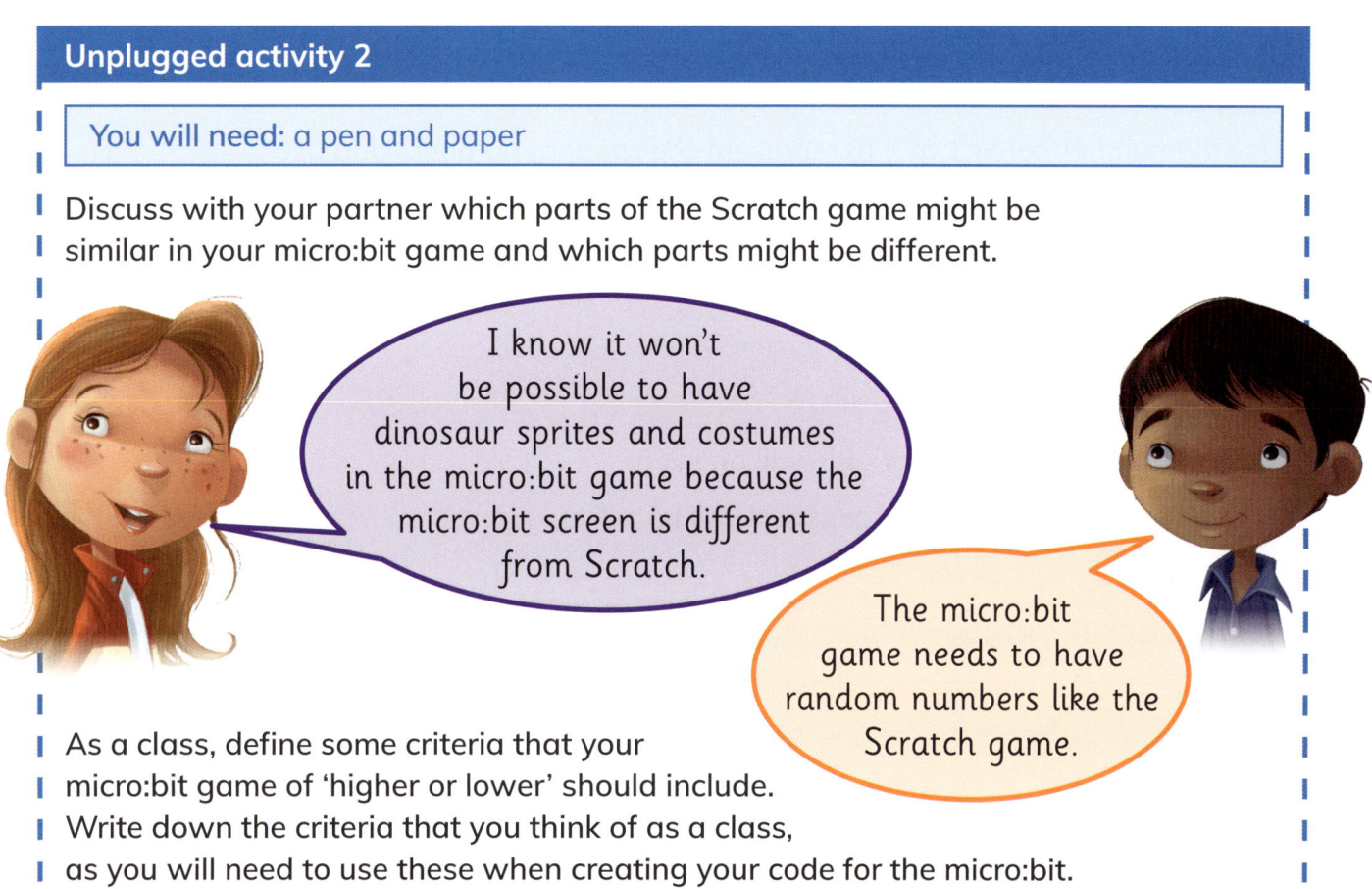

I know it won't be possible to have dinosaur sprites and costumes in the micro:bit game because the micro:bit screen is different from Scratch.

The micro:bit game needs to have random numbers like the Scratch game.

As a class, define some criteria that your micro:bit game of 'higher or lower' should include. Write down the criteria that you think of as a class, as you will need to use these when creating your code for the micro:bit.

Before starting a complex programming task, it is important to understand what you want your program to do at different points, for example when a user starts the program or provides an input.

One way to do this is to act out your code. This means going through the program step by step and 'performing' or 'telling the story' of what should be happening. If there are points in your program that you don't fully understand, this gives you a chance to discuss what the solution might be before you begin programming.

# 1 Computational thinking and programming

## Unplugged activity 3

> **You will need:** Resource sheet 1.16, three containers, a large, clear space on a table

Act out your code.

Cut out the number cards on Resource sheet 1.16.

Use the number cards 1 to 9 to represent the random numbers and use three spaces or containers on your table to represent the variables. Tell the story of how your code will run during the game.

Use these sentence starters if you need them:

- When the user begins the program . . .
- The score variable will be set to . . .
- The Random number variable will be set to . . .
- The Next random number variable will be set to . . .
- The user will be shown . . .
- If they think the next number will be higher they will . . .
- If they think the next number will be lower they will . . .
- If they input their choice as lower, the program will . . .
- If they input their choice as higher, the program will . . .
- If they were correct, the program will . . .
- If they were incorrect, the program will . . .

### How am I doing?

Give yourself a mark from 1 to 5 for the following statements.
1 is 'not confident' and 5 is 'very confident'.

- I understand how I am going to use variables in my program.
- I know how the user will choose higher or lower.
- I know what will happen if the user guesses correctly.
- I know what will happen if the user guesses incorrectly.

1.6 Using variables with a physical device

## Using sub-routines in MakeCode

In Scratch, you can create sub-routines using the 'broadcast' block. In the Scratch 'higher or lower' game, the 'Incorrect guess' sub-routine runs when a user makes an incorrect guess, and the 'broadcast' block is used.

There is no 'broadcast' block in the MakeCode interface . Instead, you need to use a *function*. A function is a separate section of code that runs when it is called from the main code. It may be called several times when a program runs. This is very similar to how a 'broadcast' block works.

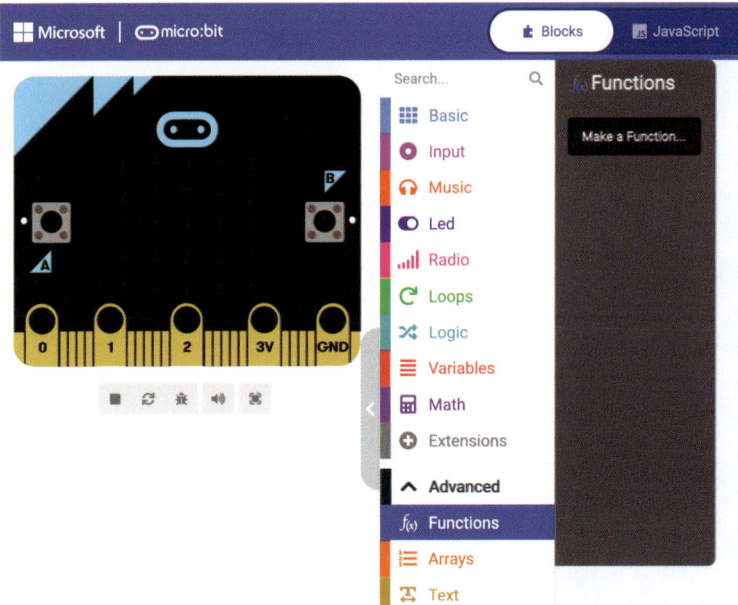

Programmers use functions in their code to:
- make the code clearer to read
- reduce the amount of repetition (so the same blocks of code aren't repeated again and again). This makes programs shorter and more efficient
- make it easier to fix bugs – a function only needs to be checked and corrected once, instead of having to correct the same error lots of times where code is repeated.

# 1 Computational thinking and programming

If Sofia and Marcus's Scratch game didn't include sub-routines, it would be one long stack of code with lots of repeated blocks!

> **Did you know?**
>
> You can create your own functions in Scratch using the 'Make a Block' button.

## Programming task 2

**You will need:** a desktop computer, laptop or tablet, access to the internet and source file **1.22_function_example**

### Part A

Look at the code below. Discuss with your partner what you think it does. Try to include the words 'function', 'sub-routine' and 'broadcast' in your discussion.

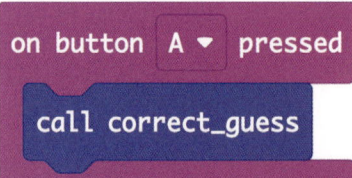

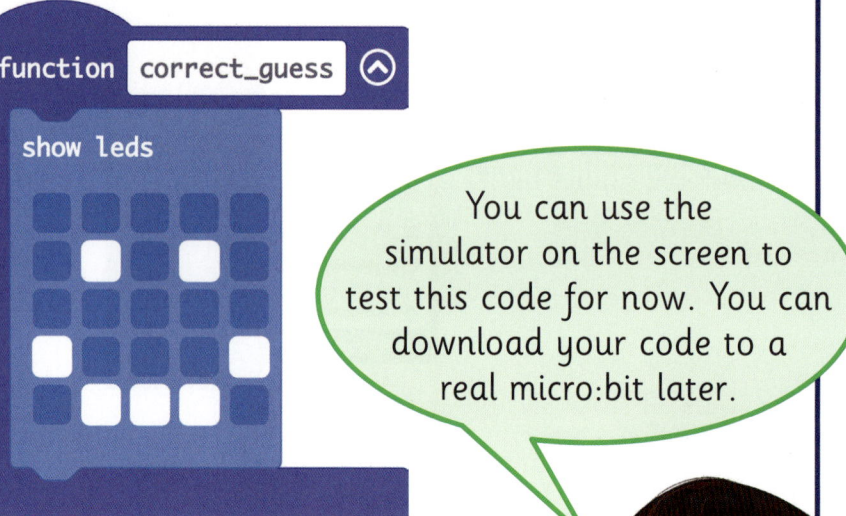

> You can use the simulator on the screen to test this code for now. You can download your code to a real micro:bit later.

Go to the MakeCode website, click 'Import' and open source file 1.22_function_example. Run it using the micro:bit simulator on the left side of the screen.

1. What happens when you click button A on the simulator?
2. What happens when you click button B?
3. How can you reset the program?

1.6 Using variables with a physical device

## Continued

### Part B

Click the 'Edit' button at the top of the screen to modify the program.

Add another function that will do something different when the user presses button B.

Under 'Advanced', click 'Functions' and then 'Make a Function . . .'. Give your function a name, tell the program what it should do when it is called, then program it to be called when button B is pressed.

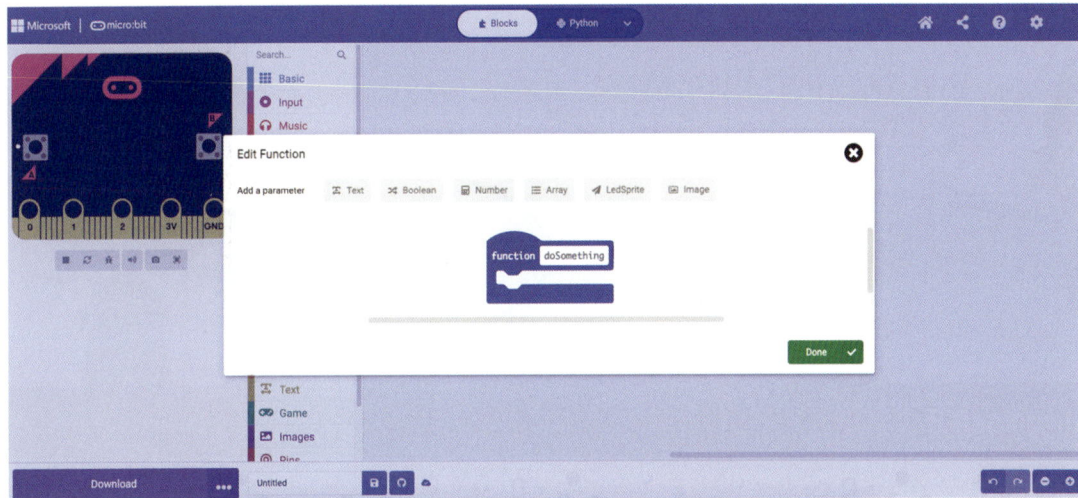

Use the simulator to test your program. When you are happy with your program, download it onto a micro:bit and test it.

### How are we doing?

Swap your program with a partner and test each other's programs. Check the following:

- The program has a function for button B.
- The function is called when button B is pressed.
- The program works on the micro:bit.

# 1 Computational thinking and programming

## Planning your game

Now that you understand how functions work, it's time to program your 'higher or lower' game for the micro:bit. Before you begin, it is a good idea to decompose the project into smaller parts. Programmers decompose complex projects and then decide who will work on the different parts.

My first task is to get the micro:bit to show a random number when the program starts. I will focus on that first and then move onto the next task.

Let's get coding!

### Programming task 3

> You will need: a desktop computer, laptop or tablet, access to the internet, your list of criteria from Unplugged activity 2 and source file **1.23_higher_or_lower**

Open source file 1.23_higher_or_lower. In this project, one of the functions and some of the variables have already been created, but others still need to be created. Most of the functions are not complete so the program is not finished. Click the 'Edit Code' button to work on this project and develop your own 'higher or lower' game for the micro:bit.

**How am I doing?**

Look at the criteria you thought of as a class in Unplugged activity 2. Does your game meet all of the criteria?

If your game doesn't meet all the criteria, what else do you need to do?

1.6 Using variables with a physical device

> **Continued**
>
> If your project does meet all the criteria, how could you extend your game?

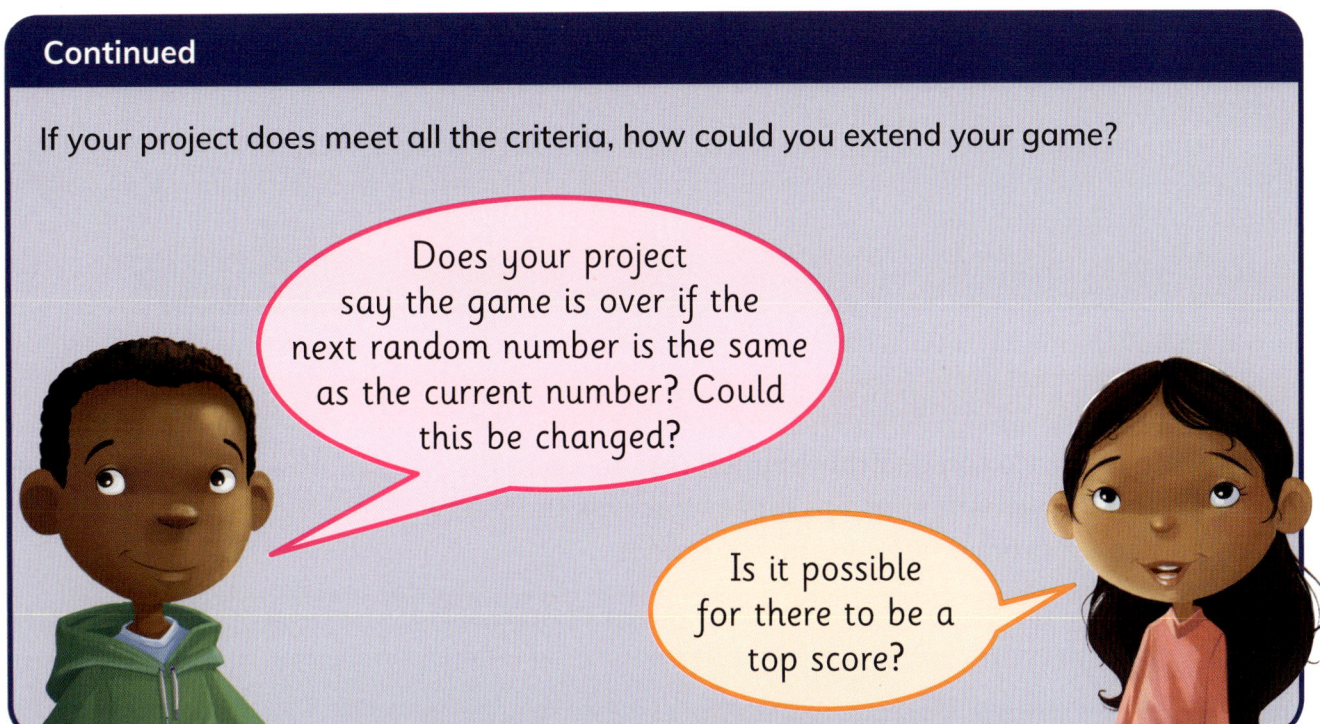

> Does your project say the game is over if the next random number is the same as the current number? Could this be changed?

> Is it possible for there to be a top score?

### Activity 4

> **You will need:** a desktop computer or laptop, a micro:bit, a mini USB cable and access to the MakeCode website; or a tablet, a micro:bit, a battery pack and access to the MakeCode app, your 'higher or lower' game from Programming task 3 and a cable to connect the micro:bit to the computer

Once your game is working, download the program onto your micro:bit. Attach a battery pack to your micro:bit so that you can take your game around with you.

Take your higher or lower game with you at break time and let other learners play your game. Make sure you ask your users for feedback after they have played your game.

- What did users like about your game?
- What did users think could be improved?
- Share your feedback with the rest of the class.

91

**1** Computational thinking and programming

You have developed programs in MakeCode for the micro:bit and in Scratch. Which coding environment do you prefer to use and why?

Discuss your answer with a partner and then share your ideas with the rest of your class.

### Did you know?

Many other games can be programmed for the micro:bit. The MakeCode website contains lots of tutorials that show you how to program different types of games.

### Look what I can do!

- ☐ I can develop a 'higher or lower' game for the micro:bit that uses inputs and variables.
- ☐ I can develop a game for the micro:bit that generates an output.

1.6 Using variables with a physical device

> **Project**
>
> **Create a Scratch quiz**
>
> With a partner, you are going to create a quiz in Scratch. Using what you have learnt throughout this unit, complete the following tasks.
>
> - Write a list of success criteria for your program.
> - Draw a flowchart algorithm for the program.
> - Create a project plan for the program.
> - Create a prototype of the program.
> - Develop the program.
> - Test and evaluate the program.
>
> Here are some ideas for what you could include in your quiz:
>
> - a score variable
> - different levels with different backgrounds
> - questions that become more difficult as you progress through the different levels
> - different reactions when the user gets a question correct or incorrect
> - sprite animations
> - a timer or countdown for answers.

# 1 Computational thinking and programming

## Check your progress

1. In a flowchart, what shape are decisions? (Hint: They usually have a 'Yes' and 'No' arrow coming from them.)

2. What three data types did you explore earlier in the unit?

3. In Scratch, which block would you use if you wanted to include a conditional statement in your program?

4. A variable in Scratch contains information that always stays the same. Explain whether you agree or disagree with this statement and give an example.

5. Explain what the green 'join' block does in Scratch.

6. In Scratch, event blocks are used to start a program. For example, 'When green flag clicked' is an event block. Write down as many other event blocks as you can remember.

7. Explain what a sub-routine is and why it can be useful in programming.

8. How might a sub-routine be used in a quiz?

9. What does IPO stand for?

10. Give some examples of inputs and outputs on a micro:bit.

# 2 Managing data

## > 2.1 Capturing data

**We are going to:**

- identify the different computing tools that you can use in a statistical investigation
- explore how to plan a statistical investigation
- explore how to collect continuous data
- design an appropriate form to collect continuous data.

---

collaborate
continuous data
criteria
questionnaire

question type
statistical investigation
validation rules

---

**Getting started**

**What do you already know?**

- What a statistical investigation is.
- The range of tools that can be used in a statistical investigation, including:
    - data loggers, such as sensors recording temperatures every hour
    - spreadsheets, which can be used to keep track of data such as expenses
    - databases, such as a collection of information about where people like to go on holiday
    - other productivity software, such as a word processor for writing up the investigation.
- How to collect categorical and discrete data.

## 2 Managing data

> **Continued**
>
> **Now try this!**
>
> Look at these descriptions of statistical investigations.
>
> 1. An investigation to find out the temperature of a home throughout the day
>
> 2. An investigation to find out who is the oldest in a class
>
> 3. An investigation to find out the most popular type of drink in the school canteen
>
> What type of data is collected in each investigation – discrete, categorical or continuous data?
>
> How could you collect the data in each investigation?

# Statistical investigations

A statistical investigation is the collection of data to help you find the answer to a question. For example, Sofia might want to find out the mean number of goals she scored in every football match she played in a month. Sofia could look at each match and then work out the mean.

Remember, you can calculate the mean by adding all of the numbers up and dividing the total by the number of numbers you have!

| Match | Number of goals |
|---|---|
| 1st | 3 |
| 2nd | 5 |
| 3rd | 1 |
| 4th | 2 |
| Mean | 2.75 |

2.1 Capturing data

Arun might want to find out how many different birds he sees in his garden in an hour. He could count the birds he sees over the space of an hour to find this out. This is another example of a statistical investigation.

## Different types of data

There are three types of data: categorical, discrete and continuous data.

Categorical data can be grouped into categories. It is usually an opinion, a description of something or a range of numbers. Examples include favourite cupcake flavour, colour of pet, favourite type of cat, favourite lesson, favourite book and age group such as 7 to 11.

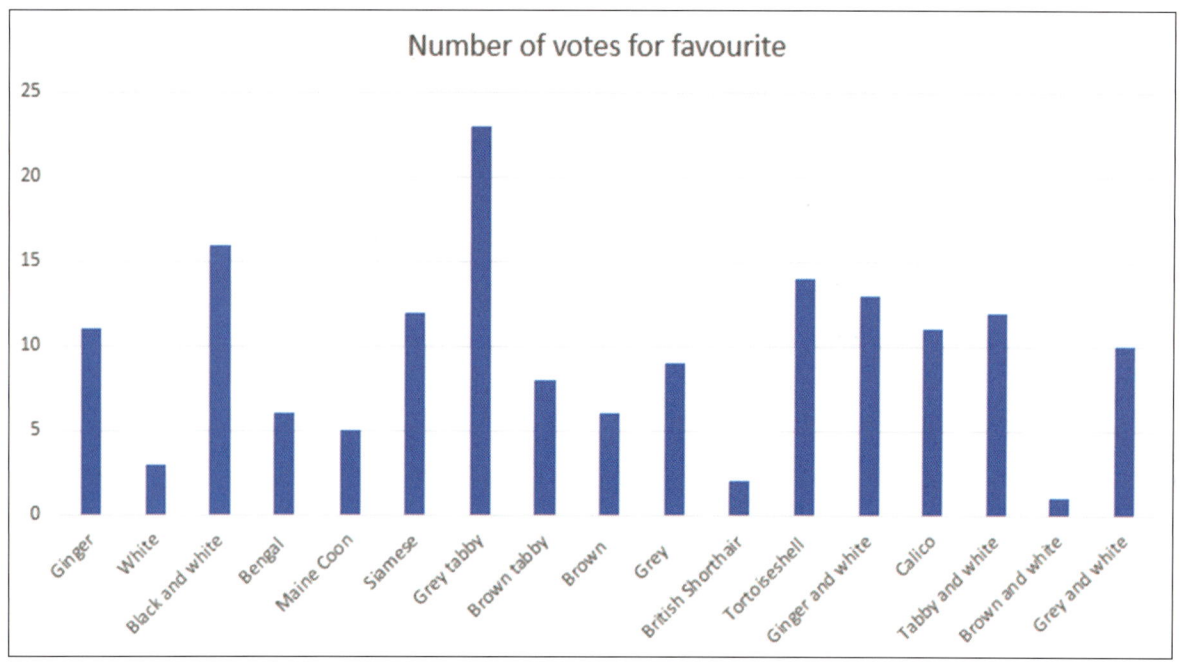

Continuous data is numerical and can have any value, not just whole numbers (like discrete data). This means it can be really precise. It is not usually countable (you cannot use your eyes to find out the number). Examples include temperature, length, height, weight, amount of rainfall and time in a race.

> Continuous data can be a number with a decimal point, like 1.5 or 17.75.

## 2 Managing data

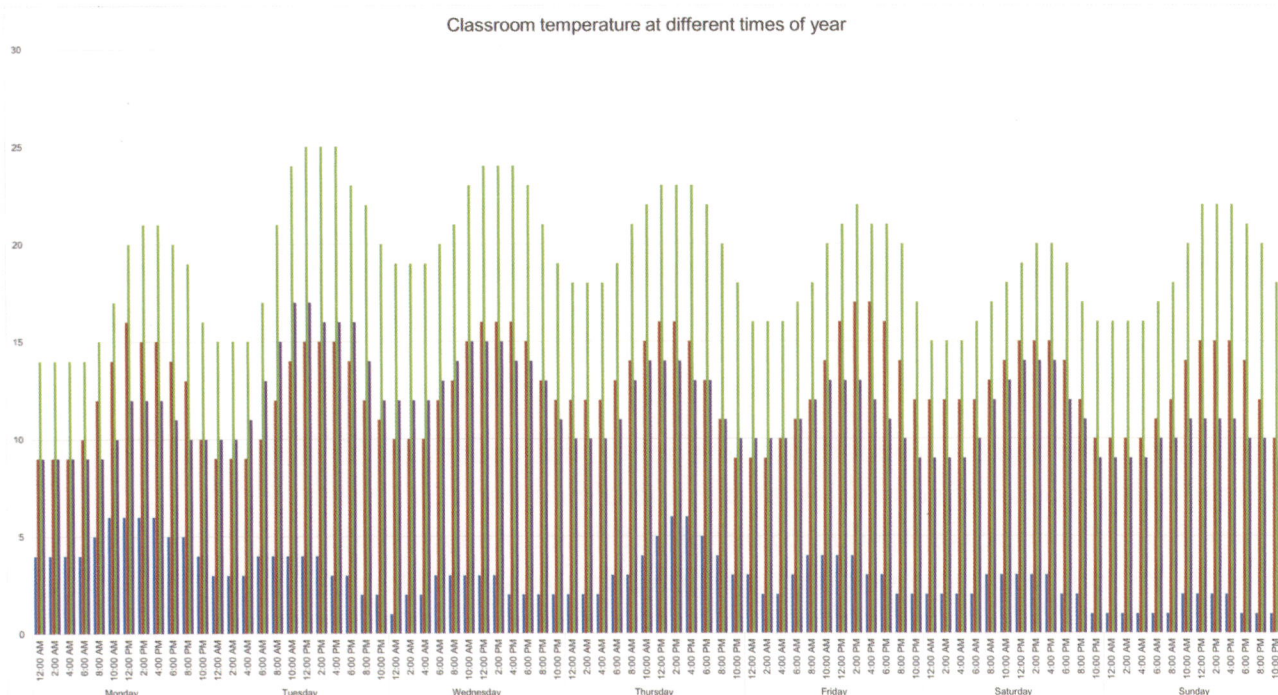

Discrete data is numerical but can only have whole values like 0 or 1. For example, you can't have half a person! It is often countable, like the number of people in a room. Examples include number of learners in the class, number of customers in a shop, number of pets and age.

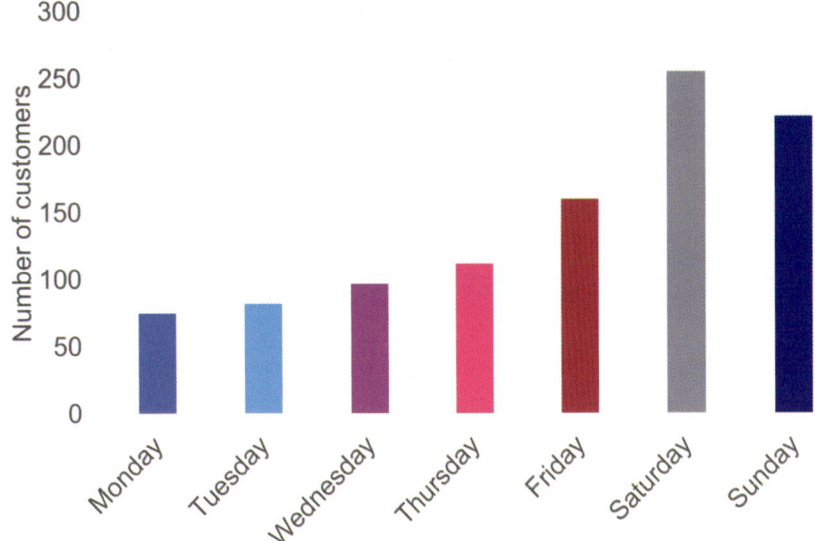

2.1 Capturing data

## Planning an investigation

When planning a statistical investigation, you need to think about the following questions:

- **What do you want to find out?** For example, you might want to find out what sort of pets people in your class have.

- **What questions will help you to find out this information?** Any questions you ask must give you exactly the information you need. You need to think about what sort of answers you will receive. Do you want to give a choice of answers, or for people to answer freely?

- **Who will you ask?** This is linked to what you want to find out. If your question is specific, you will know which group of people you need to ask. For example, 'Which pets do people in my class have?' is specific. 'Which pets do people have?' is not specific.

- **How will you collect the data?** This depends on the data you are trying to collect. If you are asking a simple question such as 'What is your favourite food?', you might use a questionnaire. If you are measuring the temperature of something every 10 minutes, you might use a data logger (see next page) and a table or a spreadsheet.

## 2 Managing data

- **How will you analyse the data?** Depending on the type of data you have collected, you might use a suitable chart or graph.
- **What tools will you use throughout the process?** For example, if you are collecting data on temperatures or light levels, you might use a data logger.

There is a range of different tools that you can use to collect data in a statistical investigation, for example:

- data loggers
- spreadsheets
- databases
- other tools like questionnaires or online forms.

# Data loggers

A data logger is a device that uses sensors to collect data over time. A data logger is one way of collecting continuous data. A weather station is an example of a data logger. This is used to record the temperature and wind speed for the location of the station every hour.

The weather station could be in that position for months or even years.

Some schools use data loggers in their lessons. You might use a data logger to test acid levels in drinks in science, or to check how voltage affects volume, like the learners on the next page! You might use one to check changes in your heart rate during sports lessons.

100

## 2.1 Capturing data

Can you think of a time when you used a data logger in school?

Often, a data logger can collect data on its own. It does not need a person to be there every time data needs to be collected. This means it can be left alone or put in a place that is difficult for a person to access, like Antarctica or a volcano.

### Did you know?

Every year there are between 12 000 to 14 000 earthquakes in the world. These are measured using a type of data logger called a seismograph. You can see information about earthquakes around the world using weather station websites.

### Unplugged activity 1

**You will need:** a pen and paper

Write down three statistical investigations where you would collect continuous data.

#### How are we doing?

Swap your three investigations with a partner.

Were all three of your partner's suggestions examples that would use continuous data? Give them a mark out of three, one mark for each correct suggestion. If they lost any marks, work together to come up with a new suggestion.

## 2 Managing data

# Spreadsheets

You may have learnt about how spreadsheets are used in statistical investigations before. A spreadsheet is a useful tool for statistical investigations because you can use it to store data. You can use spreadsheets to perform a range of calculations on the data, like finding the average, dividing, multiplying, adding and subtracting.

> Remember that * is the symbol for multiplication and / is the symbol for division in a spreadsheet!

You can also use spreadsheet software to present data visually as a chart or a graph. This is known as a representation of the data. Charts and graphs often make it easier to understand the data you have collected.

Look at the two images below. They show the same data but the data is represented in different ways. Which is more useful for identifying the most popular type of cat?

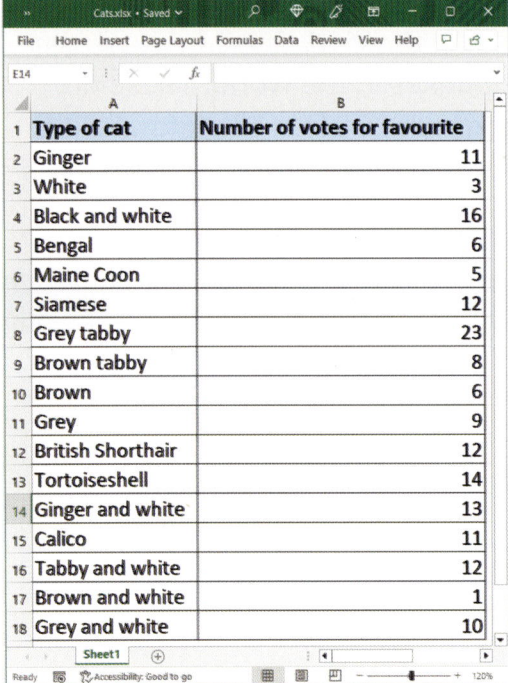
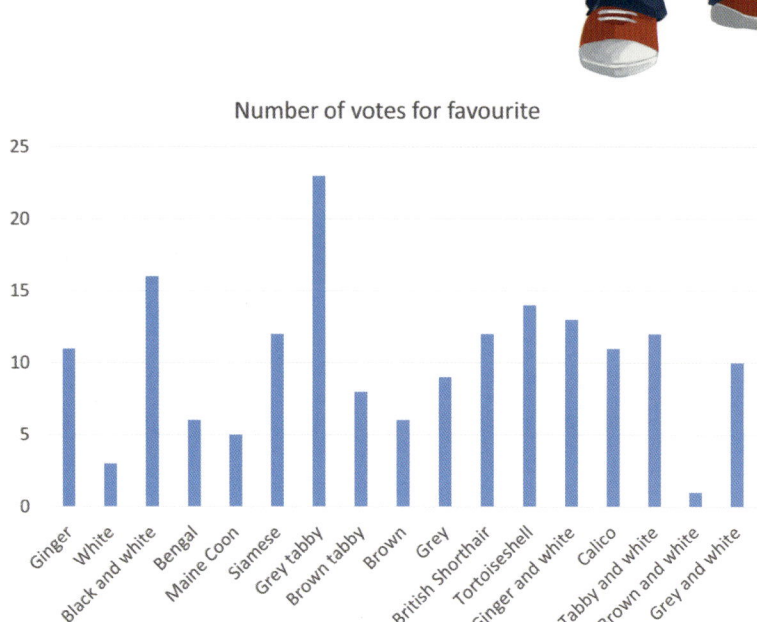

## 2.1 Capturing data

### Activity 2

> **You will need:** a desktop computer, laptop or tablet, spreadsheet software, a pen and paper, a thermometer

Investigate the temperature of your classroom to see how it changes during the day.

Place the thermometer in a sensible place in your classroom, such as on a shelf or table. Your teacher might have a good suggestion.

Create this table in a spreadsheet:

| Time | Temperature |
|---|---|
|  |  |
|  |  |

At the start of the school day, take the temperature on the thermometer and record this in your table. Do the same at the end of every lesson until the end of the school day.

The following day, enter the results into a spreadsheet. Use the headings from the table in your spreadsheet.

Select the data in the spreadsheet and create a suitable chart to represent the data. You may be familiar with this from previous learning. Make sure you have added a suitable title to the chart and included a key.

Print out your spreadsheet and chart and stick it in your exercise book.

Under the chart, describe what the results tell you. For example, when is the hottest time in the classroom? Why do you think this is? Is it easier to view this information in a chart? Why? Discuss this with a partner first before writing your explanation.

## 2 Managing data

# Databases

A database is a useful way of storing, organising and analysing data. For example, if your database stores a list of people and their favourite fruit, you can search or filter the data to answer questions such as 'Which people like pineapple?' This is what the database might look like before you filter the data:

|   | A | B |
|---|---|---|
| 1 | **Name** | **Favourite fruit** |
| 2 | Arun | Mango |
| 3 | Zara | Banana |
| 4 | Sofia | Pineapple |
| 5 | Marcus | Papaya |
| 6 | Zain | Banana |
| 7 | Afrin | Apple |
| 8 | Yasmeena | Pineapple |
| 9 | Khalid | Apple |
| 10 | Leanne | Banana |
| 11 | Farah | Pineapple |
| 12 | Simba | Banana |
| 13 | Usma | Papaya |

*I wonder how many people in my class like pineapple.*

This is what the database would look like if you used a filter to only see the people who like pineapples:

|   | A | B |
|---|---|---|
| 1 | **Name** | **Favourite fruit** |
| 4 | Sofia | Pineapple |
| 8 | Yasmeena | Pineapple |
| 11 | Farah | Pineapple |

104

## 2.1 Capturing data

The database can tell you which people meet these criteria. Criteria are requirements. For example, search criteria are requirements for the type of information you are looking for when you search a database or the internet.

We can use spreadsheet software, such as Excel or Google Sheets, to create simple databases and analyse the data in them. Remember that spreadsheet software can be used for many other tasks too!

Database software, such as Access, is only used to create databases and to analyse the data within them.

An example of a database could be a record of all the car licence plates in a particular country. People can search the database to see who a car belongs to.

## Other tools

When planning an investigation, you can use a mixture of other tools. You might consider a word processor to write up the investigation or to produce a list of questions you want to ask people. This is a useful tool as it automatically checks your spelling, and you can email the document or print it.

## 2 Managing data

You could use an online form to create a questionnaire for people to fill in. A questionnaire is a series of questions that you want to ask people. Creating a form online means you do not have to print out lots of paper copies to hand out, and you can ask people far away to fill it in for you. You can even post a link to your form on a website, or email people a link to the form.

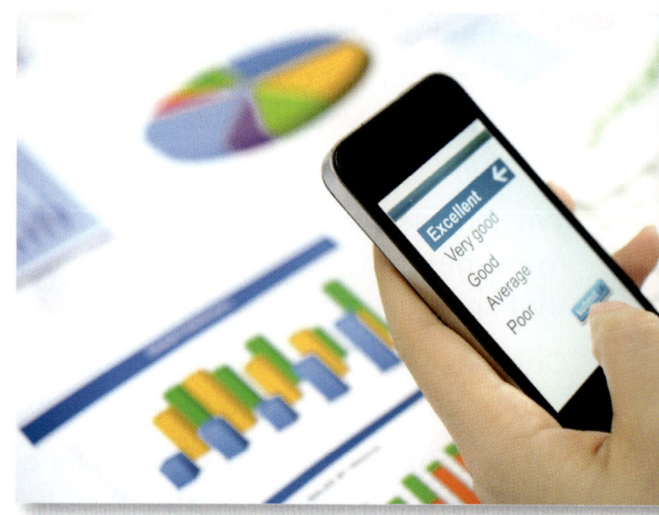

Online forms automatically provide the results of your questionnaire in a spreadsheet for you.

### Unplugged activity 3

**You will need:** a pen and paper

Copy the following table. Write down which data collection tool would be the best to use for each investigation.

| Investigation | Best tool to use |
|---|---|
| Measure the rainfall in a month | |
| How many people visit the supermarket on a Monday | |
| The test results of everyone in your class for the year | |
| The amount of time you spend on your device in a day | |

1. Work with a partner. Select one of the investigations from the table and explain to your partner why you chose a particular tool to collect data.
2. What might the disadvantages be of using an online form to collect data?

## Planning a form

People are often asked to fill in forms requesting their personal details. For example, this might happen when they move to a new school or enter a competition.

They might also be asked to fill in a form asking for their opinion on an item they have recently bought or on a hotel they have recently stayed in. Business owners like to have people's feedback so they know if their customers are happy or if they need to make any improvements.

## Creating a form to collect continuous data

When creating a form to collect continuous data, you need to think carefully about the following things.

- Phrase your questions precisely.

    If you are asking someone for the temperature every day in a classroom at midday each day last week, you should make sure you include all of these elements in the question, like in the first example here:

    ✓ What was the temperature in your classroom at 12:00 p.m. on Monday?

    ✗ What is the temperature?

    You should also make sure that you do not allow people to type their own text answers, and that you only accept answers in the format you want.

- How often should data be entered?

    If you want data to be recorded three times a day, you should specify this and make sure there is space in your form to add three lots of data per day.

> **Stay safe!**
>
> As you get older, you might start using social media. Think carefully about what information you share online about yourself. You never know who might see it or what it could be used for.

## 2 Managing data

- Over what period should the data be entered? If you want data every day for a week, make sure this is clear. Again, make sure there is space in your form to add data every day.

- What measurements are you going to use? (such as mm, cm, kg or lb)?

  Your form should specify the measurements you will accept answers in.

- How precise should the data be?

  For example, you could request that answers have one or two numbers after a decimal point.

### Unplugged activity 4

**You will need: a pen and paper**

Work with a partner for this activity.

Zara and Arun have each decided to make a form to collect data on everyone's height in the class so they can help their teacher decide where everyone should stand for the school photo.

Take a look at Zara's form:

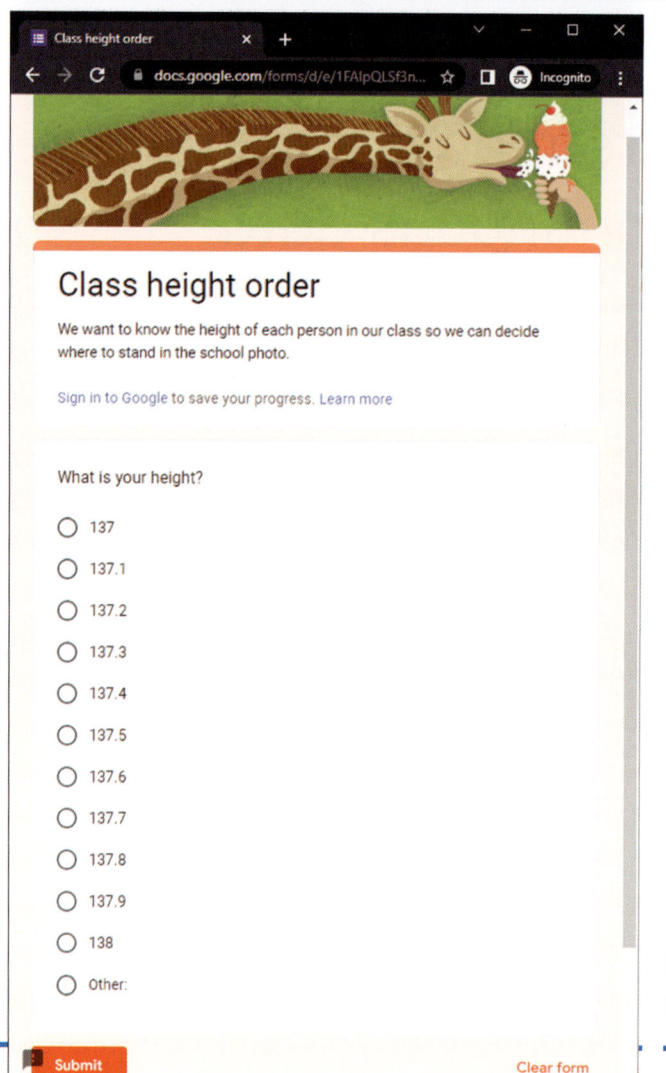

108

## 2.1 Capturing data

### Continued

Now look at Arun's form:

Whose form is better?
Think about:

- question type
- preciseness of the question
- whether all necessary questions have been asked
- whether everyone in the class could complete the form with their data.

Once you have decided which form is more appropriate, think about any further changes you could make to make it even better. Try to come up with two suggestions.

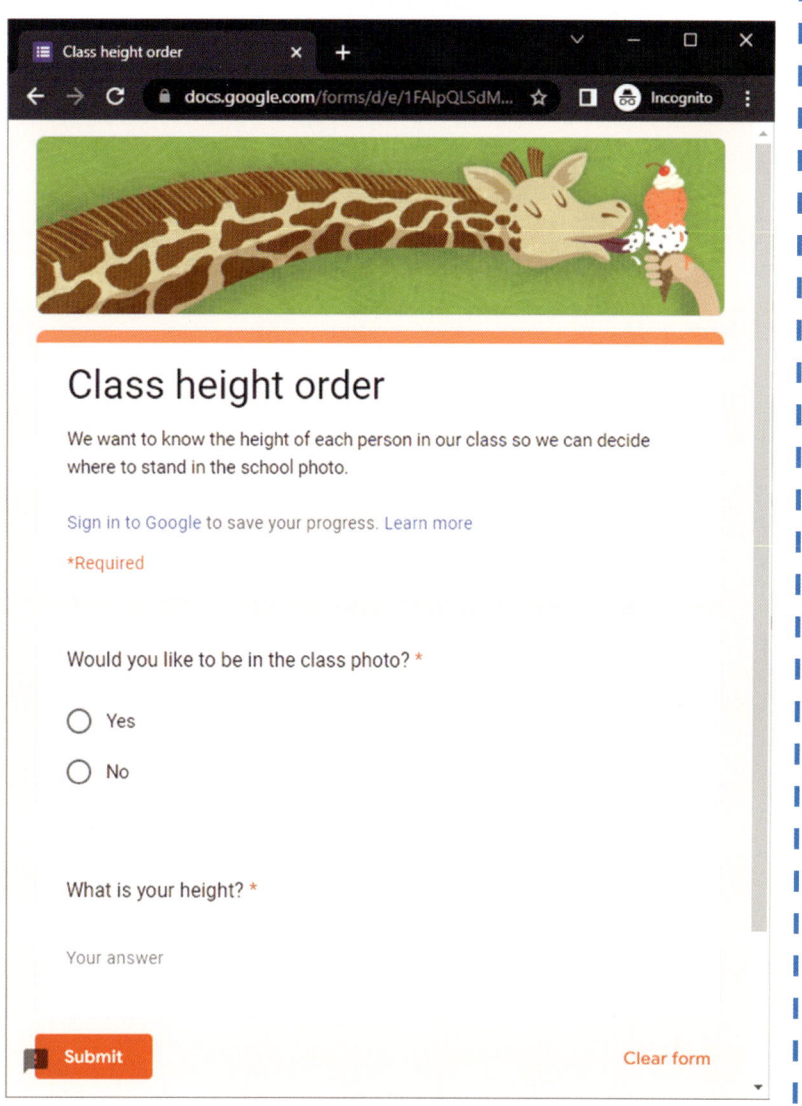

How do you make sure that you listen to your partner properly?
How might you improve your communication in future activities?

How did you make sure you agreed on your chosen questions?

If you worked together again, how could you improve your partnership?

**2** Managing data

# Creating a form

There are many different ways to create an online form.
One popular way is to use an online form creator, like Google Forms.

This is an example of an online form.

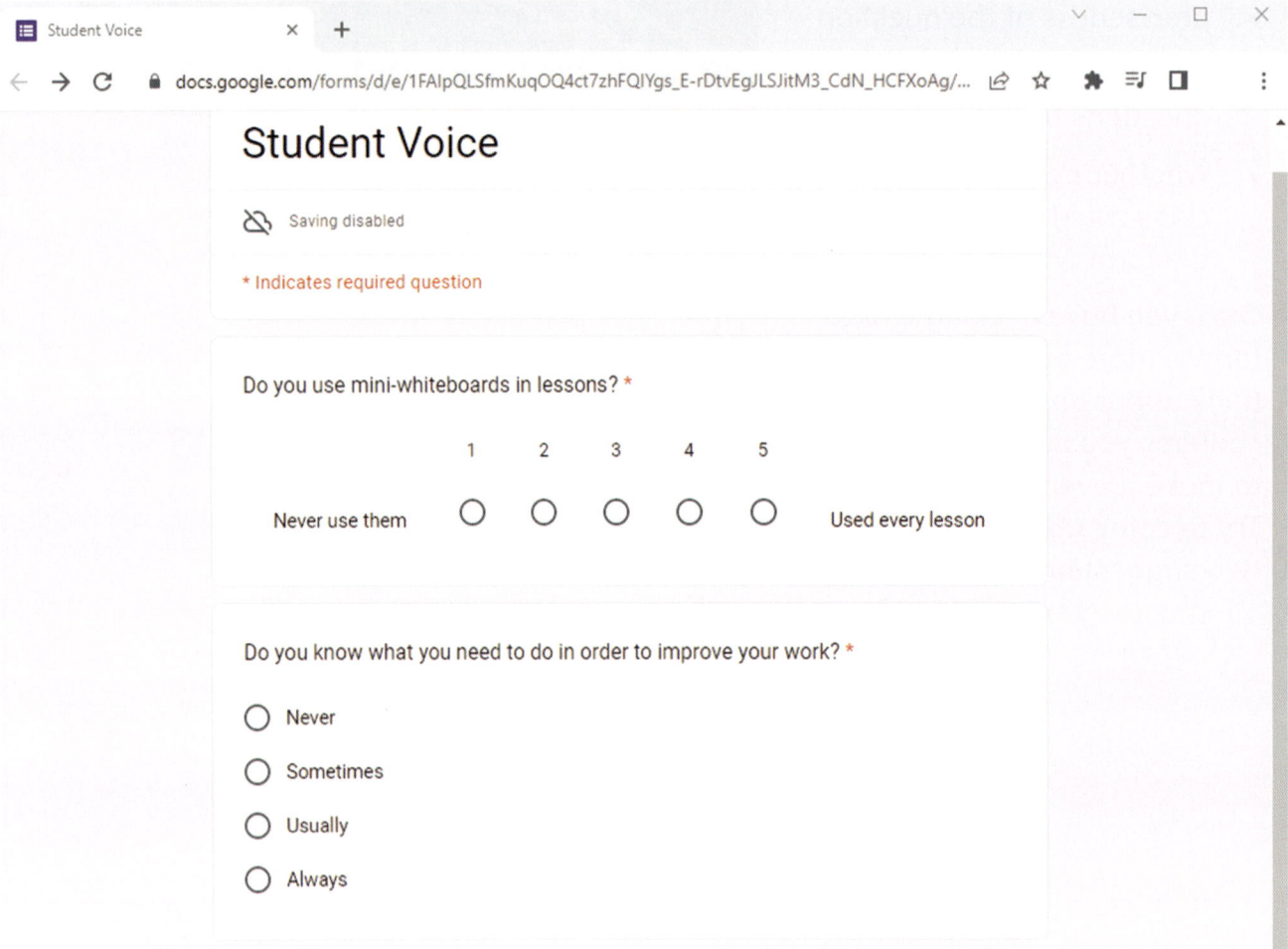

2.1 Capturing data

Online form creators are very easy to use. They also allow you to collaborate (work with other people) on the same document at the same time with a partner or group and share the finished form with anyone.

Online form creators give you lots of options when choosing question type (the way in which you ask your question). For example, you can choose to insert an open text question, a multiple choice question, a ranking question or another type of question. Some online form creators even allow you to add images.

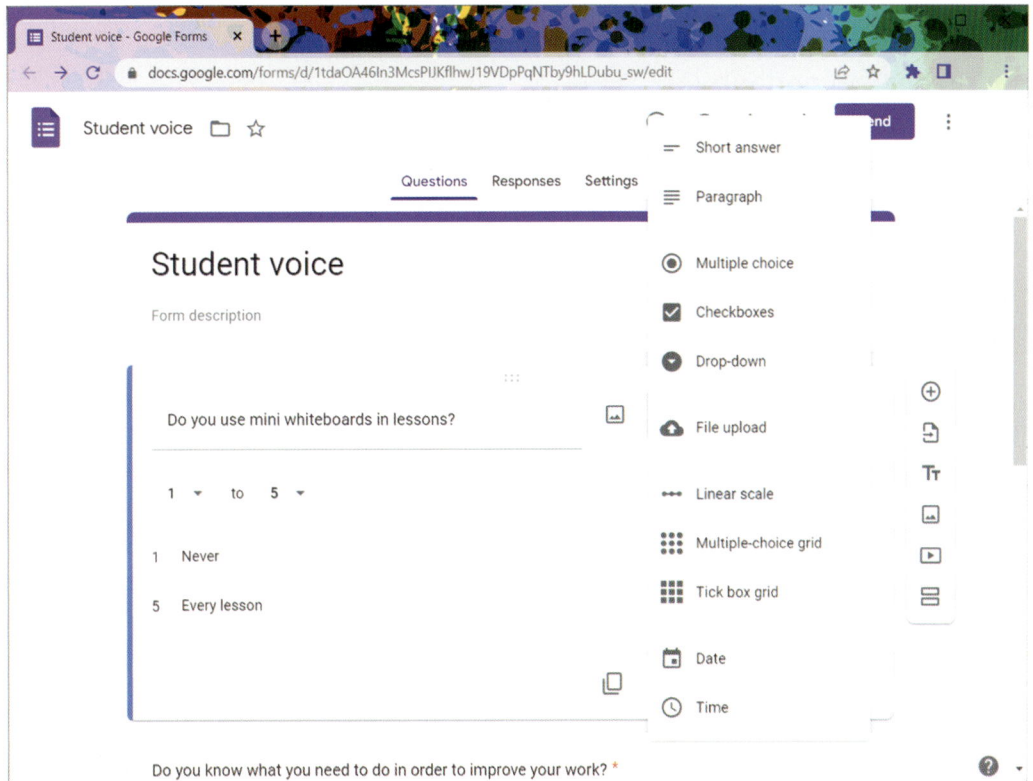

# Question types

Imagine you want to find the heights of everyone in your class so you can decide who stands where in the class photo. What question types would help you to collect this continuous data?

## 2 Managing data

## Open text questions

Open text questions allow people to write their own answer, but they might not submit their answer in the correct format or with the correct type of measurement. To prevent this, you could allow a written answer with validation rules. Validation rules are restrictions that make sure that only certain types of answer are accepted, like only words or only symbols. You may remember validation rules from lessons in previous years.

Examples of open questions:

- Why do you like reading?
- What is your favourite lesson and why?
- What is your opinion on the local library?

## Multiple choice questions

Multiple choice questions allow people to pick from a range of answers. However, because continuous data is numerical data that can have any value, it would take forever to add answer options to cover every possibility. You could limit the options you provide, but this would mean that some people would not be able to enter their data.

Examples of multiple choice questions:

- Do you like to play tennis?
  Yes ☐    No ☐
- What is your favourite colour?
  Red ☐    Yellow ☐
  Pink ☐    Green ☐
  Orange ☐    Purple ☐
  Blue ☐    Brown ☐
  Other ☐

112

## Ranking questions

Ranking question types allow the person to select their response on a scale, for example 1 to 5 where 1 is the worst and 5 is the best. This type of question is useful when asking people their opinions about something, but it will not allow you to collect continuous or discrete data.

Example of a ranking question:

- How would you rate today's lunch on a scale of 1 to 5, with 5 being excellent?

    1 ☐   2 ☐   3 ☐   4 ☐   5 ☐

## Other questions

You also need to remember to ask important questions about the person completing the form. For example, you might need to know the name of the person answering the questions. If you were collecting data on pets, you would need to know if the person answering the questions has a pet. If not, they would not need to answer the rest of the questions!

## 2 Managing data

### Unplugged activity 5

**You will need:** a pen and paper

Work with a partner for this activity.

Write questions for a form which will allow respondents to record continuous data. Choose one of these investigations to focus on:

- You want to investigate who the tallest person is in your class.
- You have a friend in Norway. You want to compare the average temperature at midday across a period of a week between where you live and Norway.
- You want to find out who in your class has made the best paper plane by seeing whose flies the furthest. You fly them three times each to get accurate results.
- You want to know who in your class has the heaviest school bag.

Think about:

- whether the data changes over time and needs to be entered multiple times
- when the data should be recorded
- what measurements should be used
- the wording of your questions.

Write your questions down on a piece of paper. Think about how you want your form to look, too.

> Remember, continuous data can change over time. It can be any data that is measured and can take any value, like the time it takes to finish a race.

## 2.1 Capturing data

### Activity 6

**You will need:** a desktop computer, laptop or tablet with access to the internet and source file **2.1_class_height_order**

Sofia has made some changes to Zara and Arun's forms.

Open source file 2.1_class_height_order, which is a Google Forms document, to see what she has done. Remember that you will need to open the form in a web browser once you have access to the weblink.

What happens when you try the following?

- Leave question 1 blank, scroll to the bottom of the page and press the red 'Next' button.
- Select 'No' for question 2, 'Would you like to be in the class photo?'.
- Enter the number 7 for question 3.

Why do you think Sofia designed the form to react in these ways? What is the benefit?

Suggest two reasons why Sofia's form is more appropriate than Zara's or Arun's.

## Benefits of an online form creator

Using an online form creator rather than a word processor has many advantages.

A word processor will allow you to format the questions so the form looks presentable and clear, but an online form creator will do much more:

- You can add as many questions as you need.
- The response options are automatically arranged for you.
- The results are automatically saved, analysed and sent to you.
- You can easily share the link to the form with anyone in the world.
- Users do not need special software to complete the form. They only need an internet connection and a web browser.

## 2 Managing data

Using an online form creator means someone from another country could complete your form. This is very useful when you want to collect data from all over the world!

> **Stay safe!**
>
> When creating and sending an online form, think about how you share the form. Your teacher will show you how you can change the settings so that only specific people can access your form.

### Practical task 1

**You will need:** your questions from Unplugged activity 5, a desktop computer, laptop or tablet with an internet connection, a Google account

You are now going to create an online form using your questions. Work with your partner. Use your paper plan to help you.

1. Log in to a Google account and go to Google Forms.
2. Under 'Start a new form' press 'Blank'.
3. Create your form. (A template for the first question will appear automatically.)
   a. Give your form a title.
   b. Select the question type you want to use (for example, short answer or check boxes).
   c. Type in your question text.
   d. If you have selected multiple choice or check boxes, type in the answer options.
4. To add another question, press the plus (+) in a circle in the toolbar on the right.

You might need to slightly change the question types that you planned to use as there is a limited number of question types in Google Forms.

All changes to your form are saved automatically.

2.1 Capturing data

> **Continued**
>
> 5   When you are both happy with the form, share it with others in your class:
>     a   Press 'Send' in the top right corner of the screen.
>     b   Press on the link icon next to the envelope.
>     c   Press 'Copy'.
>     d   Share the link with your classmates.
> 6   To complete a form:
>     a   Paste the link into a new web browser tab.
>     b   Fill in the form then press 'Submit'.
>
>
>
> *If you are all using the same computer, you can all fill in the form one after the other. Just press 'Submit another response' after each person submits their answers.*
>
> **How are we doing?**
>
> Hold up a red, yellow or green card to show how confident you are with writing questions for a form.
>
> • Red means you do not really understand and you need more help.
> • Yellow means your confidence is increasing but you need support or more practice.
> • Green means you are confident enough to teach others.
>
> If you held up a green card for one of the questions, find someone who held up a red or yellow card for that question. Help them to understand the things they are not sure about.

## 2 Managing data

Did you both agree on what question types to use when creating the form? Why/why not?

How easy was the form to fill in? What made it easy or difficult? What would you do differently next time?

## Questions

1. Describe an advantage of using an online form creator.
2. Suggest two question types that would not be appropriate for collecting continuous data.
3. List three computing tools that can help with statistical investigations, with examples of how they can be used.

### Look what I can do!

- [ ] I can describe the role of different tools I can use in statistical investigations.
- [ ] I can plan a statistical investigation.
- [ ] I can explain how continuous data can be collected.
- [ ] I can create an appropriate form for collecting continuous data.

# > 2.2 Creating a spreadsheet

**We are going to:**

- explore the features of a spreadsheet
- design a spreadsheet with different features and functions
- select some data for a given purpose.

> AVERAGE  spreadsheet
> cell reference  SUM
> formula  unique

**Getting started**

**What do you already know?**

- How to add data into a spreadsheet.
- How to use simple operators in a spreadsheet, including +, -, *, and /, for calculations.
- How to use simple formulas in a spreadsheet.
- How to use built-in functions including SUM and AVERAGE.

## 2 Managing data

**Continued**

**Now try this!**

Look at the spreadsheet. It shows the cost of different items that are sold in a stationery shop and how many of each item the shop has.

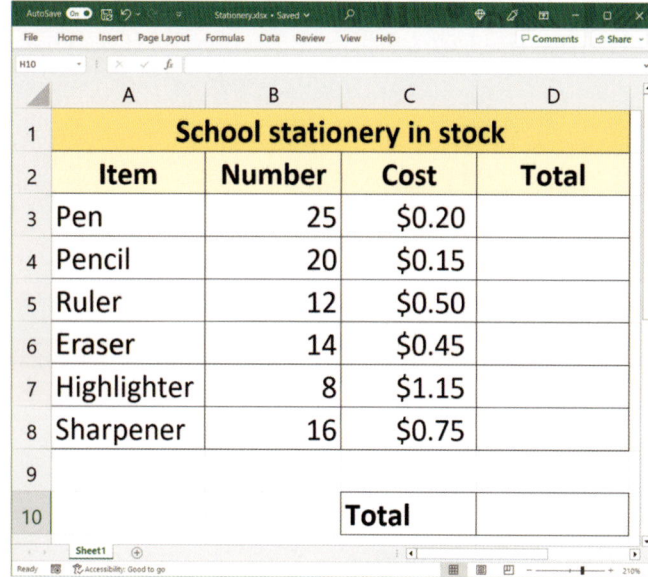

With a partner, discuss how you could answer the following questions:

1. What formula could you use to work out the total cost of the pens?
2. How could you calculate the total cost of all the items in the shop?
3. How could you fill the 'Total' cell with data?
   What calculation would be needed?
4. What other calculations could you do with this data?

# Features of a spreadsheet

A **spreadsheet** is a document that is split into a large grid. Each box in the grid is called a cell. The cells are organised in rows and columns.

Each row has a **unique** number and each column has a unique letter. Unique means it is not like anything else, and that there is only one of them – like you!

## 2.2 Creating a spreadsheet

You can use a spreadsheet to store data or information. However, spreadsheets can do much more than store data! They are powerful computing tools that we can use to carry out complex calculations. Spreadsheets are often used to analyse data such as sales, stocks of goods in a shop, or financial information.

## Cell references

Each cell has an address made up of a letter and a number. This is known as a *cell reference*.

In a cell reference, the letter tells you how far *along* the cell is from left to right (which column the cell is in). The number tells you how far *down* the cell is (which row it is in).

Look at the spreadsheet in the picture. The selected cell has a cell reference of B3.

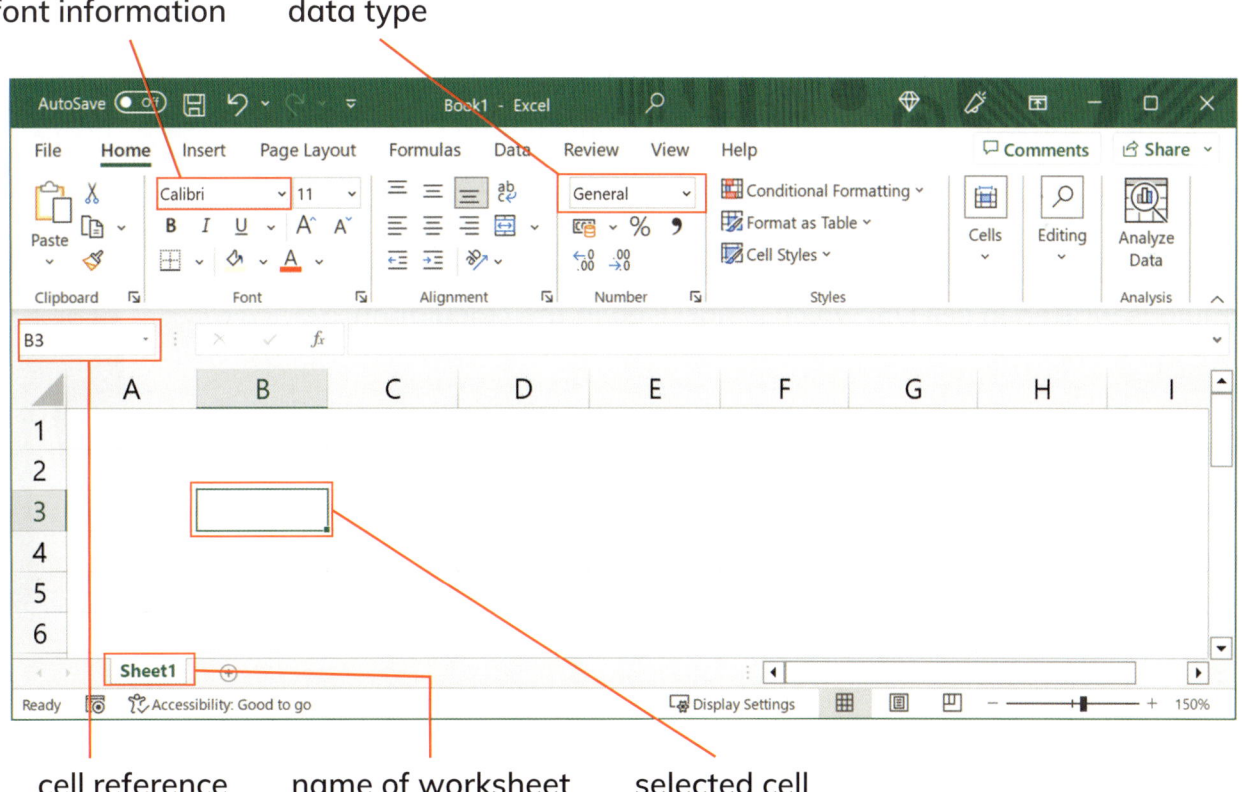

121

# 2 Managing data

Cell references make it really easy to make calculations, because we can use the cell reference to find values by just typing in the cell reference.

## Formulas

To make a calculation in a spreadsheet, we need to use a formula. A formula is an instruction to do a calculation. Spreadsheet formulas combine cell references with arithmetic operators. Remember, arithmetic operators are the symbols we use to do maths, such as + (plus), − (minus), * (multiply), / (divide).

You might already know how to use a formula in a spreadsheet with numbers and arithmetic operators, like this: =6+1664.

In this topic, you will use cell references to make calculations.

*I need to remember to include = at the start of my formulas.*

For example, =C3*D4 is an example of a simple formula that multiplies the value in C3 by the value in D4. If the cell C3 contained the number 2 and the cell D4 contained the number 4, the formula would return 8. A formula must begin with =. This is so the spreadsheet software knows you are doing a calculation.

You must put the formula for the calculation you want to do in a separate cell (not either of the cells you are trying to use in the calculation). Look at the spreadsheet below. You can see that the formula is written in cell D5, which is not used in the calculation.

## 2.2 Creating a spreadsheet

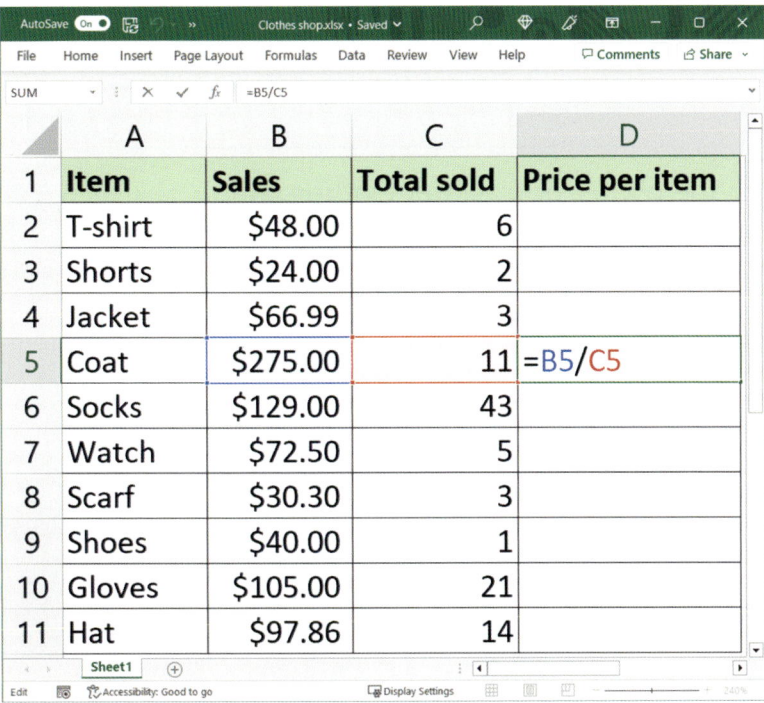

When writing a formula, you can type directly into a cell. Click on an empty cell to start typing into it. To change part of the data already in a cell, double-click on the cell before typing. Alternatively, you can type into the formula bar at the top of the spreadsheet. You only need to click in the formula bar once before you start typing.

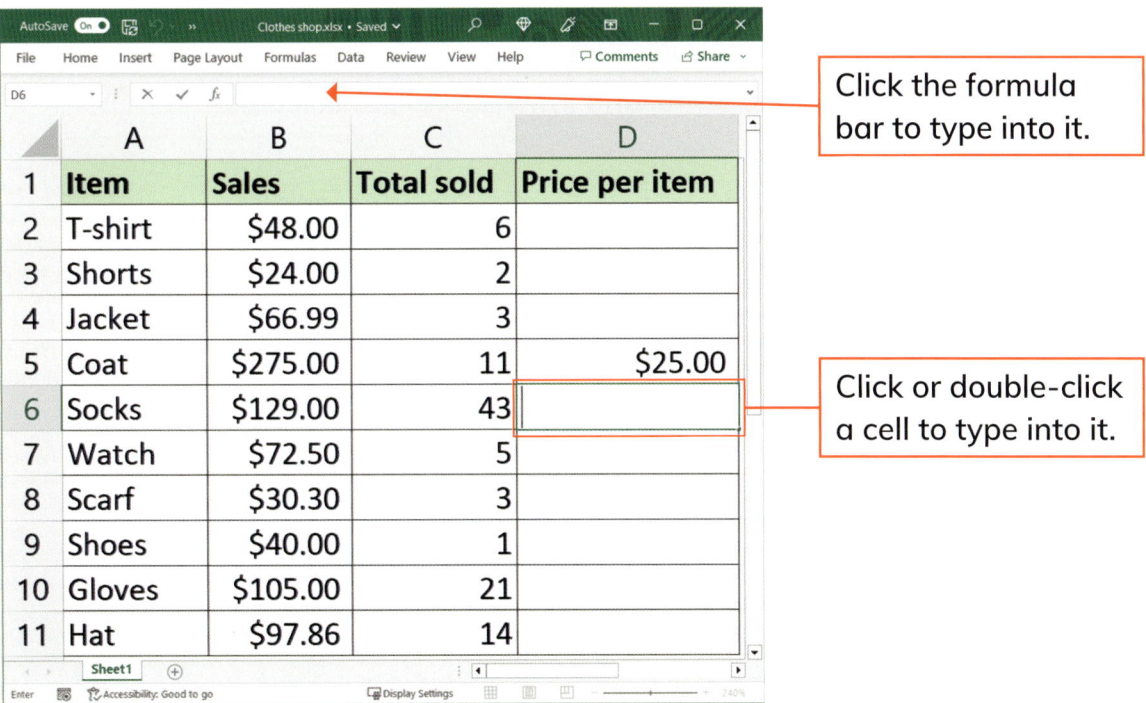

Click the formula bar to type into it.

Click or double-click a cell to type into it.

123

## 2 Managing data

**Unplugged activity 1**

**You will need:** a pen and paper

Look at this spreadsheet belonging to the owner of a winter clothes shop. The owner knows how many items she sold and what she sold, but forgot how much she sold them for!

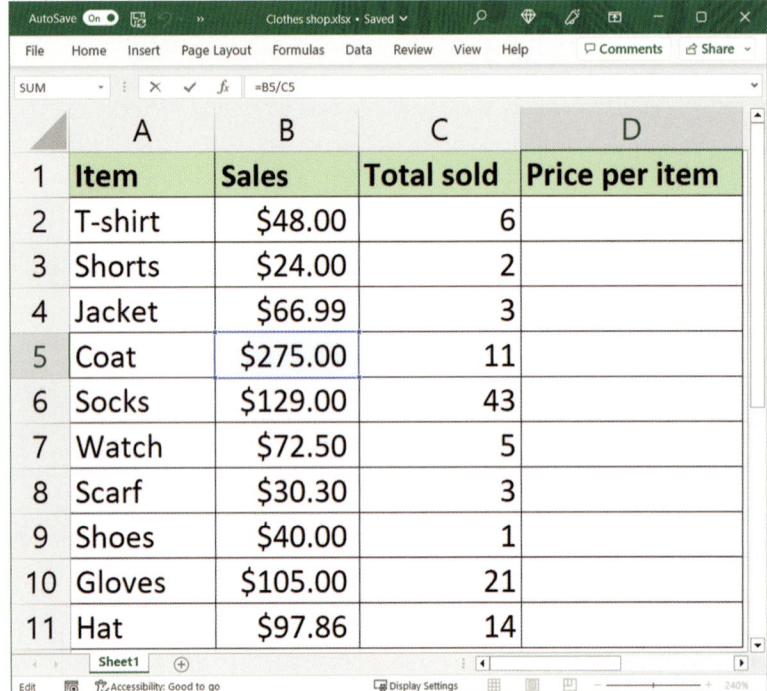

1. What formula would you need to write, and in which cell, to calculate the price per item for:

   a hats?   b gloves?   c socks?

2. Write a formula to calculate how much it would cost to buy 127 of each item listed above.

# Functions

Just like in programming, a function is a sub-routine in the spreadsheet software's code. There are lots of different functions that are ready for us to use in a spreadsheet. Each function contains a hidden formula that has already been written for us. We can call a function by using its name. We will focus on the functions SUM and AVERAGE.

## 2.2 Creating a spreadsheet

When we want to use a function in a formula, we follow these steps:

1. start with an equals sign: =
2. add the name of the function we want to use, for example SUM or AVERAGE
3. type the cell references we want to use in the function in brackets: ( ). This is so that the spreadsheet software can tell the difference between the function name and the rest of the formula.

## SUM

The SUM function calculates the total of the values in the selected cells.

For example, if we want to add up all the values in the cells A1 to A10, we could use the following formula: =SUM(A1:A10)

'SUM' comes straight after = because that is the function we are using. The cells we want the sum of are written within brackets. The colon (:) means 'to'. So, the formula will calculate the sum of the cells from A1 to A10 (A1, A2, A3, A4, A5, A6, A7, A8, A9 and A10).

Remember to add in the colon so that the spreadsheet software knows which values to add together.

## AVERAGE

The AVERAGE function calculates the mean of the values in the selected cells. You can calculate a mean by adding together all of the values and dividing the answer by the number of values.

We can calculate the average in a spreadsheet using the following formula: =AVERAGE(A1:A10)

Again, we must remember to include the colon (:) so that the spreadsheet software knows which values to use in its calculation. We also must remember to use the function name 'AVERAGE' before we type in the cell references. Otherwise, the spreadsheet software will not know what to do with the values!

## 2 Managing data

### Unplugged activity 2

**You will need:** a pen and paper

With a partner, identify the incorrect formulas in the following list.

1. =SUMB5:B10
2. =(B5:B10)
3. =SUM(B5:B10)
4. AVERAGE(B5:B10)
5. =AVERAGE(B5-B10)
6. =B5/B10
7. B5*B10
8. =AVERAGE(B5B10)
9. SUM=(B5:B10)
10. =AVERAGE(B5:B10)

Why is each formula you have identified incorrect? Write them again, correctly.

### Did you know?

There are a maximum of 1,048,576 rows and 16,384 columns in Microsoft Excel, which gives us 17,179,869,184 cells in total.

There are at least 475 functions, depending on which software you are using, which are built in for you to use in a spreadsheet!

## 2.2 Creating a spreadsheet

### Activity 3

You will need: a desktop computer, laptop or tablet, spreadsheet software and source file **2.2_winter_clothes_shop**

Open source file 2.2_winter_clothes_shop.

You will see that there are three empty cells: B14, C14 and D14. You are going to do calculations in these cells using formulas.

Type a formula in B14 to calculate the total sales (money customers paid for items).

Type a formula in C14 to calculate the total number of items sold.

Type a formula in D14 to calculate the average price per item in the shop.

#### How are we doing?

Compare your answers with a partner.

- Did your calculations give you the same output?
- If not, can you identify whose is correct and why?
- Did your partner use the SUM and AVERAGE formulas, or did they use a different formula?

Give your partner's spreadsheet and calculations a rating from 1 to 3:

1. means the spreadsheet was perfect – the answers were correct and they used the SUM and AVERAGE functions.
2. means the spreadsheet was good but there was room for improvement. Maybe your partner used a different formula but got the right answers. Maybe they used the appropriate formula but made a mistake.
3. means your partner did not get the right answers and did not use SUM or AVERAGE.

If your partner scored 2 or 3, work together to ensure their spreadsheet is correct.

# 2 Managing data

## Questions

1. Why is it useful to use cell references?
2. Why should you use a formula? Give two reasons.
3. What advantage is there to using a built-in function in a spreadsheet?
4. What formula or function would you use to calculate the total value of cells D3 to D40?

## Planning a spreadsheet

In Topic 2.1, you planned the questions you wanted to ask your class before you created an online form.

When you want to create a spreadsheet, you also need to carefully plan what it is going to look like and what you would like it to do. You need to think about the formulas you could use and the type of data the cells might contain.

When you create a spreadsheet, ask yourself these questions:

- What data do I want to use?
- What headings will the data have?
- How will I organise the data so that is it easy to understand?
- What format will the data be in?
- What calculations do I want to do on the data?
- What formulas or functions can I use to perform these calculations?

> **Stay safe!**
>
> As with any document, you should be careful opening spreadsheets if you are not sure where they come from. This is because they can include hidden code that can damage your computer.

I want to know the total number of hours I watch TV in a week, so I know I need a blank cell where I can make this calculation.

## 2.2 Creating a spreadsheet

**Unplugged activity 4**

**You will need:** a pen and paper

Work in pairs to plan a class outing to the local park for a picnic.

You need to decide what food and drink you will need for the picnic and the amount of each item you need.

Copy the following tables onto paper. Everyone in your class should choose one drink and up to three food items they would like to eat from the lists below. They can only choose items from the lists. Each person in the class can vote for their choices. Your teacher will help you with this.

| Food | Number |
|---|---|
| Tandoori turkey sandwich | |
| Spring rolls | |
| Crisps | |
| Bhaji | |
| Bao bun | |
| Fruit salad | |
| Crackers | |
| Chicken sticks | |
| Chocolate | |
| Sugar cookies | |
| Cake | |
| Pakoras | |
| Kebabs | |

## 2 Managing data

> **Continued**
>
> | Drink | Number |
> |---|---|
> | water | |
> | milk | |
> | soda | |
> | juice | |

## Selecting data for a purpose

Spreadsheets often contain large amounts of data. This means it is very useful to be able to select particular pieces of data that allow you to answer a question or complete a task.

A supermarket might have a huge amount of data on what they sell each day, but if they want to answer questions about how much of an item they have sold, they need to select particular pieces of data.

> You selected data for a purpose in Activity 3 when you chose the data you needed to make the SUM and AVERAGE calculations.

They might decide to group the data into different categories, such as fruit, and calculate how many of each item they have sold. Or they might select sales at different times of day to calculate how many customers they had in a specific hour.

## 2.2 Creating a spreadsheet

The owner of the supermarket might not just want to know how many apples have been sold that day, but they might want to know how many apples are left in stock.

All these different scenarios can be worked out in a spreadsheet by selecting specific data and using a suitable formula.

To work out how many apples are left, the owner might use a formula that uses subtraction, but to work out how much money they will make from selling all the apples, they might use a multiplication formula. However, whether they get useful results depends on them selecting the correct data to use in the calculations.

To select data in a spreadsheet to use in a calculation, you can either:

- type cell references into a formula
- click and drag the cells you want to use.

We already know how to type cell references into a formula from the Functions section of this topic.

### Activity 5

> **You will need:** a desktop computer, laptop or tablet, spreadsheet software and source file **2.3_weather_data**

Look at source file 2.3. The spreadsheet shows weather data for one month. The data was collected by a data logger at 9 a.m. every day.

Use the spreadsheet to calculate:

1. the mean maximum temperature for the month
2. the mean minimum temperature for the month
3. the mean humidity for the month
4. the mean pressure for the month.

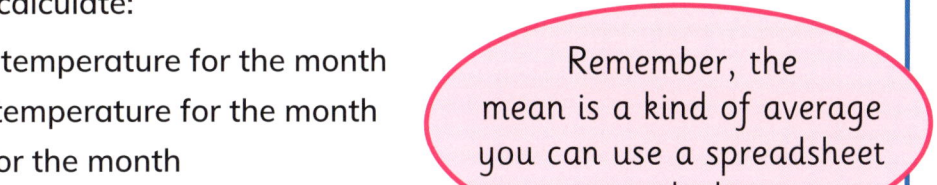

Remember, the mean is a kind of average you can use a spreadsheet to calculate

Discuss with a partner how you could make these calculations. Why would you not perform any calculations on the wind direction?

Complete the calculations in the spreadsheet.
Show your partner what data you selected to perform each calculation.

Selecting data for a purpose in an existing spreadsheet can sometimes be difficult because you need to familiarise yourself with the data before you know that to select.

## 2 Managing data

Designing your own spreadsheet helps with this, because you will know where to find the data you need for your calculations.

> **Unplugged activity 6**
>
> **You will need:** a pen and paper and your completed tables from Unplugged activity 4
>
>
>
> With the same partner you worked with in Unplugged activity 4, you are going to plan a spreadsheet to record what is needed for the class picnic.
>
> You can only buy the five most popular food items for the picnic. You need to make calculations to find out:
>
> - how many people are attending the picnic
> - what the five most popular food items are (you should use only these five food items in your calculations)
> - how many of each drink you need
> - how much drinks will cost in total
> - how much food will cost in total
> - what the average cost is for each person attending the picnic
> - how much the picnic will cost in total.

## 2.2 Creating a spreadsheet

### Continued

The price lists for the food and drink are as follows.

| Food | Cost for 1 serving |
|---|---|
| Tandoori turkey sandwich | $1.07 |
| Spring rolls | $0.87 |
| Crisps | $0.59 |
| Bhaji | $1.13 |
| Bao bun | $1.52 |
| Fruit salad | $1.87 |
| Crackers | $0.61 |
| Chicken sticks | $1.01 |
| Chocolate | $0.43 |
| Sugar cookies | $0.65 |
| Cake | $0.85 |
| Pakora | $1.15 |
| Kebabs | $0.98 |

| Drink | Cost for 1 serving |
|---|---|
| Water | $0 |
| Milk | $0.41 |
| Soda | $0.99 |
| Juice | $0.81 |

Your spreadsheet plan should also show how you will use the following at least once:

- formulas (with cell references and arithmetic operators)
- the SUM function
- the AVERAGE function.

## 2 Managing data

### Continued

You should also show what data you will select when you use formulas and functions.

As you work on your plan, think about these questions:
- What headings will the data have?
- Are you organising the data into columns or rows?
- What format will the data be in?

### Activity 7

> **You will need:** a desktop computer, laptop or tablet, spreadsheet software, your plans from Unplugged activity 6

Work with the same partner as you did in Unplugged activities 4 and 6. Use your plan from Unplugged activity 6 to create your picnic spreadsheet.

Remember to use formulas and the SUM and AVERAGE functions.

#### How are we doing?

Once you have completed your spreadsheet, share it with another pair. Explain how you have created your spreadsheet.

Ask the pair for feedback on your spreadsheet.

Look at the spreadsheet from the other pair. Check the following:
- Has all the relevant data been included?
- Have they used the SUM and AVERAGE functions?
- Have they used formulas correctly, with cell references and arithmetic operators?
- Did they select the correct data to perform their calculations?

### Look what I can do!

- ☐ I can explain the different features of a spreadsheet, including how to use a range of formulas and functions.
- ☐ I can design a spreadsheet with different features and functions.
- ☐ I can select data in a spreadsheet to use in calculations.

# > 2.3 Creating a database

## We are going to:
- design a single table database
- create a single table database
- search for information in a database using a phrase.

> attribute  filter
> database  phrase searching
> data type  record
> field

### Getting started

**What do you already know?**

- You can find data that matches a single keyword.
- Data can be edited and updated.
- Changing data input into a spreadsheet impacts the calculated outputs.
- The difference between physical (paper-based) and digital databases.
- How to use a database to answer a single question.
- The different parts of a database table, including what a record is and what a field is.
- A database is one tool that can be used in a statistical investigation.

## 2 Managing data

> **Continued**
>
> **Now try this!**
>
> Look at this database. It shows a range of information about some cars.
>
>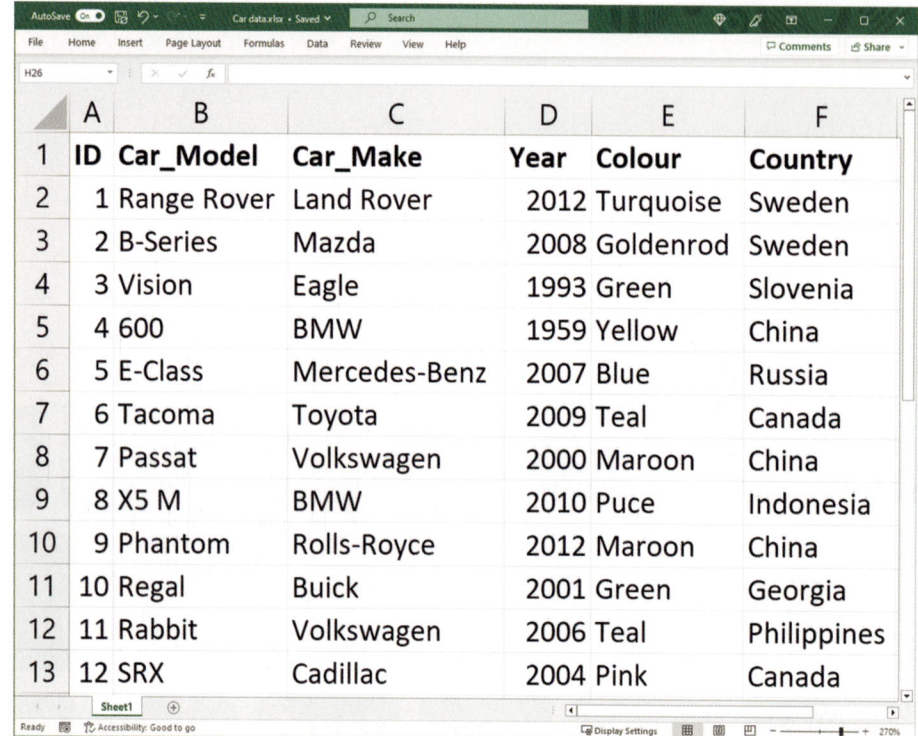
>
> With a partner, discuss how you could use the database to answer the following questions:
>
> 1. How many cars are green?
> 2. What steps would you take to find a specific car?

# What is a database?

A database is an organised set of data. Databases are really useful because data is much easier to use when it is organised.

A database is made up of records and fields.

## 2.3 Creating a database

A record provides all the data about one thing. For example, the record below provides all the data about the car that Marcus's mum drives:

Colour: red

Car make: Toyota

Fuel type: petrol

Age (in years): 5

Each record in a database is made up of different fields. A field is a category of data within a record. For example, in the record above, the fields are:

- Colour
- Car make
- Fuel type
- Age (in years)

A record is complete when all fields are filled with data.

In a database, records are usually organised as rows, and fields are usually organised as columns. But this is not always the case!

An attribute is the data found in one field of a record in a database. Look again at the record above for the car that Marcus's mum drives.

The attributes in this record are red, Toyota, petrol and 5.

> If my teacher had a database with all the learners in our class, I would be a record in it. The fields the teacher might have could include my name, my address and my birthday.

137

## 2 Managing data

## Questions

Look at this record about a country.

> Country: Oman
>
> Size (in km²): 309 500
>
> Population: 4 576 298
>
> Language: Arabic
>
> Currency: Omani rial

1. What are the fields in the record?
2. What are the attributes of the record?

### Did you know?

AllMusic.com is an online database that contains information for over 30 million music tracks and 3 million albums. You can search for music based on the type, artist or other individuals that were involved in any of the tracks.

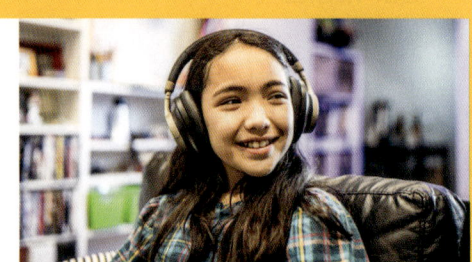

## Data types

We can store the data in a database in the form of different data types. A **data type** tells us the way that data is presented, for example as text or numbers.

You may have previously learnt about two types of data: number and text.

In Unit 1 of this book, you learnt about integer, character and string data types.

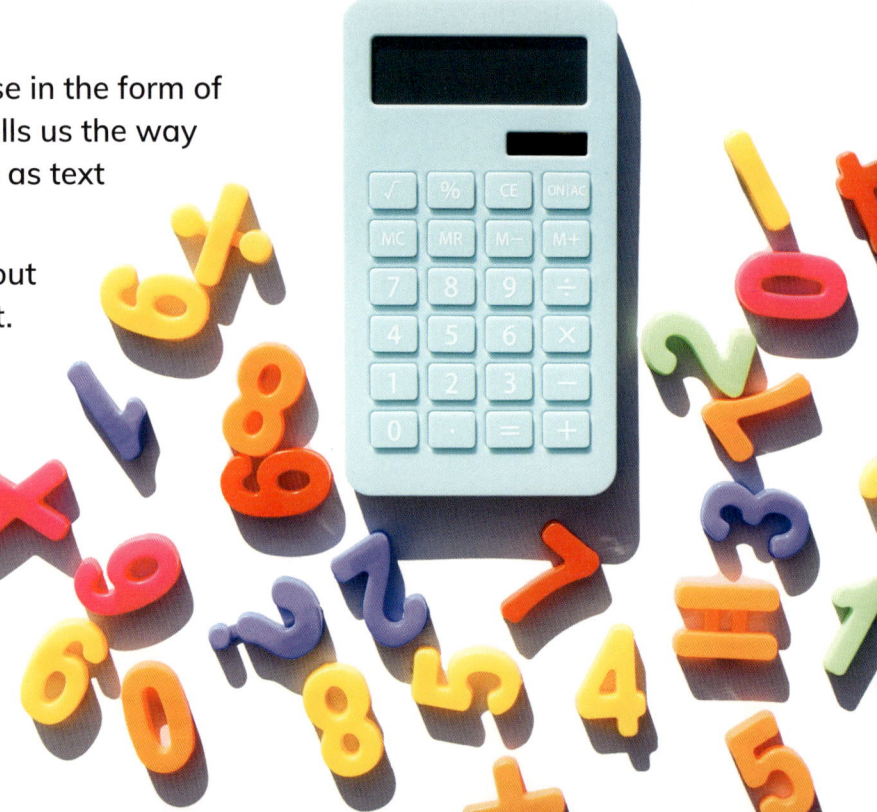

## 2.3 Creating a database

Look at this table for some information about database data types.

| Data type | Description | Example |
|---|---|---|
| Integer | Whole numbers only | 500 |
| Text | Words only | mustard |
| Character | A single letter, number or symbol | R |
| String | More than one character joined together (can include any character) | marcus_42* |

## Question

3 Identify the data types used in the attributes of the following record:

   a   Country: Oman
   b   Size (in km$^2$): 309 500
   c   Population: 4 576 298
   d   Language: Arabic
   e   Currency: Omani rial
   f   Have you visited this country?  ✓

## Formatting data

In a digital database, we can use formatting tools to make sure the data appears in the way we want it to. For example, if the data type is an integer (a whole number), we need to make sure the data will be displayed without a decimal point.

## 2 Managing data

We can format our data as text, number, currency, date, time, percentage or fraction. There are also lots of other categories we can use!

For example, if you type '21' into a cell that is categorised as the currency US dollars, the spreadsheet automatically changes the data to $21.

Look at the table. It shows the common ways we categorise data in a spreadsheet and how the spreadsheet formats this data.

| Data category | How does the spreadsheet format the data? |
|---|---|
| Number | Only a number can be entered. We can specify if the number has any decimal places. |
| Currency | Data is automatically formatted as money, for example $3, £3 or €3. |
| Date | This puts the data into the format of a date, for example 12/03/23. |
| Time | This puts the data into the format of a time, for example 07:36:00. |
| Text | Any text can be entered. A good example of this is headings or labels. |
| Percentage | This puts the data into a percentage format, for example 0.75 shows as 75%. |
| Fraction | This puts the data into a fraction format, for example 0.5 shows as 1/2. |

When entering data into a spreadsheet database, the data is automatically categorised as 'General', which means you can enter anything. The software will automatically decide how to treat the data unless you format the data yourself. For example, if you entered $5, the spreadsheet would treat it as currency. Sometimes spreadsheets can get confused if we use multiple kinds of numbers in the same column or row, like a number and a date, so it is useful to know how to change the formatting yourself.

2.3 Creating a database

### Practical task 1

**You will need:** a desktop computer, laptop or tablet and source file **2.4_formatting_data**

You are going to practise formatting data so that a data type is displayed correctly.

1. Open source file 2.4_formatting_data.
2. Select the data you wish to format.
3. Open the menu as shown in the image below.

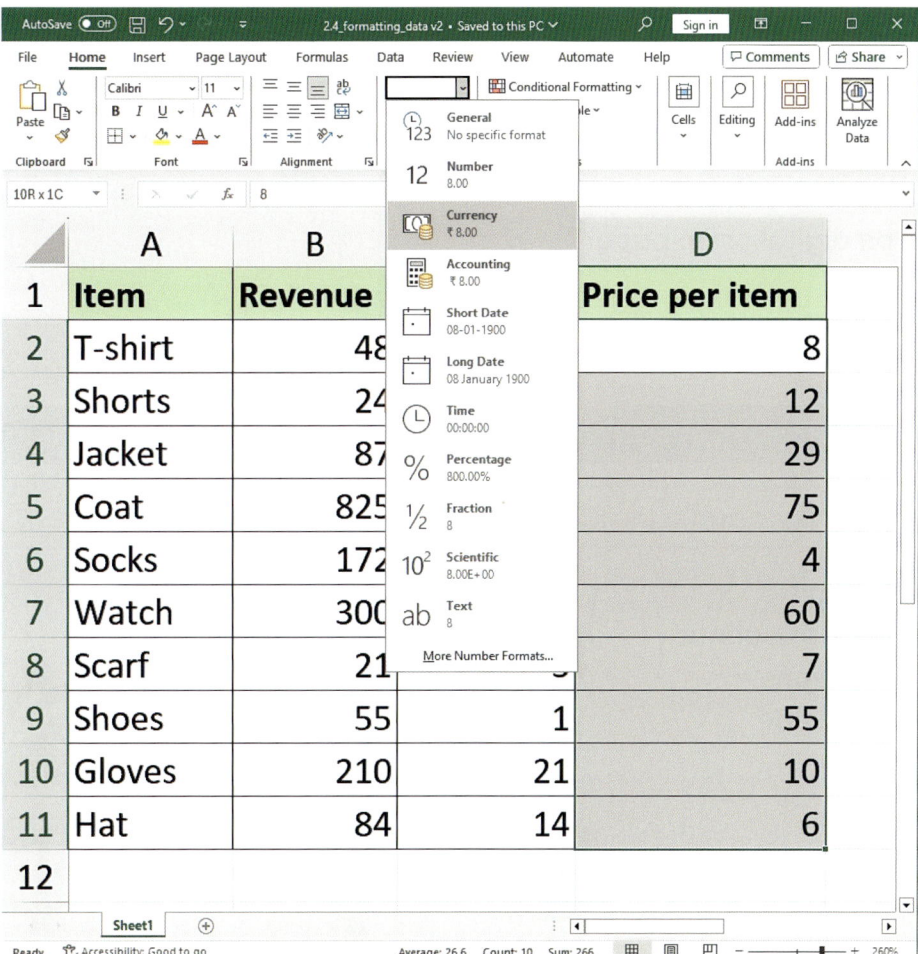

4. Choose the formatting option you want to use.
   The spreadsheet will format the cell as requested.

141

## 2 Managing data

# Designing a database

When we want to design a database, first we need to think carefully about the data that we want to collect. This helps us to identify the records, fields and attributes that will make up the database.

When designing a database, we need to think about these questions:

- What records, fields and attributes do we need?
- How many records will there be? How many fields will there be?
- How will the records and fields be arranged into rows and columns?
- What will the titles of the columns be?
- What data types will be used in each of the fields?
- Will the database be digital or on paper?

You can design a database by making notes and sketches to collect your ideas.

### Unplugged activity 1

**You will need:** coloured pens and a large piece of paper

Work in a group to design a database that provides data about different holiday destinations. Your database should include five records.

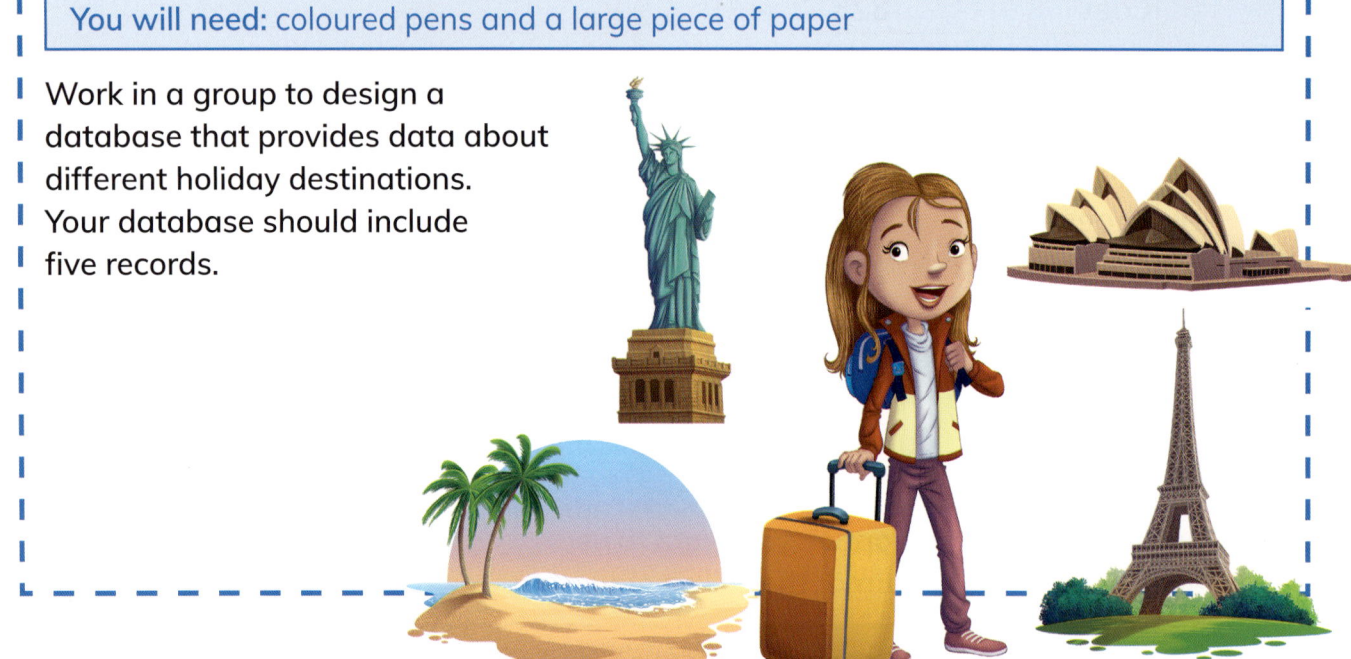

2.3 Creating a database

> **Continued**
>
> - Use the questions on the previous page to help you.
> - Write and sketch your ideas on a big piece of paper.

*I think two of the fields should be currency and language because this is important data to know if you are visiting a country!*

# Creating a database

Once you have designed a database, you can create it.

Databases can be created on paper or digitally.

## Creating paper databases

Paper databases can be created very simply by making paper records.

A paper record contains data for a number of different fields. Look at the paper record below. It shows data for a character called Splashy.

*This particular record is used in a card game where you have to try and beat your opponent by picking the field with the best score. Have you ever played one of these games, like Pokémon, or Top Trumps?*

143

## 2  Managing data

> **Activity 2**
>
> > **You will need:** a desktop computer, laptop or tablet with access to the internet, a pen and paper, Worksheet 2.6 and your database design ideas from Unplugged activity 1
>
> You are going to create a simple paper database to organise data about different holiday destinations.
>
> Create a paper record for each holiday destination. Use your ideas from Unplugged activity 1 and the record card template to help you.
>
> Use the internet to help you find information to add to your paper database.
>
> Your record cards might look something like this:
>
> Country name: Oman
> Area: 309 500 km²
> Population: 4 576 298
> Language: Arabic
> Flag:
> Currency: Omani rial

## Creating digital databases

You can create a digital database using specific software.

For example, you can use:

- spreadsheet software, such as Excel or Google Sheets
- database software, such as Microsoft Access or Oracle. These programs are designed specifically for creating databases.

You only need to know how to create databases using spreadsheet software.

## 2.3 Creating a database

### Practical task 2

**You will need:** a desktop computer, laptop or tablet, spreadsheet software such as Excel or Google Sheets, your ideas from Unplugged activity 1, your paper database from Activity 2 or source file **2.5_countries**.

You are now going to create a digital database. You can use the data you recorded in Activity 2, or you can use source file 2.5_countries.

To create a simple database:

1. Open your spreadsheet or database software.
2. Create headings for each column of your database. The headings for each column should match your field titles from Unplugged activity 1, Activity 2 or source file 2.5_countries. For example:

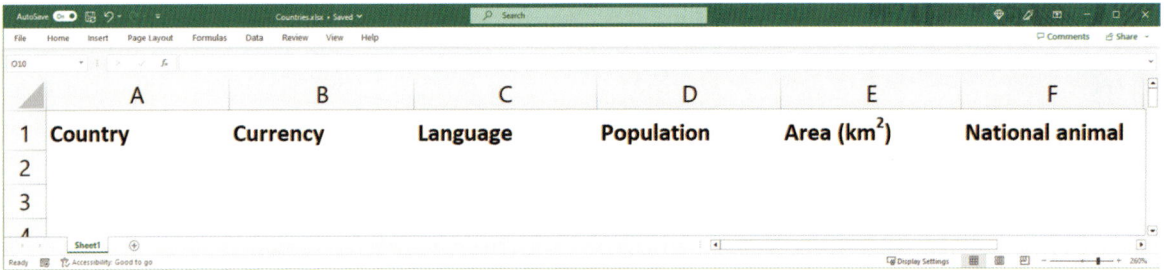

3. Type the data for each record into the database.
4. Now format your cells according to the data type in them, to ensure that all the data is displayed correctly (see Practical task 1).

## 2 Managing data

# Searching a database

We already know that databases are made up of data that is organised.

Searching organised data in a database is much quicker and more efficient than trying to search for data by reading through lots of separate record cards!

There are different ways of searching for specific data in a database. One way is to apply a *filter*, which allows you to hide data that does not meet your criteria, so the database only shows data you want to see. You may have learnt about filters in previous years.

Another way is to search for data that matches a single keyword, which you might have done previously.

One other way to search data is to use *phrase searching*. This means searching for data that matches a series of words.

For example, your school probably has a database about all the learners who attend the school. If a member of staff needs to contact your parent or carer because you are unwell, they can do a phrase search of the database, using your full name as the search criteria. A single keyword search (your first name) would not work here, as there might be more than one learner with the same first name as you.

The phrase search will bring up all records that match the criteria (your full name). That record will include a contact number for your family.

## 2.3 Creating a database

### Practical task 3

**You will need:** a desktop computer, laptop or tablet, spreadsheet software such as Excel or Google Sheets and source file **2.6_countries_database**

You are now going to use phrase searching to find specific phrases in a database.

1. Open source file 2.6_countries_database.
2. To search for a phrase, find the search tool in your software. In Excel, this is found in the Home menu, under Find & Select.

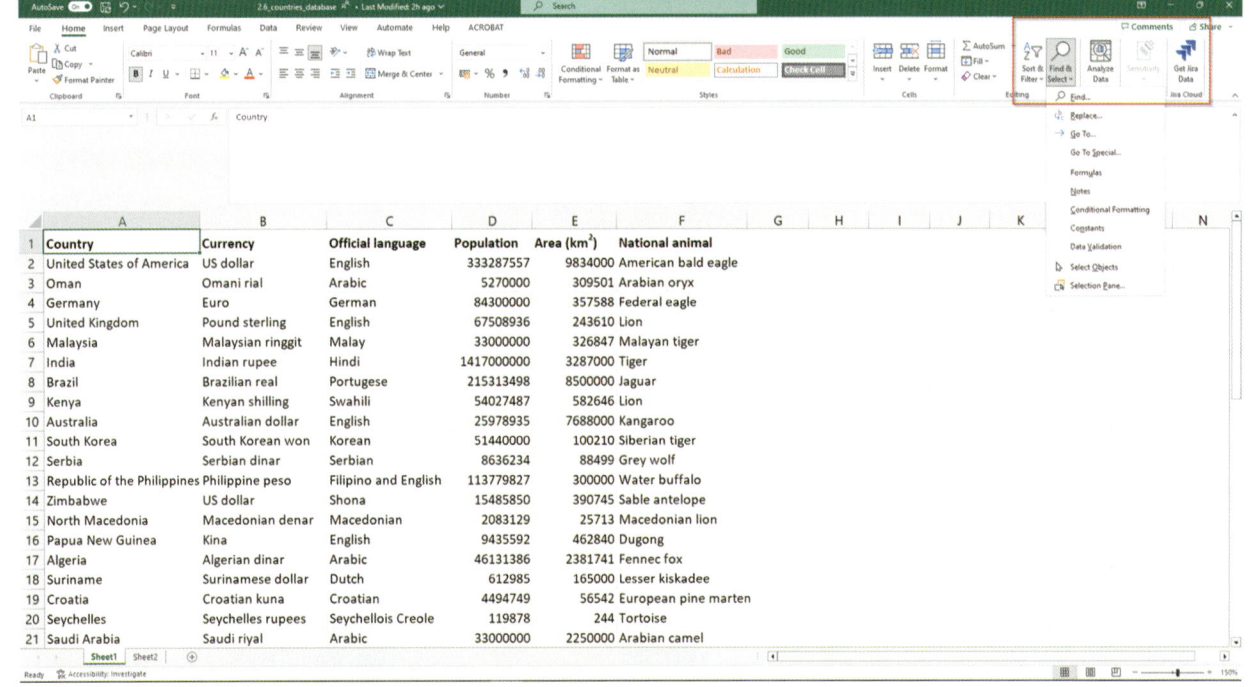

3. Click 'Find'. Type the phrase 'Malayan tiger' and press Enter.
4. The phrase you have searched for will be highlighted in the database.

## 2 Managing data

> **Continued**
>
> Use phrase searching to find the answers to these questions:
> - Which country uses pound sterling as currency?
> - Which three countries have a lion as their national animal?
> - Which country has a population of 51440000?
> - Which country has the federal eagle as their national animal?

## Question

4   How do you search a database for a specific phrase?

| **Look what I can do!** |
| --- |
| ☐   I can design a single table database. |
| ☐   I can create a single table database. |
| ☐   I can search for information in a database using a specific phrase. |

# > 2.4 How is data used?

**We are going to:**

- explore how data can be used to solve problems
- look at how data can be used to solve problems in healthcare, manufacturing and retail.

> healthcare    retail
> manufacturing    trends

**Getting started**

**What do you already know?**

- How to use a database to answer a single question.

## 2 Managing data

### Continued

**Now try this!**

Look at this database. It shows sales data for a café over one week.

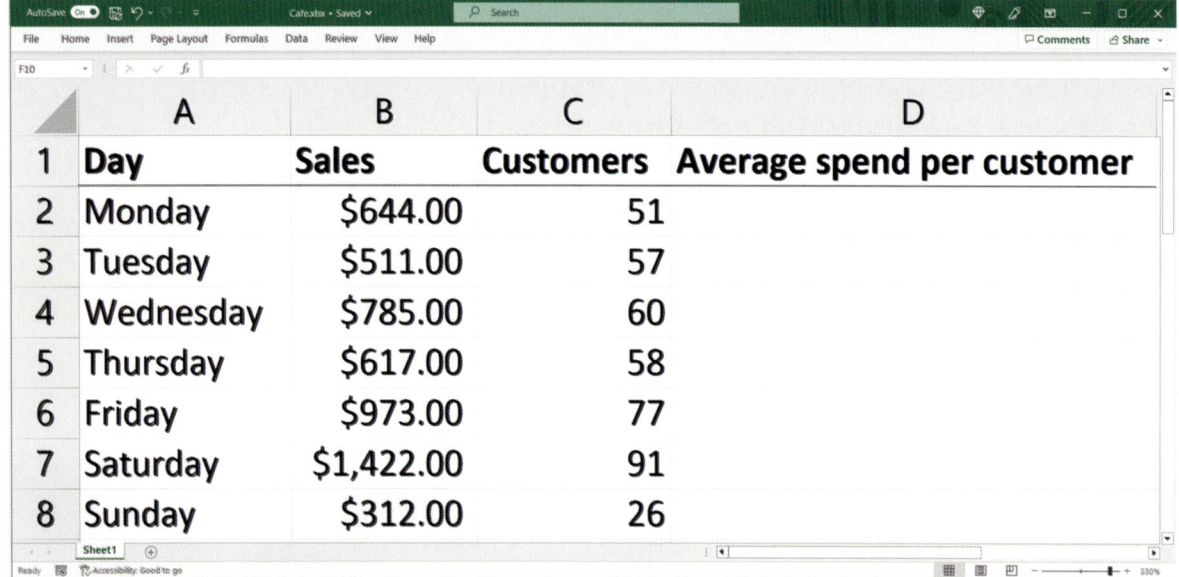

Work with a partner to answer the questions.

1. What type of data is shown in column C?
2. What function would you use to calculate the average spend per customer?
3. What would happen to the average spend if the café owner changed any of the numbers in the spreadsheet?
4. What other useful data could the owner collect and how could they format it? (Hint: Think about date, staff costs)

## Using data to solve problems

We can use sets of organised data to help solve a range of problems.

By looking at the data, we can identify patterns, for example how often something occurs. Patterns in data are sometimes called trends.

2.4 How is data used?

For example:

| Problem | How data can help |
|---|---|
| Farmers can't harvest in the rain because the crops are wet and may go mouldy. | Farmers can look at weather trends to see when it is likely to rain so they know the best time to harvest crops. |
| Supermarkets might run out of popular products and customers might shop somewhere else. | Supermarket owners could look at sales trends to find out what the most popular products were during a particular month to make sure they stock the same items again. |
| A teacher has noticed that not everyone is finishing their school lunches, and some children are hungry. | The school could look at data showing which meals are eaten and which are left, so that they only provide meals that students enjoy. |

## Solving problems in retail, manufacturing and healthcare

Sets of organised data are very useful for solving problems in retail, healthcare and manufacturing.

Retail means selling items, for example clothes, cars, food or games.

Healthcare means an organised way of looking after the medical needs of individuals or a community.

Manufacturing means making lots of products using machinery.

### Using data to solve problems in retail

Data can be used in retail to solve problems such as:
- a shop not selling enough
- a shop not making enough money
- a shop which doesn't have many customers.

I wonder what the data can tell you about me and how I am doing in school?

## 2 Managing data

For example, the manager of a shop can look at the monthly sales and see which products are selling well and which are not. They might choose not to stock the least popular items again, or to stock smaller amounts of them. The price of items that have been in stock for a while but are not selling might be reduced.

## Question

1. Describe two ways that a shop could use data to increase sales.

### Activity 1

**You will need:** a desktop computer, laptop or tablet, word processing software, spreadsheet software, a pen and paper and source file **2.7_cars_in_stock**

The owner of a car showroom is running out of space! He might need to reduce the amount of cars he has by removing ones that do not sell well to make space for ones that do sell well. He has asked you to look at some sales data to help choose which ones he removes.

Look at the data in source file 2.7_cars_in_stock. It lists all the cars that the showroom has bought second-hand and how much each car has sold for.

The owner has asked you to investigate the data to see if there are any trends, and to make any suggestions about what cars they should have in the showroom.

Use the data to answer these questions:

1. Which kinds of car are not selling second-hand?
2. Which cars make the most profit when sold second-hand?

Note down the answers to these questions on paper.

Create a short digital report for the owner of the showroom. Your report should include:

- their questions
- your answers
- your recommendations for how the business could improve sales and increase profit.

## 2.4 How is data used?

# Using data to solve problems in healthcare

Data can be used in healthcare to make improvements such as:

- identifying the most successful treatments for particular illnesses
- diagnosing new types of illness
- reducing how long people have to wait for treatment
- identifying patterns in illnesses
- saving more lives.

For example, data from medical trials can help scientists find out which treatments are the most successful at curing illnesses such as an infection. Data about patients' lifestyle and symptoms over time can help doctors find patterns. When lots of people have similar symptoms but doctors do not know what the illness is, recording data about the symptoms could help medics find a new diagnosis, or identify a new illness.

## 2 Managing data

**Unplugged activity 2**

You will need: a pen and paper

Doctors have found a new disease, but they don't know which medicine is best to treat it. They have decided to use two types of medicine to see which one works best.

A doctor assessed each patient before treatment and gave them a wellness score out of 10 (where 10 is very well and 1 is very unwell).

Two months after treatment, patients had another assessment and received another wellness score.

Look at the data with a partner.

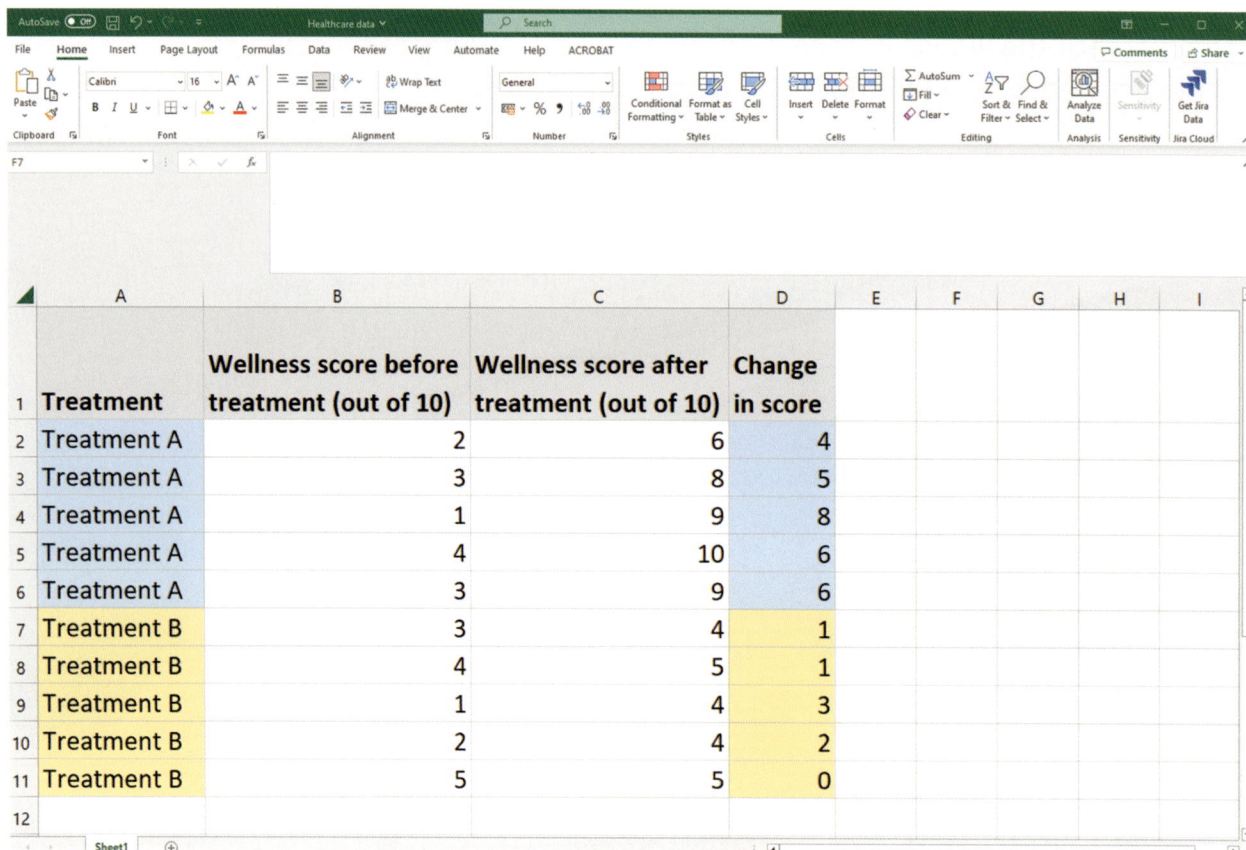

| Treatment | Wellness score before treatment (out of 10) | Wellness score after treatment (out of 10) | Change in score |
|---|---|---|---|
| Treatment A | 2 | 6 | 4 |
| Treatment A | 3 | 8 | 5 |
| Treatment A | 1 | 9 | 8 |
| Treatment A | 4 | 10 | 6 |
| Treatment A | 3 | 9 | 6 |
| Treatment B | 3 | 4 | 1 |
| Treatment B | 4 | 5 | 1 |
| Treatment B | 1 | 4 | 3 |
| Treatment B | 2 | 4 | 2 |
| Treatment B | 5 | 5 | 0 |

Which treatment would you recommend the hospital uses to help treat the disease in the future? Write down any ideas you have.

Explain your recommendations to a different pair of learners.

2.4 How is data used?

# Using data to solve problems in manufacturing

Data can be used in manufacturing (making goods in a factory) to solve problems such as:

- products not being good quality or not lasting very long
- low sales
- the number of accidents happening during the manufacturing process.

For example, a manufacturing company could keep data about all the accidents that happen during the manufacturing process. By analysing this data, they could find ways to keep their staff safe and reduce costs. When accidents happen, businesses often have to pay money to the injured staff. Staff being off work also costs the business money because they have to pay sick pay and hire someone else to do the job.

### Activity 3

> You will need: a desktop computer, laptop or tablet, presentation software such as PowerPoint or Prezi and source file **2.8_accident_data**

Look at source file 2.8_accident_data. It shows data a manufacturing company has collected about accidents that happened during the manufacturing process over one month.

Work in a group. Review the data. Decide how the factory owner could use this data to solve problems. Come up with at least three ways that the data could be helpful.

## 2 Managing data

> **Continued**
>
> Present your findings as a digital presentation.
>
> **How am I doing?**
>
> Work individually. Using a scale of 1 to 5, where 1 is the least confident and 5 is the most confident, score yourself on these points:
>
> - I could identify ways the safety data could be used to solve problems.
> - I could explain ways that the safety data could be used to solve problems.

How did you work as a team?

What roles did each person have in the group?

If you worked as a team again, what would you change?

> **Unplugged activity 4**
>
> **You will need:** a pen, coloured pencils and paper
>
> Pick one way in which data can be used to solve problems in either retail, manufacturing or healthcare.
>
> **Part A**
>
> Using the information in the Learner's Book, research how data is used to solve problems within your chosen area. Note down your findings.
>
> **Part B**
>
> Use what you find out to create a paper leaflet explaining the advantages of using data to solve problems in your chosen area.

> **Look what I can do!**
>
> ☐ I can explain how data is used to solve problems in healthcare, retail and manufacturing.

2.4 How is data used?

## Project

A local children's clothes store has recently opened, and the owner has asked for your help. She doesn't know what to sell!

She wants to know what kinds of clothes local children prefer, so she can sell them. She particularly wants to know if there are any data trends in children of a certain height or age. The owner has asked you to collect and analyse data about the preferences of people in your class.

Work in a small group. You will need to consider the following things:

- How could you use data to help the manager solve her problem?
- What data do you want to collect?
- What computing tools will you need?
- How will you collect the data?
    - What type of form will you use?
    - What kinds of questions will you ask?
    - Who will you ask?
- How will you design and create a spreadsheet or database to organise the data?
- Can you see any patterns in your data? If so, what are they?
- What recommendations can you make to the manager to help her solve her problem?

*I wonder if slightly older children prefer different colours?*

*I think the manager would like to know how tall an average 10 year old is so she can position clothes at the right height.*

157

## 2 Managing data

### Check your progress

1. What is a statistical investigation?
2. What is continuous data?
3. What does a data logger do?
4. What type of question would you use to collect continuous data using a form?
   - a  Multiple choice
   - b  Open text
   - c  Ranking
5. What operator do you use in a spreadsheet for division?
6. What function do you use in a spreadsheet to calculate a mean value?
7. Will this formula work in a spreadsheet? How do you know?

   SUM(A2:A5)
8. How can you select data to use in a spreadsheet formula? Give two ways.
9. What is a data attribute in a database?
10. Describe how to use phrase searching to find information in a database.
11. Describe one way that analysing data can help in the healthcare industry.

# 3 > Networks and digital communication

## > 3.1 Storing and transferring data on a network

**We are going to:**

- understand what kinds of data can be stored on a server
- explore how data can be transferred wirelessly through wi-fi and cellular networks
- discuss the effect of bandwidth on the performance of a network
- explore what happens if there are too many devices connected to a network.

antivirus software
bandwidth
encryption
GPS (Global Positioning System)
intranet
malware
network overload

packet
radio waves server
server farm
streaming
wi-fi
wireless

**Getting started**

**What do you already know?**

- Servers are used to store data, including websites.
- A range of devices can be connected to a network.
- Data is sent via packets over a network.
- Data can be sent using a cellular network.

## 3 Networks and digital communication

> **Continued**
>
> **Now try this!**
>
> You have already learnt about the role of a server. The photo shows a server in a **server farm**, which is a group of connected servers.
>
> With a partner, discuss the following:
>
> 1   What other devices are connected to a server?
> 2   What can you store on a server?
> 3   Why is a server used as part of a network?

## Storing data on a server

Remember, a **server** is a networked device that 'serves' data to other devices on the network. Other devices on the network can ask the server for data. Having a server means you don't need to store everything on your device. For example:

- an email server holds all of your emails, meaning they don't need to be stored on your computer

- a web server hosts websites that other devices can then access. You access all websites through a server.

160

3.1 Storing and transferring data on a network

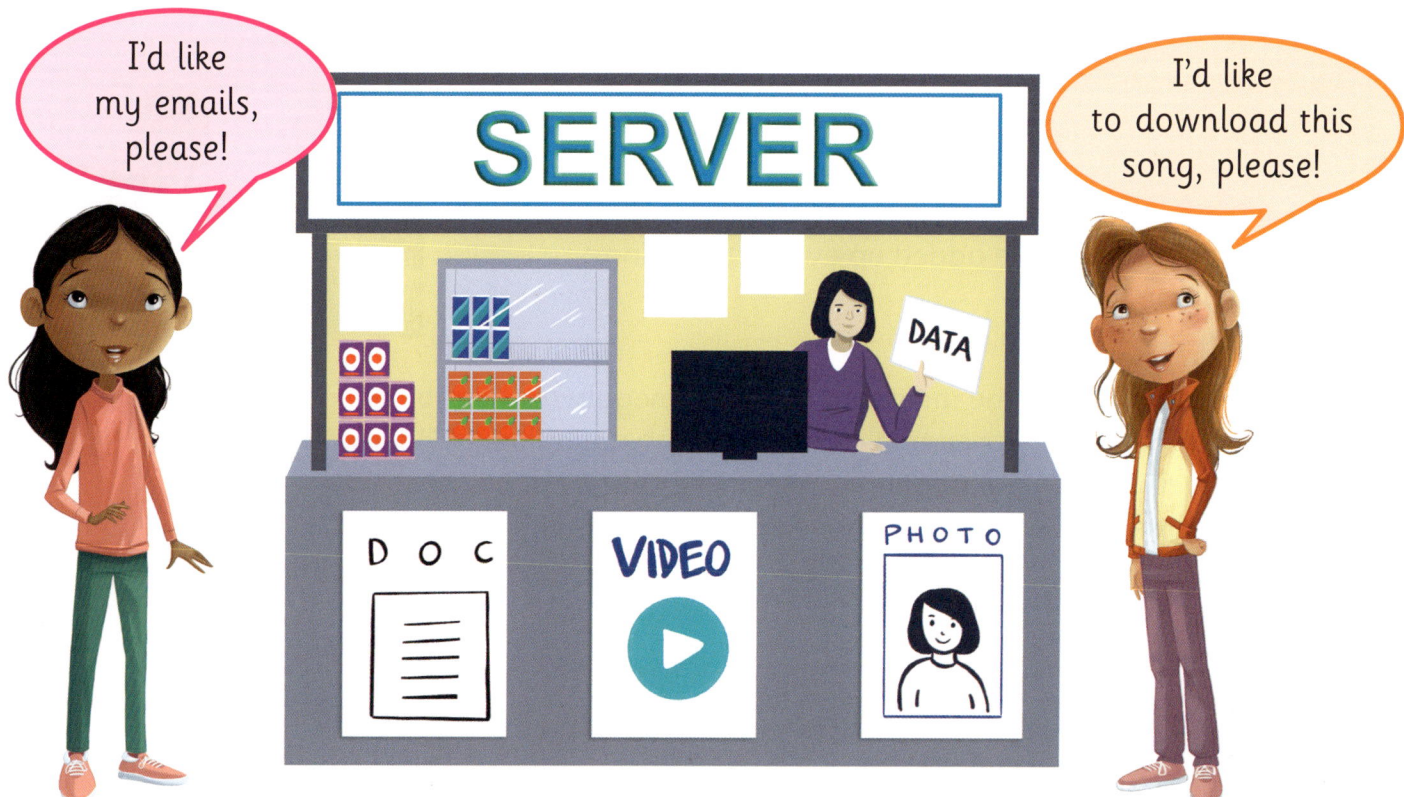

You can also save files to a server. These files can then be accessed from any other device that is connected to the same network. For example, if you saved a document to Google Drive or OneDrive, anyone on the same network (in this case, anyone with an internet connection!) could access the document if they are sent a link.

## Streaming services

Have you ever streamed a film on your TV or some music onto your phone? A specific server in a network can be used for streaming large files such as films or music. Streaming is where a video or sound file is played over an internet connection. The file is not stored on the device that plays it. This type of server needs a large storage capacity as high-quality media takes up a lot of space. You might have learnt about storage capacity previously.

161

# 3 Networks and digital communication

> **Did you know?**
>
> Netflix users across the world spend around 164 million hours per day watching videos! That is around 1 hour 11 minutes per registered user. Imagine how many hours it would be if we added up every streaming service's use time!

Files on a computer can be measured in bytes, megabytes, gigabytes and other larger sizes. For example, a typical high definition (HD) film might use between two and four gigabytes of storage space, whereas a presentation might only use 10 megabytes of space.

## Messaging services

Using digital devices allows users to send messages to other users. This is known as direct messaging.

162

3.1 Storing and transferring data on a network

Large companies might also have a dedicated specific server that allows direct messaging between employees or between customers and employees. This is a quick way of communicating as people do not have to keep checking their emails.

A private network that is only available within an organisation is known as an intranet. A school will have an intranet so that the staff in the school can easily share messages.

## Questions

1. Why might people use streaming services rather than storing a file on a device?
2. What types of data could you retrieve from a server during your school work?

---

**Unplugged activity 1**

*You will need: some pens and a large piece of paper*

Consider the server(s) in your school, and the services it supplies to other devices in the school network.

Work in a small group to draw your school network. This is known as a network map.

---

163

> **3** Networks and digital communication

**Continued**

Here is an example:

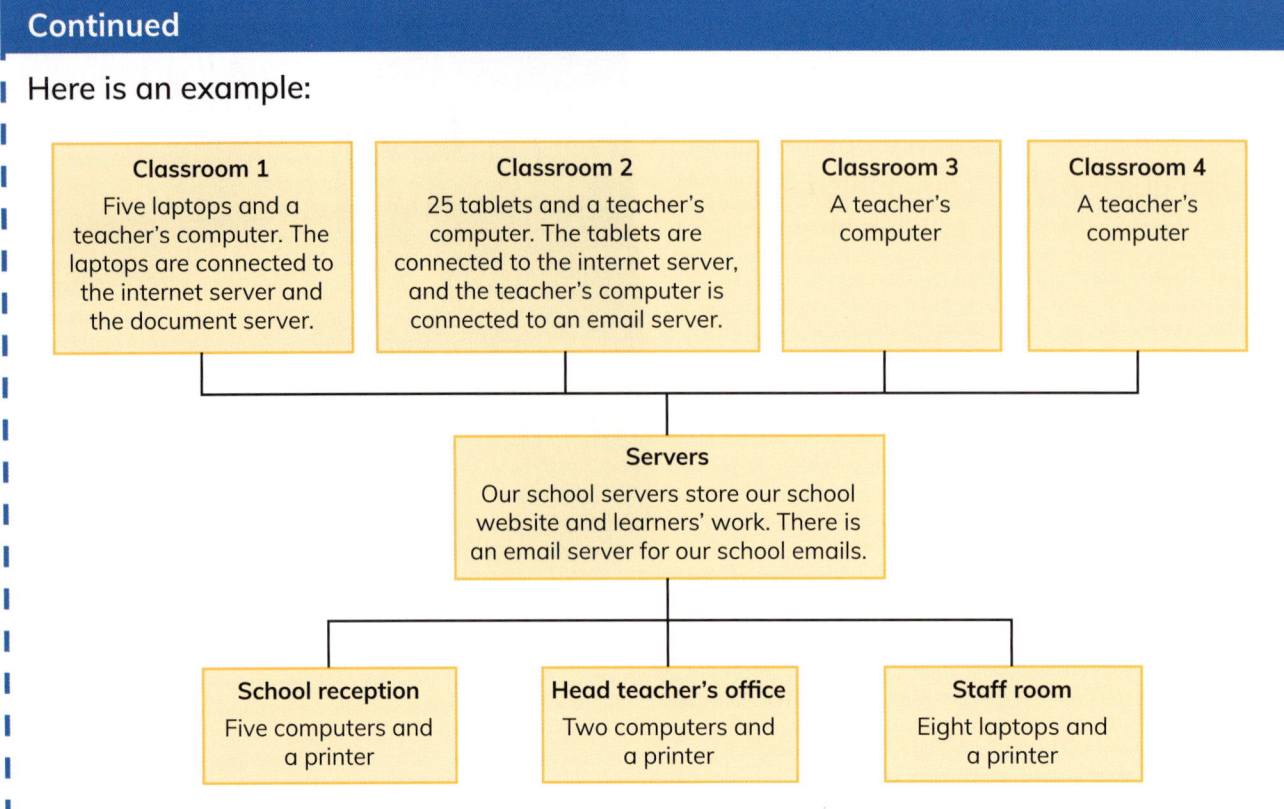

Consider the following:

- Do you have a school website? If so, you might need a web server (a server for hosting websites).

- How does your school communicate with your parents? Email? Messaging? Do you need an email server?

- How many rooms are in your school and how many devices in them are connected to the server?

- What are the connections between the server and the devices? (Every device needs to be connected to the network somehow.)

For two of the rooms, explain why the devices are connected to the server. What service does the server provide?

Don't forget, your map can cover your whole school, so think about all the rooms in your school, including any offices, the canteen and the library. It might be a good idea if each member of your group focuses on a specific area of the school.

3.1 Storing and transferring data on a network

# Transferring data

We can send data between devices using two different kinds of connection: wireless (without using wires) or wired.

Data can be transferred using wires via Ethernet cables like this one. You may have one connecting your router to a device in your home network.

Data can also be sent wirelessly. One way that data can be sent wirelessly is by radio waves. A radio wave is a form of energy that can be used to send data such as text or sounds from one place to another. Radio waves are transmitted through antennas like those shown in the image below.

165

# 3 Networks and digital communication

## Cellular networks

A cellular network is a massive network of communication towers that cover almost the whole world. A mobile phone works by connecting to the cellular network.

> **Did you know?**
>
> Over 85% of the world's population have a mobile phone. That's over 7 billion people!

When there is no internet connection available, a mobile phone will connect to the nearest cell tower and use this tower to send and receive all kinds of data.

Imagine you have gone out of the house and taken your digital device with you. When you use a digital device like a smartphone when you are out, the device is constantly in touch with the nearest cell tower via radio waves. This constant connection enables the device to send and receive messages and emails, browse the internet, stream music and make phone calls.

Phones can also use a combination of cellular internet and GPS to enable map apps to tell us where to go – this is known as satellite navigation (or satnav). **GPS (Global Positioning System)** is a network of satellites that phones can use to track their location. It can help us when we are lost or need directions.

## Wi-fi

We also use radio waves in our homes. Most homes have access to the internet by using **wi-fi** (the technology that allows digital devices to communicate without wires) through a router. A router is a networking device that allows users to access the internet from an internet service provider. Any digital device in the home sends and receives data to the router either using an Ethernet cable or wirelessly using radio waves.

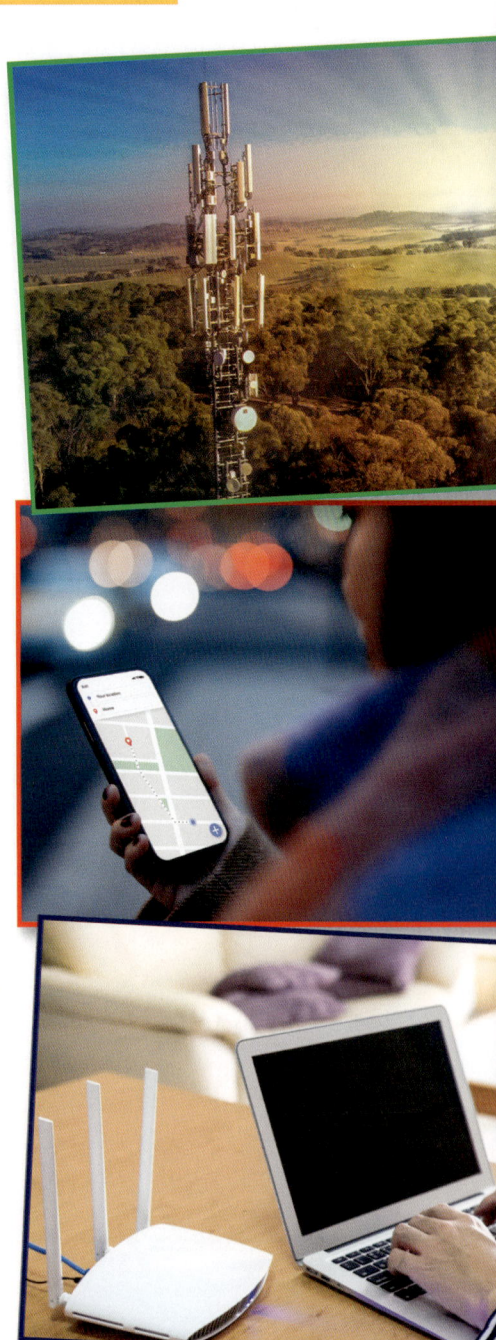

### 3.1 Storing and transferring data on a network

When data is sent over a computer network, it is not sent as a whole file. Instead, the data is split up into pieces, each known as a packet, and then sent. If someone wanted to stop the data from reaching its destination, they could steal some of the packets. If the packets do not have any encryption on them, then someone can try to put the pieces back together. If the data packets have encryption on them, then this is very difficult to do.

### Unplugged activity 2

**You will need:** a pen and paper

Work with a partner to list as many digital devices as possible that you have at home.

Decide how each of the devices you have listed can transfer data.

For each device, answer the following questions:

- Can it transfer data with a network cable?
- Can it transfer data wirelessly? With wi-fi? With a cellular network? Both?

**How am I doing?**

Using smiley faces, where a sad face ☹ is not very confident, a neutral face 😐 is quite confident, and a happy face ☺ is very confident, answer each of questions below:

- describe the range of digital content that can be stored on a server.
- explain how digital devices can transfer data wirelessly.

### 3 Networks and digital communication

## The effect of bandwidth on a network

**Bandwidth** is the maximum amount of data that can be transmitted between two points in a network in a specific amount of time.

The smaller your bandwidth is, the longer it takes to download a file from the internet or for a video to load so you can stream it. The larger your bandwidth is, the quicker the network performs.

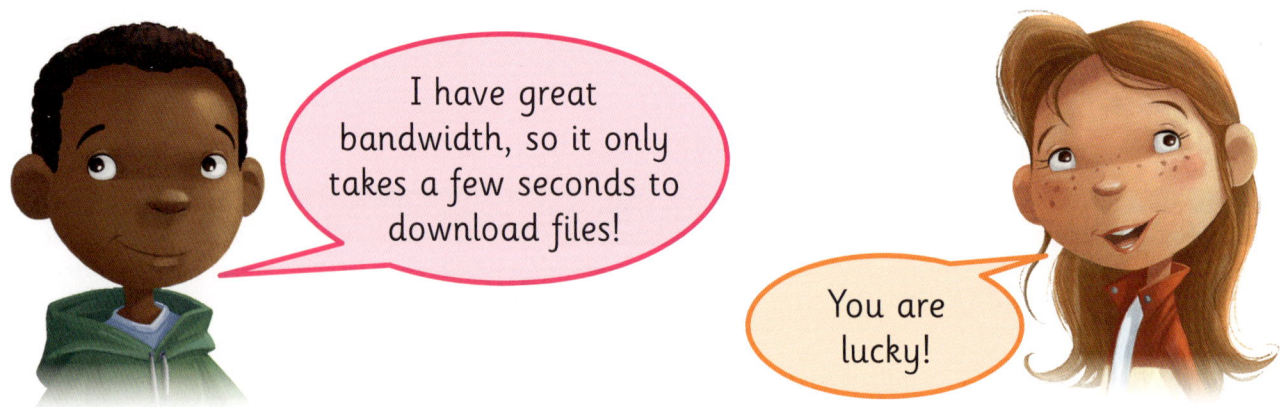

I have great bandwidth, so it only takes a few seconds to download files!

You are lucky!

Bandwidth is a bit like a straw. If you have a narrow straw, you won't be able to drink as quickly as you would with a really wide straw. It would take someone with a wide straw a lot less time to drink the same amount as someone with the thin straw!

3.1 Storing and transferring data on a network

### Activity 3

**You will need:** a desktop computer, laptop or tablet with access to the internet and source file **3.1_speed_test_website**

Have you ever noticed that when you are using a digital device it seems to take a long time to open a web page? You can check what your current network speed is using certain websites.

Go to the website your teacher will show you to find out the speed of the connection you are using.

When you have the results, share them with your teacher.

With a partner, consider the following discussion points:

- Do you think the speed will change if you do the test at a different time of day?
- Do you think the speed will change if you do the test on a different device?

The number of devices using the network can also affect the speed of data transfer. Even if you have lots of bandwidth, downloading and uploading data may still be slow.

Does your favourite TV show pause when you watch it online?

This often happens when other people are downloading or streaming content, which uses a lot of bandwidth. Your home internet connection has a limited amount of bandwidth that has to be shared out among all devices on the network. So if other people are connected to the internet and are trying to stream or download a file, the bandwidth is divided between all active devices. It is possible to pay for more bandwidth if the bandwidth needs to be shared between lots of active devices. However, there is still a limit on the amount of devices that can be connected at once.

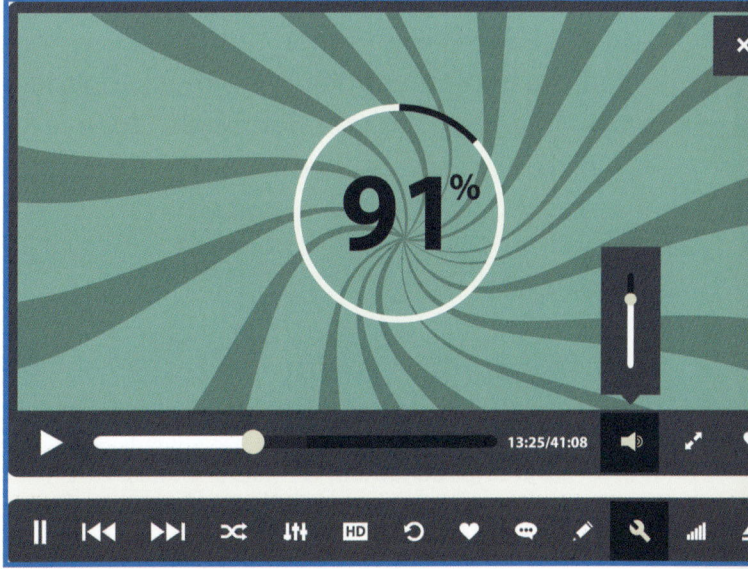

169

### 3 Networks and digital communication

Even browsing the internet, which does not require a lot of bandwidth, can affect speed if there are lots of devices doing it. This will not just include digital devices, such as a mobile phone, but other internet-enabled devices such as a smart TV, smart lights, smart plugs, or other smart devices. Too many devices can lead to **network overload**.

Network overload happens when too many devices try to access data at the same time. When a network is overloaded, the network stops working properly: data moves extremely slowly, pictures can get stuck when they are loading and error messages might appear. If some devices are demanding a lot of bandwidth for streaming or downloading, a network overload can happen with even just a few devices connected! Look at this example of an overloaded network.

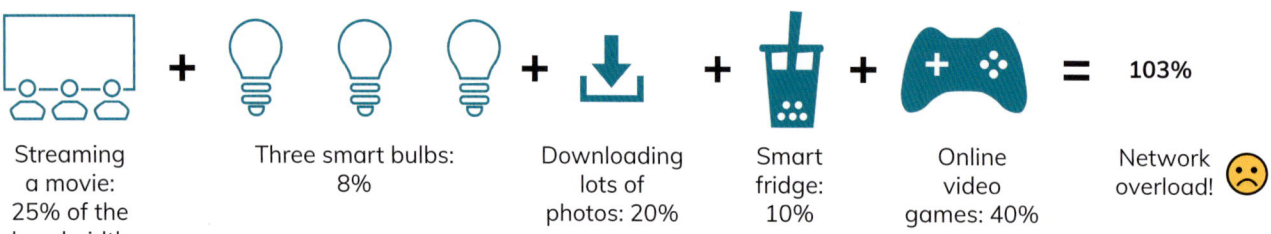

Streaming a movie: 25% of the bandwidth | Three smart bulbs: 8% | Downloading lots of photos: 20% | Smart fridge: 10% | Online video games: 40% | Network overload! = 103%

If the person watching the movie on this network stopped, then they would have enough bandwidth for everything else, though it might be slow. They could also turn off the smart fridge, but their food might go rotten!

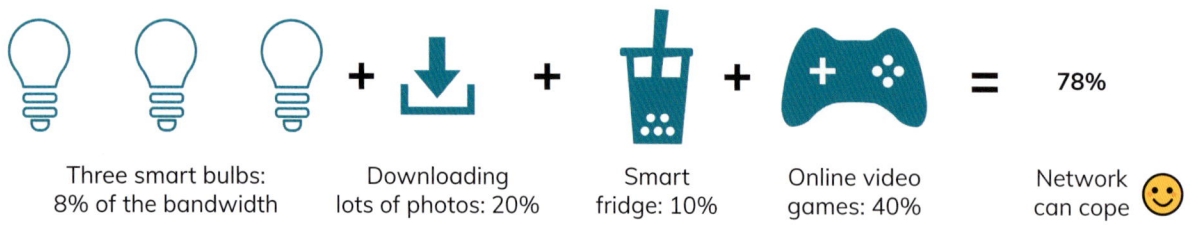

Three smart bulbs: 8% of the bandwidth | Downloading lots of photos: 20% | Smart fridge: 10% | Online video games: 40% | Network can cope = 78%

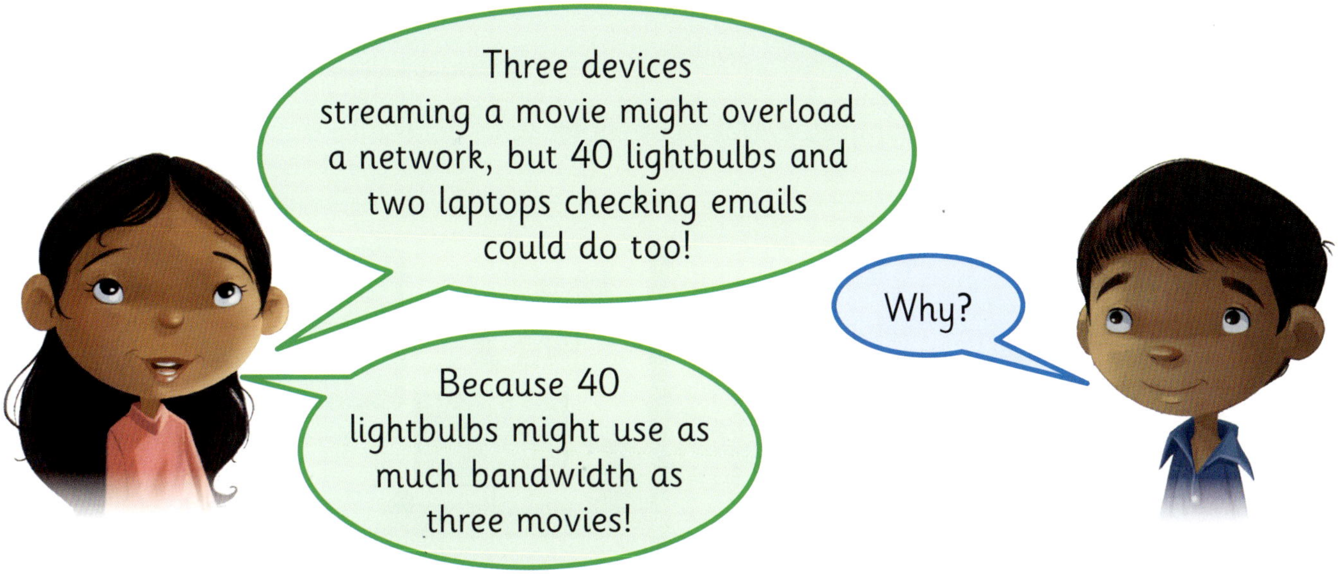

## 3.1 Storing and transferring data on a network

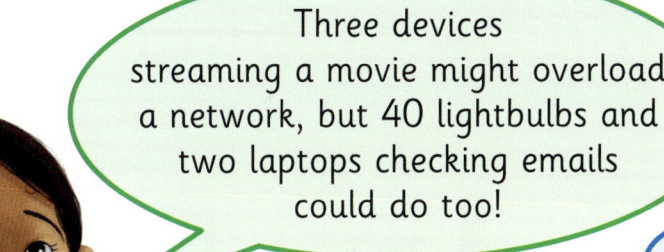

"Three devices streaming a movie might overload a network, but 40 lightbulbs and two laptops checking emails could do too!"

"Because 40 lightbulbs might use as much bandwidth as three movies!"

"Why?"

You could think of bandwidth as a pie. The more people the pie has to feed, the smaller your slice will be. The more people using bandwidth, the smaller each person's piece of bandwidth will be. If there are too many people, some people will not get any bandwidth at all!

Or you could think of bandwidth as a road. The more cars on a road, the more time it takes to travel to where you need to be because the cars go slowly. There is no problem with the road – there are just lots of cars!

## 3 Networks and digital communication

### Activity 4

**You will need:** a desktop computer, laptop or tablet with access to the internet, a pen and paper

Research and list as many devices as possible that could be connected to the internet in a home. Think about kitchen and bathroom appliances as well as devices you use for fun!

Compare your list with a partner's.

Discuss with your partner which devices are the most important.

The most important devices need to be able to connect to the wi-fi over the other devices. Which devices could be stopped from connecting in order to prevent a network overload?

Would your list change based on the day of the week? For example, would you have different priorities on a Wednesday and a Saturday?

### Stay safe!

Sometimes when a device is infected by **malware** (software designed to disrupt or harm a computer system), it can use up a great deal of your bandwidth without you realising. It is always a good idea to use **antivirus software** (software that identifies, removes and prevents malware) on a regular basis to check for any malware that might have been installed on your devices, and to keep the antivirus software up to date.

## Questions

3  Explain what bandwidth is.
4  Explain what causes network overload.
5  What steps could you take to prevent a network overload?

### Activity 5

**You will need:** a desktop computer, laptop or tablet with word processing software

Your neighbours have asked you to help with a network problem. They are a family of four who are having problems with streaming in their house, especially in the evening and at the weekend.

They have three smart TVs, a laptop, two games consoles, five tablets, two e-readers, a smart fridge, 20 smart lightbulbs and 27 smart plugs. They also have a wi-fi-enabled alarm system and a smart doorbell. One of the family members streams her favourite TV show for two hours a day.

Create a short report that gives them some advice on how to solve the issues.

### Look what I can do!

- ☐ I can describe the different digital content that a server can store.
- ☐ I can explain how data is transferred wirelessly.
- ☐ I can discuss how bandwidth impacts the performance of a network.
- ☐ I can explain what network overload is.

# 3 Networks and digital communication

## > 3.2 Securing data

**We are going to:**

- explore why it is important to keep data secure when it is sent to another device or person
- explore how a user's identity can be confirmed
- discuss the range of methods that can be used for user authentication.

> authentication secure
> facial recognition spam
> hack transmission
> password username
> phishing

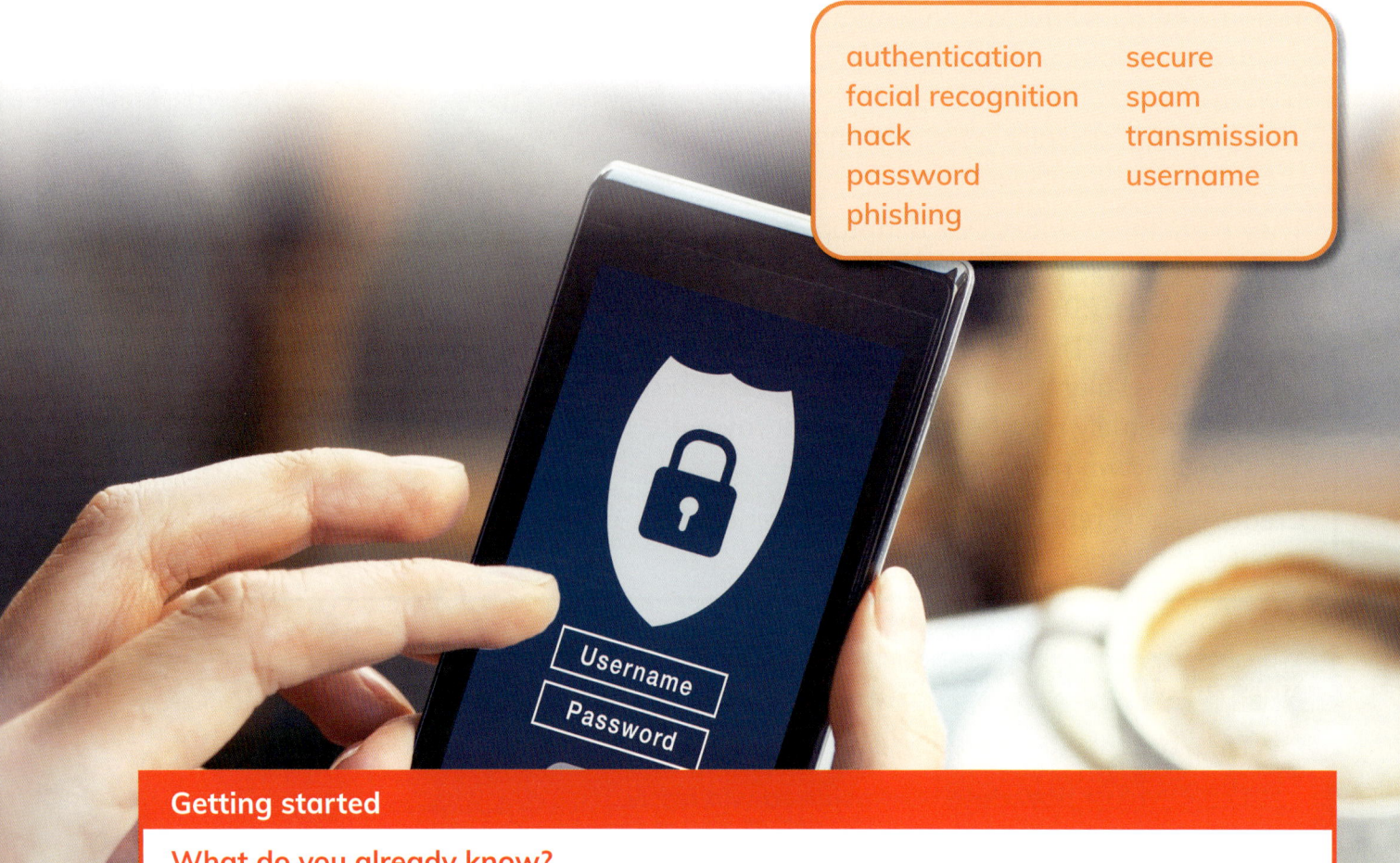

### Getting started

**What do you already know?**

- Where encryption is used in a digital system.
- Why encryption is used in a digital system.
- How ciphers are used to keep information secret.

## 3.2 Securing data

> **Continued**
>
> **Now try this!**
>
> Decode the following message:
>
> **Mywzedsxq sc wi pkfyebsdo celtomd.**
>
> Use the Caesar cipher, which is given below.
>
>
>
> Julius Caesar used a similar cipher so his military plans could not be read by the enemy.
>
> To decode the message, you will need to use a right shift by 10 letters.
>
> | Alphabet | A | B | C | D | E | F | G | H | I | J | K | L | M | N | O | P | Q | R | S | T | U | V | W | X | Y | Z |
> |---|---|---|---|---|---|---|---|---|---|---|---|---|---|---|---|---|---|---|---|---|---|---|---|---|---|---|
> | +10 shift | Q | R | S | T | U | V | W | X | Y | Z | A | B | C | D | E | F | G | H | I | J | K | L | M | N | O | P |
>
> Discuss with a partner why keeping data secure is important.
>
> Feed back your reasons to the rest of the class.

# Keeping data secure

Every day, trillions of packets of data are sent over the internet. The sending process – the transmission – needs to be secure because the data being sent is often private. Secure means safe and accessible only by those with permission to access it.

Data that needs to be kept secure includes:

- personal information, like your address or date of birth
- financial information, such as bank details
- health information, like test results.

As we know, data is split up into packets when it is sent. If enough of these packets are lost or stolen, someone who should not be allowed to read the data could see it. These people might then use that data illegally (in ways that are against the law).

## 3 Networks and digital communication

Data that has been stolen can be used for a range of purposes:

- fraud (where someone tries to trick others, usually to gain money)
- identify theft (where someone uses your personal information to pretend to be you)
- phishing attacks (where someone tries to trick you into revealing personal data such as account details)
- account takeover (where someone tries to get into an account such as your email account and locks you out).

### Did you know?

Around 333.2 billion emails are sent each day. This works out at about 47 per person, though some people might send 100, but others might send 0. Over 85% of all sent emails are spam (junk mail) or phishing attempts. The more active you are online, the more spam emails you may receive.

### Activity 1

> You will need: a desktop computer, laptop or tablet with access to the internet, software such as Publisher or Canva to create a poster

Work in a group of four. Discuss what stolen data can be used for. You might want to do some internet research into each use.

Produce a poster that explores three types of misuse.

Your poster might include:

- how each type of misuse can affect a person
- how each type of misuse could affect a business.

3.2 Securing data

What challenges did you and your group have?
How did you overcome the challenges?
What new skills did you learn?

# User authentication

There is a range of ways to protect user data.

The most common way is to make sure only the user that the data belongs to can access it. This can be done through user authentication, which means checking that the user is who they say they are. There are lots of ways to authenticate a user.

## Username and passwords

Having a username and password means that anyone trying to get into your account needs to know both before they can get access. A username is the unique name for each user of a system. A password is a secret string of words, numbers and characters that you set, like a special code you can use to prove a username is yours.

If someone can guess your passwords they can easily hack (access something they are not allowed to) your accounts. Passwords are easy to guess if people use numbers in a predictable order, the word 'password' or information that has meaning for them, such as their own name, a pet's name or their birthday. These can be easy to guess or find out if you know someone. A strong password should contain three random words and no personal information such as your pet's name or your birthday. Even though security has improved and it is not good practice any more, many organisations may ask that your password also contains:

- a combination of letters, numbers and symbols
- lowercase and uppercase letters in random places.

> Websites such as passwordmonster.com can be used to check how good a password might be.

177

## 3 Networks and digital communication

> **Unplugged activity 2**
>
> **You will need:** a pen and paper
>
> Arun was born in 2014 and has a cat named Pancake. Arun's favourite colour is purple.
>
> Below is a list of passwords that Arun likes to use:
>
> - Pomegranate23
> - Arun123
> - Arunspassword
> - Arun2014
> - hoTel@23
> - purple123
> - Pancake1
> - jewelpowdergenerous
> - chocolateflowerzoologist
>
> 1 Decide whether each password is strong or weak on a scale of 1 to 5, where 5 is very strong and 1 is very weak.
> 2 Explain why you have made this decision.
> 3 For any weak passwords, suggest how they could be improved.

# Fingerprints

Fingerprints can be used to unlock digital devices with a fingerprint scanner.

When using a fingerprint to unlock a digital device, the scanner checks for the unique pattern of ridges on the fingerprint. The scanner software compares the scanned fingerprint with the fingerprint that is stored in the device. If the two fingerprints match, the digital device is unlocked. If the two fingerprints do not match, the device stays locked.

3.2 Securing data

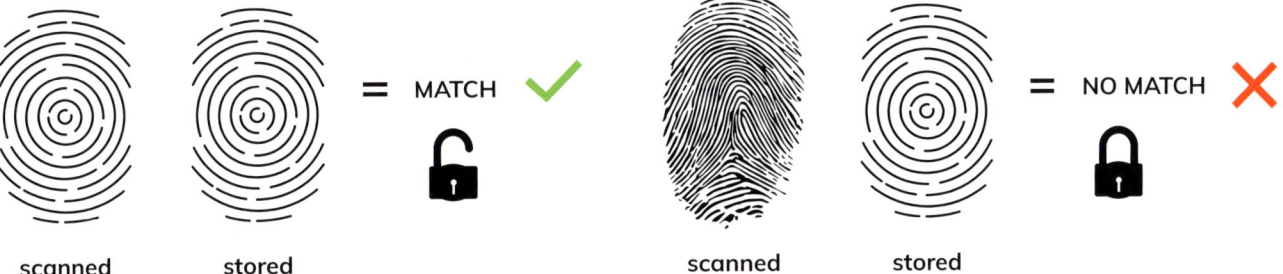

scanned  stored  scanned  stored

Fingerprints are a good way of authentication because every person has a unique set of fingerprints. This means that no two people have the same fingerprint. It is very difficult to hack this type of authentication.

### Did you know?

Our fingerprints are made up of three different types of pattern: loops, whirls and arches. These patterns are what make each fingerprint unique. Even identical twins have different fingerprints. However, there are some rare genetic conditions which cause people to have no fingerprints.

### Unplugged activity 3

You will need: a microscope, paper, paint or ink

Cover your thumb with a thick layer of paint or ink and print it onto paper. Make sure that your thumbprint is nice and clear.

Once it has dried, place your thumbprint under the microscope. What do you notice?

With a partner, look at their thumbprint. What do you notice is the same? What do you notice is different?

## 3 Networks and digital communication

## Facial recognition

**Facial recognition** is where a camera or scanner takes a 2D or 3D image of a person's face. This is then used in a similar way to fingerprints: the facial image must match a stored image before access to the data is allowed. You or your parents might use facial recognition to unlock your phones.

### Activity 4

**You will need:** a desktop computer, laptop or tablet with access to the internet and software suitable for making a leaflet (word processor or desktop publishing software)

We have looked at a range of different ways of protecting your data.

You are going to create a leaflet explaining:

- what different methods of protecting data are available
- the advantages of each method
- the disadvantages of each method
- examples of when you might use each method.

You might want to use the internet to find relevant information or extra information.

## Questions

1. Give an example of a strong password that meets the criteria for good passwords (don't use one of your real passwords!).
2. Describe why the combination of a username and password stops people from accessing your data when they shouldn't.
3. Explain one reason why fingerprint recognition is a successful method of protecting data.

### Stay safe!

You should never share passwords with someone else, even if they are your best friend or promise to keep it a secret. When you discuss passwords in class, you shouldn't talk about or share your real passwords.

## 3.2 Securing data

### Activity 5

**You will need:** a desktop computer, laptop or tablet with presentation software

Create a presentation for a parents' evening that explains why it is important to protect your data.

Your presentation should include:

- reasons why you need to protect your data
- the different ways you can protect your data
- relevant websites that can provide additional information.

### Activity 6

**You will need:** a desktop computer, laptop or tablet with internet access and presentation software

Data theft is often in the news, for example when a business has its data stolen or when an important individual leaves a device on public transport.

Using well-known news sites, research a recent example of data theft.

- What happened? When? Where? What was stolen?
- What impact was there? Who was affected?

Produce a presentation explaining what happened in the example you found.

### Look what I can do!

- [ ] I can explain why data needs to be kept secure.
- [ ] I can explain what user authentication is.
- [ ] I can describe the different methods of user authentication.

3   Networks and digital communication

## Project

### Planning a network

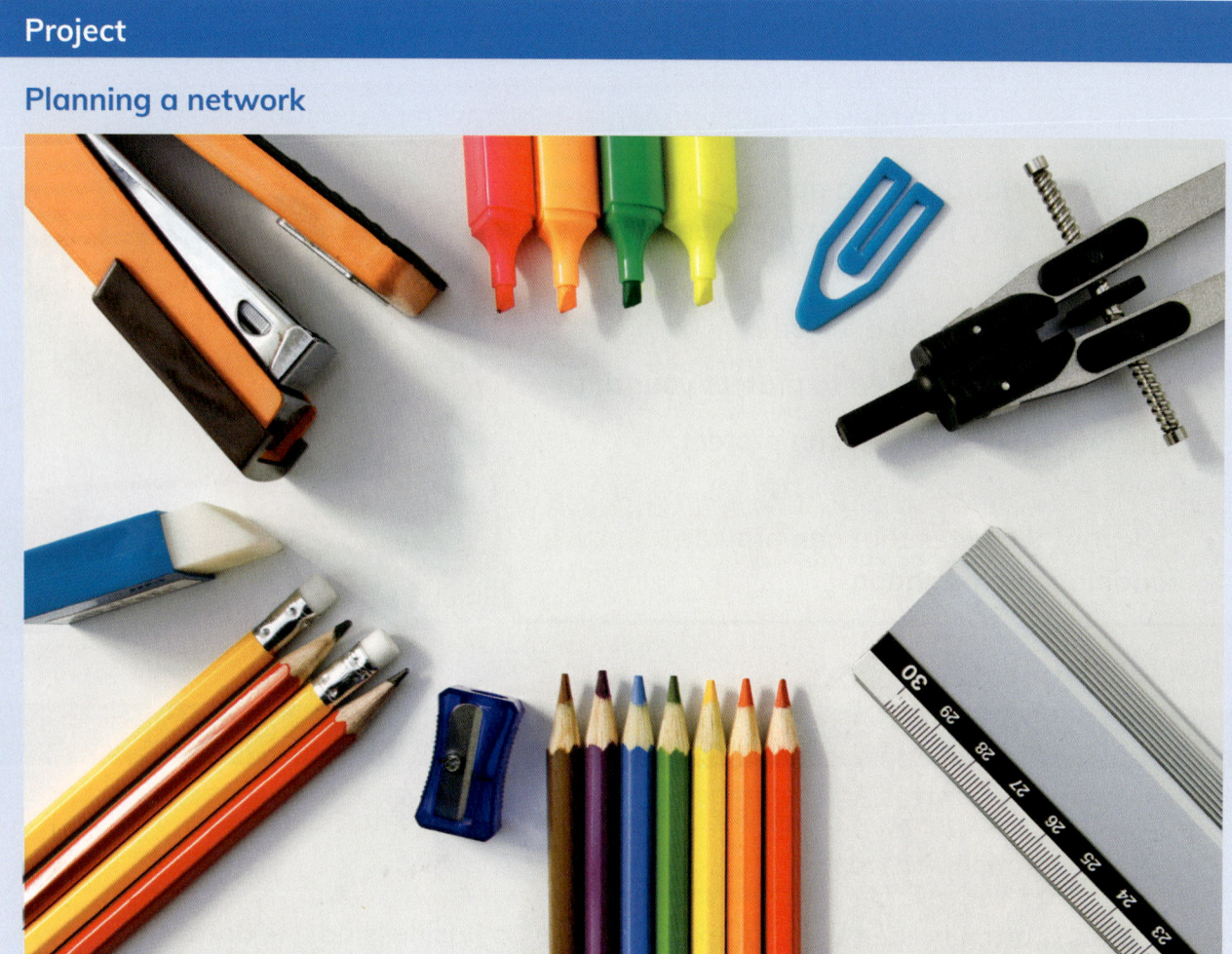

Your school is thinking of setting up a school shop in town so that parents or carers can buy all the equipment learners need for school throughout the year.

The principal tells you that:

- The shop manager needs a laptop computer which can connect to the internet wirelessly. The laptop will hold information about sales that must be kept secure as the manager will sometimes be away from their laptop. The laptop should allow the manager to message the school quickly if there are any queries from parents or carers.

- The shop needs to have tablets for parents or carers to create online accounts so they can purchase items on display. They will need to enter personal details and they may wish to walk around the shop with the tablets.

- Parents can also log into existing accounts using their own devices.

## 3.2 Securing data

> **Continued**
>
> Create a report explaining what needs to be considered when setting up the computer network for the school shop.
>
> You need to include:
>
> - Information about the different devices needed in the shop (including detail about wireless and/or wired connections).
> - Consideration of bandwidth: will there need to be an increase of bandwidth for when devices are being used by parents in the shop?
> - Suggestions about how the data can be kept secure, exploring appropriate types of user authentication.

### Check your progress

1. Give one reason why data needs to be kept secure.
2. Describe one method of securing data.
3. Why is it important that a password contains no personal information?
4. Describe why fingerprint recognition is a good way of keeping your data secure.
5. Explain the different ways phishing can happen.
6. Describe how a network can become overloaded.
7. Give one example of a task that can take place on a server.
8. Describe what happens to the data in a file (such as a document or sound file) when the file is sent to a person via email.

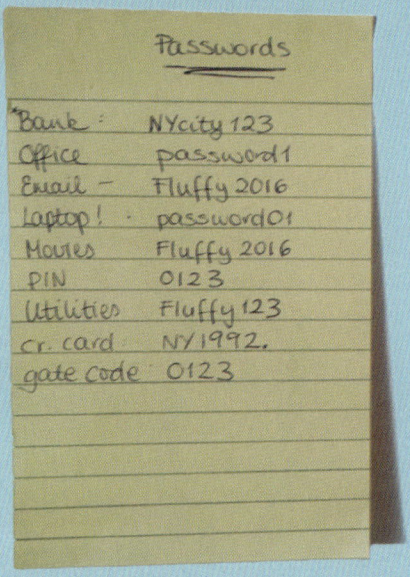

# 4 Computer systems

## > 4.1 Selecting hardware and software

**We are going to:**
- identify hardware and software components in computer systems
- discuss the key factors we consider when choosing hardware and software
- select suitable components for a computer system based on the needs of the user.

aesthetics functionality
component hardware
cost longevity
fit for purpose software
freeware upgrade

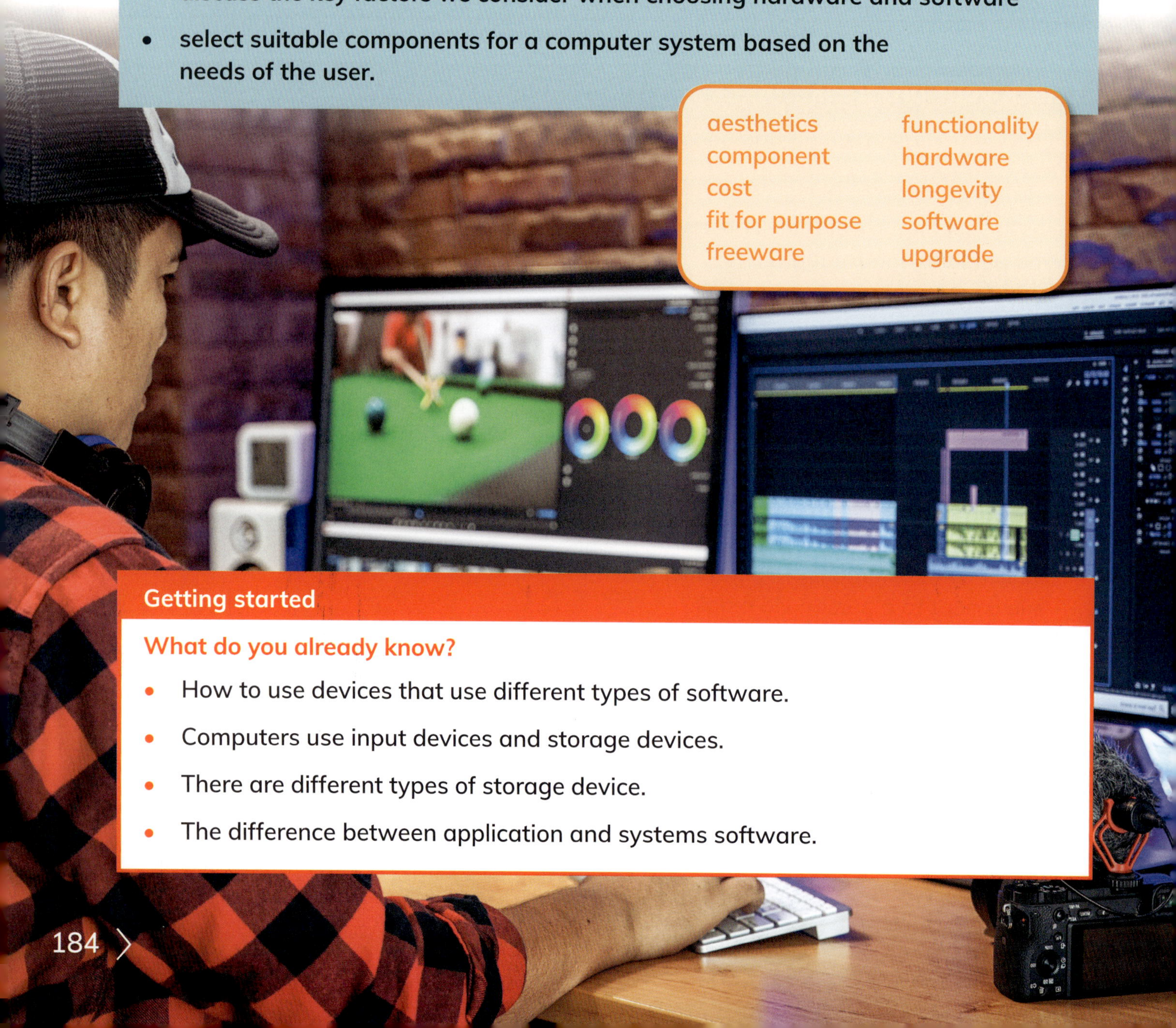

**Getting started**

**What do you already know?**
- How to use devices that use different types of software.
- Computers use input devices and storage devices.
- There are different types of storage device.
- The difference between application and systems software.

4.1 Selecting hardware and software

> **Continued**
>
> **Now try this!**
>
> Make a list of all of the digital devices you have used in the last week. Are there any other digital devices that you have seen (for example, a teacher's laptop)? Add them to the list.
>
> Look at your list of devices. Which device:
>
> - works the quickest?
> - looks the best?
> - costs the most?
> - is the one you use the most?

# Software and hardware

Every computer uses software and hardware.

Software is the range of programs you can use on a digital device.

Common software on digital devices includes:

- word processing software
- image editing software
- spreadsheet software
- web browsers
- email software
- virus checking software
- programs to manage your operating system and devices.

Software usually has to be installed on the computer. You can't touch software. It's made up of code on the computer.

185

## 4 Computer systems

> **Did you know?**
>
> The software that runs on a mobile phone can have over 10 million lines of code!

Some software can be very simple, like the program on a microwave oven or a simple calendar on a mobile device. Some software can be very complex, such as a game or word processing software. In order to run complex software, a digital device needs to have better hardware. For example a large game may need a faster CPU and more RAM to run smoothly.

Hardware is all of the physical parts of a digital device. A keyboard, a mouse, a hard drive and a game controller are all examples of hardware.

*Hardware components are physical. This means you can pick them up and touch them!*

The hardware we choose can affect how much a computer costs and how fast it can run the software.

## Components of a computer

Each physical part of a computer and each piece of software is called a component. A component is an individual part of a larger device. For example, a train is made up of many components. A door, a seat and a window are all components of a train.

The components of a computer are made up from a range of hardware and software. Each component affects how the computer runs and looks.

The following table shows some examples of hardware components.

## 4.1 Selecting hardware and software

| Component | What it looks like | Function |
|---|---|---|
| Graphics card | | Enables the computer to display pictures and images on the screen – the higher the quality of the graphics card, the more detail can be shown |
| 3D printer | | Allows you to print and create objects |
| Barcode scanner | | Allows a computer to scan barcodes in shops and post offices |
| Processor | | Carries out instructions or performs calculations (known as processing data) |

## 4 Computer systems

| Component | What it looks like | Function |
|---|---|---|
| Hard drive | | Stores data like programs and files |
| Power supply | | Provides electricity to the computer |
| Motherboard | | Connects all the hardware components together |
| Case | | Provides protection to the components to reduce the risk of accidental damage |

## 4.1 Selecting hardware and software

Software components allow the computer to carry out tasks that we want it to do. For example, word processing software allows us to type letters and other documents. Presentation software allows us to make presentations and slideshows.

### Activity 1

> **You will need:** a desktop computer, laptop or tablet with access to the internet and presentation software such as PowerPoint or Google Docs

Work with your partner to create a presentation called:
'How a computer works'.

Include these hardware components in your presentation:

- processor
- hard drive
- power supply
- touch screen
- wireless network card
- motherboard
- case
- graphics card.

For your presentation:

1. Write a sentence or short paragraph about what each piece of hardware does. You may need the internet to help you find out about some of the hardware.
2. Use the internet to find a picture of each piece of hardware and add it to the presentation.
3. Use the internet to search for the highest price you might pay for each piece of hardware. Add the information to your presentation.

#### How am I doing?

Share your presentation with another pair.

Are there any differences between your presentation and your partner pair's presentation? What differences are there? Discuss the differences.
Make one change to your presentation to improve it.

## Question

1. Laptops, mobile gaming devices and mobile phones all have similar components. How easy is it to customise and select components for a mobile phone, compared to a desktop PC? Why do you think this is?

## 4 Computer systems

# Selecting components

When you choose software and hardware components for a computer, you need to consider a number of things, such as what it can do, how it looks, and how much it costs.

## Functionality

Functionality describes the range of tasks that a device can do. For example, an oven that can roast and grill and has two cooking compartments has high functionality. An oven that can only roast has low functionality.

A computer that can complete a range of tasks has high functionality. A computer that can only do two tasks has less functionality.

You can change the functionality of a computer by adding or removing components.

## Aesthetics

We all have different opinions about how we like things to look. For example, some people might like their bedrooms to be painted yellow. Some people may like theirs painted grey.

The aesthetics of an object means how that object looks. Cars, boats and digital devices all have aesthetics.

Hardware allows people to choose the aesthetics of their computer.

For example, different people might prefer:

- a simple computer case that is red or black
- a transparent computer case that enables you to see inside
- a metal computer case.

4.1 Selecting hardware and software

Some computers have bright, colourful and attractive components. For example, some keyboards light up in different colours. The keyboard with lights does the same tasks as a simple black keyboard, but the keyboard with lights allows you to change the colour of the keyboard so it matches the colour of your bedroom walls!

## Speed

The speed of a computer means how quickly it can process data. The different components in a computer affect how quickly a computer runs.

- **Processor**

    Computer processors have different processing speeds. A faster processor helps a computer to load and use software more quickly than a slower processor. A normal computer for general use, such as in a school or in an office, does not need a really fast processor.

- **RAM**

    RAM is random access memory. RAM stores programs that are being used by the computer. If you have more RAM, your computer can do more tasks at the same time. People who want to use their computer for running very large programs or who use many programs at once need more RAM.

- **Storage**

    Storage can come in many sizes, types and speeds. People who work with very large files, like films and pictures, need much more storage.

## Longevity

Longevity is how long something remains useful for. For example, a pair of shoes that lasts for three years before wearing out has greater longevity than a pair of shoes that only lasts one year.

It is important to think about how long a computer will last when buying it.

### 4 Computer systems

We can upgrade software on a computer quite easily. Upgrade means to improve something or replace it with a better version. Upgrading software often helps to make a computer useful for longer.

Hardware is more difficult to upgrade. You often need to buy new hardware to make a computer last longer.

You will usually pay more for a computer with higher longevity. Components in a computer that last longer will be made of better-quality parts. These parts cost more money.

## Cost

The total cost of a computer depends on how much each component costs.

### The cost of software

Most computers come with general software installed, but some people need software for specific jobs. For example, a programmer needs development software.
This software would not normally be installed on a device you buy from a shop.

Development software is used to create programs.

Software can be free or cost money.

When buying a device, you should think about what software is already installed on it. Will you need to buy more software? If so, you will spend more money. Can you just use free software? This will keep the cost lower.

Software that you do not have to pay for is called freeware. Freeware does a similar job to software that costs money. Freeware is often all that people need to complete simple tasks.

Software that costs money has extra features compared with freeware. These features give it better functionality. Usually, the more money you spend on software, the higher the functionality.

# 4.1 Selecting hardware and software

For example:

- Expensive software may provide contact details for help and assistance if anything goes wrong with the software.
- Expensive software may be able to receive updates to improve the software so it lasts longer, which means it has more longevity.

Look at these two pieces of software for photo editing.
One is freeware and one is software you have to pay for.

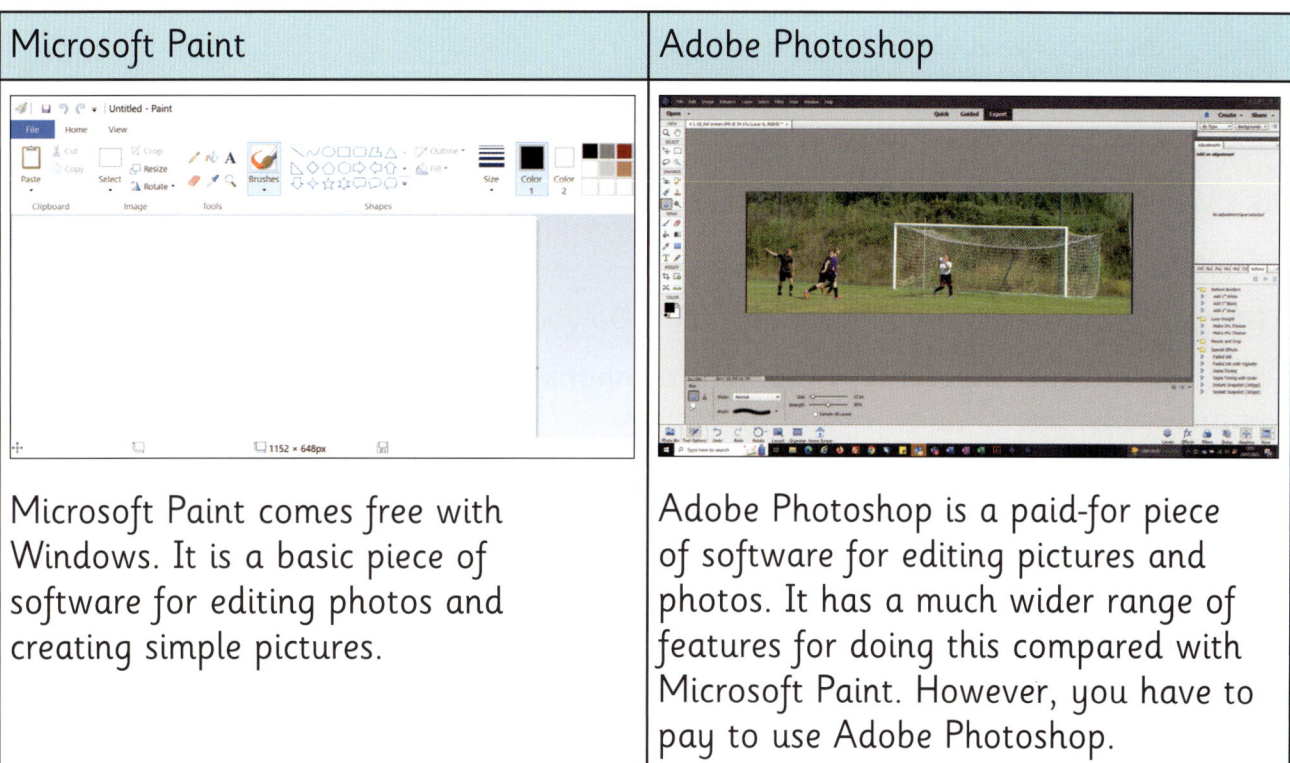

| Microsoft Paint | Adobe Photoshop |
| --- | --- |
| Microsoft Paint comes free with Windows. It is a basic piece of software for editing photos and creating simple pictures. | Adobe Photoshop is a paid-for piece of software for editing pictures and photos. It has a much wider range of features for doing this compared with Microsoft Paint. However, you have to pay to use Adobe Photoshop. |

# Questions

2   What are the advantages and disadvantages of choosing freeware like Microsoft Paint?

3   What are the advantages and disadvantages of choosing Adobe Photoshop?

## 4 Computer systems

> **Unplugged activity 2**
>
> > **You will need:** a pen, paper and Resource sheet 4.2
>
> Avast! is an example of antivirus software. There is a paid-for version and a free version.
>
> Your teacher will give you a resource sheet which shows the features of the two versions of Avast!
>
> Work with a partner. Discuss the differences between each version and write down your ideas.
>
> Imagine that you want to use this antivirus program on your computer. Answer these questions individually:
>
> - Would you pay money for it or would you just get the free version?
> - Why might you make this decision?
>
> Compare your answers with your partner's. Do you agree?
>
> Discuss with your partner why you think companies give free versions of their software.

How did you decide which version of the software you would use? What was your thinking process?

## Cost and speed

As with many things in life, the faster you want a task done, the more money it costs. For example, when you post a parcel, you can often pay more money so that it arrives more quickly.

The same is true for computers. For example:

- A faster processor helps a computer to load and use software more quickly, but faster processors cost more money because they are built from higher-quality materials.

4.1 Selecting hardware and software

- More RAM makes a computer faster, but extra RAM costs money to buy.
- Faster storage devices will allow a computer to run faster, but they cost more than slower storage devices.

Only getting one high-quality component may not make the whole computer faster!

For example, buying a really fast graphics card that costs lots of money will not make basic tasks, like making a presentation, any faster. However, it will help if you want to edit videos quickly.

# 4 Computer systems

## Cost and aesthetics

Devices that are more attractive to customers often cost more money to buy. For example, brightly coloured mobile phones, or computers with beautiful designs on them are usually more expensive than plain devices that are grey or black.

Many people are willing to spend more money on a device with the aesthetics that they like.

## Cost and longevity

Quite often, the more something costs, the longer it should last before it breaks.

Longevity affects how long it will be before you need to upgrade a computer component.

Don't forget, when we upgrade components, we often throw the old ones away. This is bad for the environment and can cause pollution. It is important to recycle old technology to help prevent pollution.

## 4.1 Selecting hardware and software

Sometimes it is better to spend more money on a computer or digital device because it has high-quality components and so it will last longer. This means you won't need to upgrade it as soon. This can help save money in the future.

> **Did you know?**
>
> It is estimated that we throw away 50 million tons of electronic waste every year. That's the same as 1 000 computers being thrown away every second!

Sofia is choosing between two processors for her new computer. Look at the table.

| Processor speed | Cost | Longevity | Cost per year | Better option? |
|---|---|---|---|---|
| Medium | $150 | 3 years | $50 | ✗ |
| Fast | $200 | 5 years | $40 | ✓ |

The medium processor costs $50 less. However, the fast processor will last for five years.

Which one should Sofia buy?

Because the faster processor will last longer, it will cost less money over time. So if Sofia can afford the faster processor, it is the better one to buy.

### 4 Computer systems

## Fit for purpose

Would you drive to school in a tractor?

Would you use a wheelbarrow to take your books into school?

Would you use a bicycle to take a caravan on holiday?

The answer to these questions is probably 'No!' Each picture shows something that is not fit for purpose. If something is fit for purpose, it is able to do the job we want to use it for.

## 4.1 Selecting hardware and software

When we buy software or hardware, we need to think carefully about whether it is fit for purpose.

Many computers and digital devices are designed to be 'general purpose'. This means that they will do most things for most people. But they will not be able to do everything that everyone wants.

Some computers need different hardware and software so they are fit for purpose for an individual.

Imagine an artist and a gamer both want new computers.

The artist spends lots of time drawing and editing pictures on a computer. The e-sports competitor spends a lot of time playing games. Needing a computer for artwork is very different to needing a computer for gaming. Each of these people have different needs and requirements, and each of these people need a computer that is fit for purpose.

### Unplugged activity 3

**You will need:** a pen and paper

#### Part A

Two different people want to buy a computer: a teacher and a teenager who plays lots of games.

Look at the table. It shows the type of device each person is thinking of buying. Each part of the device is rated as high, medium or low. High means that it is expensive and good quality. Low means that it is cheap and low quality.

| Person | Job | Processor | Storage | RAM | Monitors | Longevity |
|---|---|---|---|---|---|---|
| | Teacher | Medium | Low | Low | Medium | Medium |
| | Gamer | High | High | High | High | Short |

Work with three other classmates.

## 4 Computer systems

### Continued

Discuss the following questions in your group.
- Is the chosen device suitable for each person?
- What makes you think it is? Why or why not?
- What makes you think it isn't? Why or why not?
- What changes would you make to the device to make it fit for purpose? Why?

**Part B**

Think about what you use a computer for. Use the headings in the table to write down the sort of computer you would need. Share your answers with the other members of your group. Discuss what each person has written and ask them to explain their decisions.

### Unplugged activity 4

Work with a partner.

Ask them to imagine that they are buying a computer for a member of your family. Tell your partner what your family member wants the computer for.

1. Explain what longevity means. Describe how longevity relates to cost. Does your partner agree with your explanation?
2. Ask your partner to:
   a. recommend the components and software they would need
   b. use a low, medium and high rating when talking about the processor, storage, RAM and monitors
   c. explain why they have chosen these ratings.

Give your partner feedback on how you think they did. Now swap roles and do the activity again.

### Look what I can do!

- [ ] I can identify the hardware components and software components in computers.
- [ ] I can discuss what is important when choosing hardware and software components for computer systems.
- [ ] I can select components for a computer based on the functionality the computer needs to have for a particular user.

# > 4.2 Programming environments

**We are going to:**
- understand the difference between text-based and block-based programming languages
- identify when text-based and block-based programming languages should be used.

block-based programming language
programming environment
programming language
text-based programming language

### Getting started

**What do you already know?**
- How to use word processing software to create new documents.
- How to plan programs on paper before creating them on a computer.
- How to write programs using Scratch.

4 Computer systems

> **Continued**
>
> **Now try this!**
>
> What do you think are the differences between a block-based programming language and a text-based programming language?
>
> Write down your ideas on some paper. Think about the following questions when making your notes:
>
> - What does each one look like on the computer screen?
> - Do they both do the same thing?
> - Which do you think might be easier to use? Why?
>
> Share your ideas with other learners.

# Programming languages

There are many types of programming language. A programming language is a way of writing commands to create a program that tells a computer what to do.

We write a programming language (also known as code) inside a programming environment. The programming environment is a set of tools that are used to write and test computer programs. One tool is an editor that allows us to type the commands we want for our program. Programming environments are also known as development environments.

## 4.2 Programming environments

Different programming languages are designed for different jobs. Some languages are better for producing computer games. Other languages are much better for writing pieces of software, like word processing or spreadsheet software. There are some programming languages that exist only for doing maths calculations. Some special programming languages have been created just to make web pages.

When you learn to program, you learn about different techniques and ways to write code. Each technique does something different.

Many programming languages allow you to use these techniques – but you might write them in different ways in different languages. This is similar to learning a foreign language. You can say 'Hello!' in many different languages – you just need to learn how to say it in the language you want to use.

### Did you know?

No one really knows how many programming languages there are in the world! Some programming languages that were created in the 1950s are still in use today!

# 4 Computer systems

## Block-based programming languages

Block-based programming languages allow the user to drag and drop coloured blocks of code into a code window using a mouse. Blocks 'click' together to make larger blocks of code.

The most well-known block-based programming language is Scratch. You probably used Scratch in Unit 1.

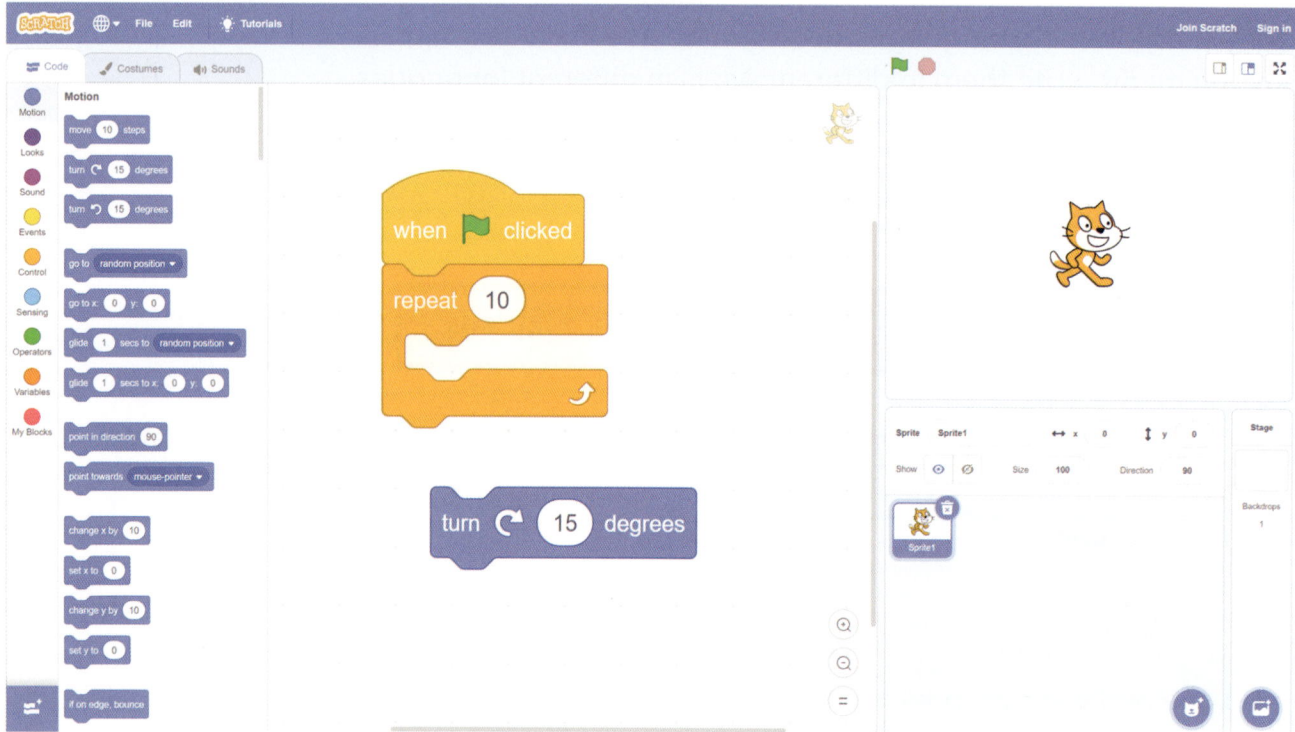

In Scratch, blocks that do similar things are grouped together by colour. For example, all the blocks that allow you to move a sprite are the same colour.

It is also possible to edit the code in some blocks.

Block-based languages can be quite easy to use because a user doesn't have to remember the names of commands. The colours also make it easier to find the right block and make the language look more fun and interesting.

Block-based languages are often used to show new programmers how to program.

## 4.2 Programming environments

Block-based languages allow users to create games and animations quickly. For example, you can create a simple game where you have to fly a rocket through space, avoiding asteroids.

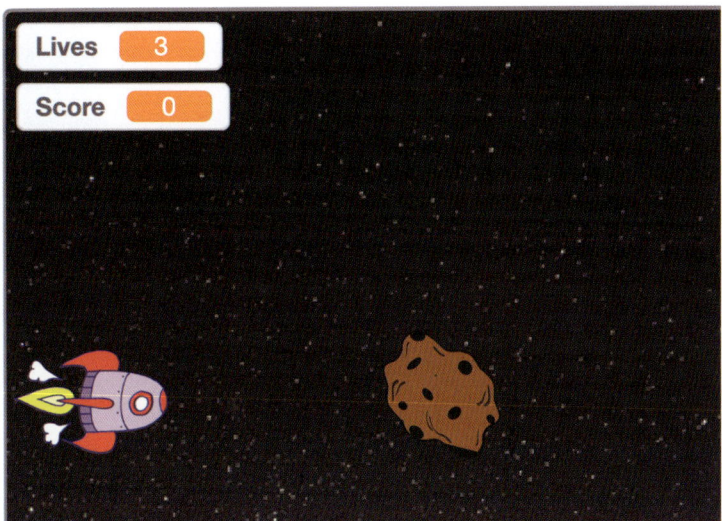

Some block-based languages allow to you make music or control small robots. However, they are not suitable for making larger and more complicated games. They are also not suitable for designing professional software such as word processing software.

### Activity 1

**You will need:** a desktop computer, laptop or tablet with access to the internet

Search for Scratch in a web browser. On the Scratch website, go to the 'Ideas' page. Pick the 'Getting Started' tutorial and try using Scratch to make a short program. Your program should display ten numbers on the screen.

#### How are we doing?

Share your program with a partner. What differences are there between your program and theirs? Do they both work in the same way?
What did you like about their program?

# 4 Computer systems

## Text-based programming languages

**Text-based programming languages** use text commands typed on a keyboard. Everything you do must be typed into a file before it can be run. This is very different to the 'drag and drop' method of block-based languages.

Text-based languages can be a lot harder to learn. This is because you need to remember the text used for each command. You need to remember what the commands do and how to spell them. If you make a spelling mistake or an error, the program will not work.

It also takes longer to get fun things to happen. Making a cat dance across a screen can take a few minutes with block-based programming. It takes a lot longer to do this using a text-based programming language.

There are advantages of text-based programming languages though. They can make much more advanced and challenging programs. They allow you to create and use many different techniques. Almost every piece of software you use was written in a text-based language.

> ### Did you know?
> The code that controls the Mars Curiosity Rover is about 5 million lines long! That's 170 000 sides of A4 lined paper!

4.2 Programming environments

> **Activity 2**
>
> > **You will need:** a desktop computer, laptop or tablet with access to the internet and desktop publishing software
>
> Use the internet to find out about the text-based programming language C# ('C sharp'). This language is used to write programs and games.
>
> Create a poster to share what you find out about C#.
>
> Include the following information:
>
> - When was it invented?
> - What does it look like? (Add a screenshot or other image.)
> - What sort of software could you create with it? (Add some pictures to show what the language might be used to create.)
> - How popular is the language? (How many people use it?)
>
> **How are we doing?**
>
> Share your poster with your classmates. Look at the posters they have made. Find one more fact about the language that you could add to your poster. Edit your poster to include this new information.

# Using programming languages

Software and digital games are written using programming languages.

Some game programs and pieces of software are very complicated, such as:

- a very realistic racing car game where players feel like they are really driving a car – the car needs complicated commands and high-quality graphics
- word processing software and presentation software with lots of tools for a user to carry out different tasks.

207

## 4 Computer systems

Complicated programs and games are written using text-based languages.

Other games and programs are very simple, such as:

- a simple subject quiz that asks a question, provides space to answer it and then gives some feedback
- a simple game where you have to dodge asteroids by moving a rocket up and down on the screen.

Simple programs and games may be written using block-based programming languages.

The text-based programming language C++ is one of the most popular languages for writing computer games!

### Unplugged activity 3

Work on your own.

Look at this list of software and games. For each one, say if you think a block-based programming language or a text-based programming language would be most suitable to create it.

- A simple spelling game where the computer plays words aloud and a learner then types in the correct spelling
- A graphics design program with lots of complicated tools to edit images
- A simple animation where a dinosaur walks onto the screen, tells a joke, and then walks off
- A complex multi-level adventure game with high-quality graphics and videos

### Look what I can do!

☐ I know the difference between text-based and block-based programming languages.

☐ I can give examples of some languages and what they might be used for.

# > 4.3 Storing data

**We are going to:**
- understand why data must be changed into numbers before a computer can process it
- identify the units used to show how large a storage device is.

analogue    continuous    gigabyte    nibble
bit         digital       kilobyte    sound waves
byte        digitise      megabyte    terabyte

**Getting started**

**What do you already know?**
- How to save documents and files to a digital device.
- Computers use binary to represent data.
- You may have recorded music or voice messages for friends, or spoken to them using video conferencing software.
- Digital content is stored on servers.

## 4 Computer systems

> **Continued**
>
> **Now try this!**
>
> Look at a digital device. See if you can write down:
> - how much storage it has
> - how much storage you have used
> - how much storage is left
> - the units that measure storage on the device.
>
> Discuss your findings with other classmates.

# Digital storage

## Digital data and analogue data

There are two types of data: digital data and analogue data.

Digital data is made up of binary digits: the numbers 0 and 1. The number 0 means that electricity is turned off, and the number 1 means that electricity is turned on.

Analogue data is different – it is not limited to the numbers 0 and 1. It is a type of signal that uses waves, such as light or sound. Analogue data is continuous. Something that is continuous keeps going without being interrupted. When talking about data, continuous means the data can take any value. A line of analogue data on a graph changes smoothly. There are no breaks in the data.

Look at the following picture. It shows what analogue data and digital data look like when the values are drawn on a graph.

## 4.3 Storing data

**Analogue**

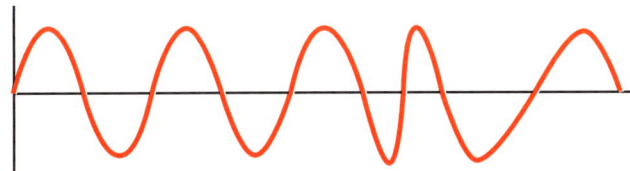

**Digital**

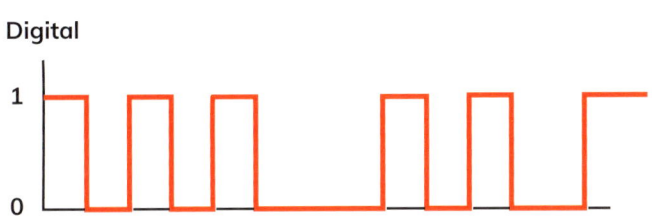

Digital devices can understand and create digital data.
Humans and animals can understand and create analogue data.

The most common analogue data is sound! Your ears hear in analogue and continuously detect sound as sound waves. Sound waves are all around us. For example, your friends talking to you, the sound of the traffic in a city, or the noise of music from a radio.

Sound waves are air vibrations – they travel through the air and our ears detect them. Our brain processes the sound waves and we hear the sound.

We can't see sound waves, but the image below shows what a sound wave looks like when we record sound on a computer.

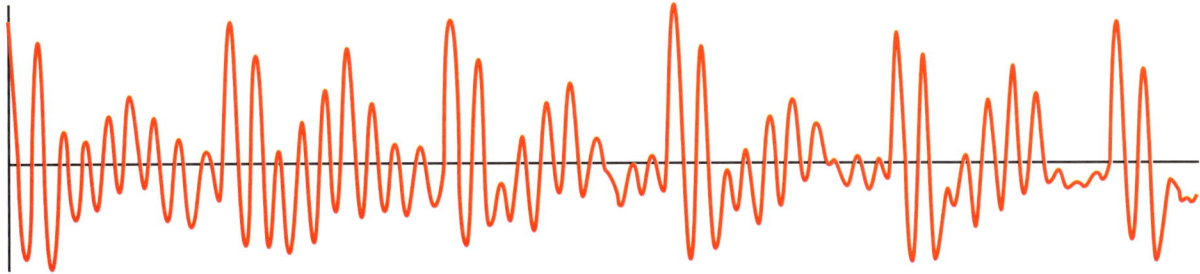

Computers cannot process analogue data. This is because computers can only understand data that is made up of binary digits: the numbers 0 and 1.

211

### 4 Computer systems

For a computer to understand, process or use analogue data such as sound, we need to digitise it. This means converting (changing) the analogue data into digital data (numbers) that a computer can process.

## Digitising analogue data

To digitise sound waves, we need a microphone. Microphones detect analogue data and a computer program then digitises the analogue data. The digital data can then be stored and used later.

Computers can detect other forms of analogue data using different sensors. For example, they can detect heat and light.

## Storing and processing data in digital format

We can only store analogue data after it has been converted into digital data.

You can do different things with the digital data. For example:

- store it on a hard drive
- share it with other people, for example over the internet
- change it using computer programs.

212

### 4.3 Storing data

We can process digital music on a computer using audio editing programs. Audio editing programs can change the digital data in different ways. For example, they can:

- make the sound louder or quieter
- add more digital data
- delete parts of the recorded sound.

> **Stay safe!**
>
> There are laws that protect most music from being copied and shared with other people. Always check to see if you are allowed to send music to other people.

#### Activity 1

> You will need: a desktop computer, laptop or tablet with access to the internet and sound recording software

Write a script to describe your understanding of how analogue data is stored as digital data.

Include the following in your script:

1. What is analogue data? Give some examples.
2. What is digital data?
3. Why do we digitise data?
4. What can we use to digitise analogue data such as sound?
5. Describe what happens when we digitise data.
6. Explain what we can do with the digitised data. Give some examples.

Record your sound file.

##### How am I doing?

Play your recording back. Did you describe digitisation of data well? Is there anything you would change about your script or recording if you did the activity again?

## 4 Computer systems

# Units of storage

Computers can only process and store digital data. Remember, digital data is stored as binary digits: the numbers 0 and 1.

Humans use a different way of counting that uses the digits 0 to 9, and the terms tens, hundreds, thousands and millions to group numbers together.

In computing, a single binary number (0 or 1) is called a bit (short for 'binary digit'). Groups of bits are given names. These are units of storage.

- A nibble is made up of 4 bits.
- A byte is made up of 8 bits.
- A kilobyte (KB) is 1000 bytes.
- A megabyte (MB) is 1000 kilobytes. These units of storage are often used when talking about the sizes of files we store on a computer. For example, a photo might be 5 MB in size.
- A gigabyte (GB) is 1000 megabytes. Gigabytes are often used when talking about how big storage devices are, like hard disks and USB pen drives.
- A terabyte (TB) is 1000 gigabytes. Terabytes are used when talking about storage space on servers, for example where web pages are stored.

Look at the table. It shows the units of storage and their size in bits.

| Unit of storage | Number of bits | Also equal to . . . |
|---|---|---|
| Bit | 1 | |
| Nibble | 4 | |
| Byte | 8 | |
| Kilobyte (KB) | 8 000 | 1 000 bytes |
| Megabyte (MB) | 8 000 000 | 1 000 kilobytes |
| Gigabyte (GB) | 8 000 000 000 | 1 000 megabytes |
| Terabyte (TB) | 8 000 000 000 000 | 1 000 gigabytes |

4.3 Storing data

> **Did you know?**
> One terabyte could store roughly 1000 hours of movies or 150 000 good-quality pictures.

**Unplugged activity 2**

*You will need: a pen or pencil, Worksheet 4.4*

Work with a partner.

Complete the worksheet by matching the units of storage with the correct box or definition on the right-hand side.

How easy did you find learning the order of the units of storage? What made it difficult? Is there anything you could use to help you remember the order more easily next time?

# Units of storage and memory size

We use units of storage to describe how large storage capacity (space) is in storage devices.

The larger the number of bits we can store, the more a computer can 'remember'. Storage devices like hard disk drives (HDDs) and solid state drives (SSDs) are often measured using terabytes (TB). One terabyte can store around 85 million pages of text or around 250 000 music files!

Many SSDs are between 2 TB and 5 TB in size.

If an SSD becomes full, we need to add more SSDs to allow the computer to store more data. You cannot make an SSD bigger once you have bought it. So it is important to think about how much storage space you need before buying it.

Storage like random access memory (RAM) is smaller. RAM is usually measured in gigabytes (GB). The most common size of RAM is 32 GB. This can store about 2000 music files. RAM comes in smaller sizes because it costs more to manufacture than SSD storage. This is because the data on RAM can be accessed much faster than on an SSD. RAM also uses more expensive components.

## 4 Computer systems

Sofia, I can't store any more pictures on my tablet!

Try upgrading! Add a 4 terabyte SSD to it!

Some secondary storage devices can store large amounts of data. Older technology like HDDs can store up to 22 TB of data. This would be more than an average person would use in a lifetime. SSDs use newer technology. However, they come in smaller sizes. The most common sizes for SSDs are 1 TB, 2 TB and 4 TB. More modern SSDs can cost three times more than older types for the same amount of storage. USB flash drives come in much smaller storage sizes. This is because they are designed to be small and carried in a pocket. The most common sizes for USB flash drives are 128 GB and 256 GB. Memory cards are often used in mobile gaming devices. Memory cards are also small and store about the same amount as USB flash drives. You will often see memory cards with 128 GB and 256 GB of storage. Portable SSDs can store much more data than memory cards, but they are larger and less easy to carry in a pocket!

### Did you know?

You can store over 17 000 hours of music on 1 terabyte of storage. That is the same as listening to music non-stop for over 700 days!

## 4.3 Storing data

## Questions

1. How many nibbles are there in one byte?
2. How many bytes are there in 2 KB?
3. How many bits are there in 2 KB?
4. How many gigabytes are there in 500 MB?
5. How many megabytes are there in 20 TB?

What is the hardest thing about converting units of storage?
What strategy can you use to help you in the future?

### Look what I can do!

- ☐ I can explain why we need to convert data into numbers before a computer can use it.
- ☐ I can identify the units used to show how large a storage device is.

# 4 Computer systems

## > 4.4 Inside a computer

**We are going to:**

- explore what a computer processor is
- describe what a computer processor does
- identify primary and secondary storage in a computer
- discuss the role of storage in a computer.

clock speed
gigahertz
hertz
persistent storage
primary storage
processor
secondary storage
transistor
volatile storage

### Getting started

**What do you already know?**

- A processor is part of a computer system.
- You know the input–process–output model.
- You understand the units of data storage.
- Computers save data on storage devices.

4.4 Inside a computer

### Continued

**Now try this!**

> You will need: a calculator and a paper/pen

Work with a partner.

One of you will complete the sums below without a calculator. One of you will use the calculator.

Time how long it takes each of you to calculate the answers.

- 423 + 143
- 213 + 124
- 105 − 53
- 3 × 41
- 25 × 50
- 126 − 83
- 125 ÷ 5
- 464 ÷ 4

How long did it take you to do the calculations?
Was it quicker working it out in your head or using a calculator?

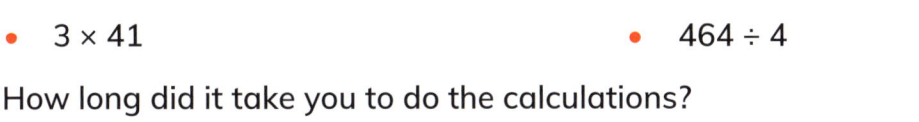

**4** Computer systems

## The processor

The processor in a computer is called the central processing unit, or CPU for short. Without the processor, a computer would not be able to process data. Many people think of the processor as the brain of the computer.

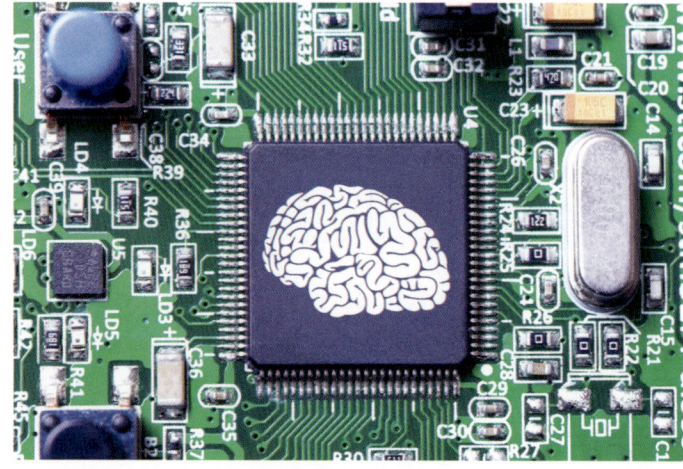

The CPU is a bit like a very small calculator made up of many small parts. Most CPUs are only around 2 cm². A transistor is a tiny device that controls the flow of electricity in the CPU. Connecting many transistors together allows the computer to carry out calculations.

> **Did you know?**
>
> Modern CPUs can have over 1.25 billion transistors in them. That's about the same number as the number of people who live in China or India!

CPU speed is measured in gigahertz (GHz).

A gigahertz is one billion hertz.

A single hertz is 'one cycle per second'. This means one calculation per second.

Therefore, a CPU that runs at one gigahertz can perform one billion calculations per second.

The number of calculations a computer can complete each second is known as the clock speed.

4.4 Inside a computer

The CPU inside a calculator works much faster than your brain. Therefore, it is a lot quicker at calculating difficult sums. The CPU inside a computer is even faster than the one inside a calculator.

This is why we use computers to process very difficult mathematical sums. For example, we would use a computer to work out the path of a planet's orbit around the solar system. To do this by hand would take a really long time, but a computer can do it very quickly.

## Primary and secondary storage

We know that computers need to store data to be able to use it. But where, and how, does a computer store data?

Computer systems usually have two types of storage: primary storage and secondary storage.

Most primary storage is short-term storage. This means the storage device usually loses the data it has stored when it is turned off. This type of storage is called volatile storage. An example of primary storage is random access memory (RAM). RAM stores all of the data that is currently being used by the computer.

Secondary storage is long-term storage. This means the device stores data even after the computer is turned off. This type of storage is also known as persistent storage (the data persists – to persist means to keep on doing something). Secondary storage is normally used for storing programs and other data we want to keep. A common type of secondary storage is a solid state drive (SSD).

## Question

1 What type of storage do you use to save your files?

## 4 Computer systems

Primary storage usually costs a lot more than secondary storage for the same amount of storage. This is because it is made of high-quality materials. This allows the CPU to access the data stored very quickly. This is important because the CPU makes billions of calculations per second. Slow primary storage can slow the CPU down.

Secondary storage can store huge amounts of data. However, it takes more time for the computer to access the data from secondary storage.

Most computer systems need both primary and secondary storage. Many devices such as mobile phones, laptops, desktop computers and smart watches all use primary and secondary storage.

### Activity 1

**You will need:** a desktop computer, laptop or tablet with access to the internet, presentation software or word processing software

Copy and complete this table using presentation software or word processing software. Use the internet to help you find an image for each type of storage.

| Feature | Primary storage | Secondary storage |
| --- | --- | --- |
| Speed | Extremely fast | A lot slower than primary storage |
| Size/capacity | | |
| Storage type | | |
| Cost per gigabyte | | |
| Physical size | | |
| Image | | |

4.4 Inside a computer

### Continued

**How are we doing?**

Share your table with a partner. Discuss any differences you have.

Edit your table with anything you learnt from your partner.

### Unplugged activity 2

> You will need: a pen and paper

Write a short poem or rhyme about primary and secondary storage.

Your poem or rhyme should include:
- what primary storage is
- what secondary storage is
- how to remember the difference between the two types of storage.

Read your poem to another learner. Ask them if this helped them to understand the difference between primary and secondary storage.

Ask for one idea to improve your poem and use the feedback to make your poem even better.

# Question

2  Why do we need both primary and secondary storage in a computer system?

### Look what I can do!

- ☐ I can explain what a computer processor is.
- ☐ I can describe what a computer processor does.
- ☐ I can give examples of types of storage in a computer.
- ☐ I can discuss the role of storage in a computer.

# 4 Computer systems

## > 4.5 Robots in industry

**We are going to:**
- explore what robots do in industry
- understand that robots can work on their own
- understand the benefits of robots.

autonomous manufacturing robot

**Getting started**

**What do you already know?**
- You know the input–process–output model.
- You understand the different roles of robots in delivery services, public transport and healthcare.
- Artificial intelligence in computers simulates human intelligence.

4.5 Robots in industry

> **Continued**
>
> **Now try this!**
>
> Your teacher will set up a maze in your classroom. Work with other learners to guide a blindfolded person through the maze. You will be timed for each try. You have three tries to get the best time you can.
>
> Answer these questions:
>
> - How did you use commands to help guide the person through the maze?
> - What worked well?
> - Did you listen to instructions from other learners?
> - What did you learn from their instructions and how did that affect your own choice of instructions?

# Robots in industry

There are many different types of robot. A robot is a machine that we can program to carry out instructions by itself. When robots work without help from humans, we say that they are autonomous. Creating autonomous robots is a very complicated process. To be able to complete tasks on their own, the robots run long, complex programs that take a long time for programmers to write.

We often use autonomous robots in industry such as car manufacturing or food production. Industry is work that involves making or selling goods or services. Remember, manufacturing means making large numbers of goods in factories using machines.

## 4 Computer systems

Look at the robots in the car factory. They are designed to do the same actions again and again. They do the same job day-by-day for 24 hours without a break!

We often think that all robots look like humans, but most robots do not look like us.

Robots come in many shapes and sizes. Some perform very difficult or complicated tasks. Some perform very simple tasks.

Some robots may be a simple robotic arm that picks a box off a shelf.

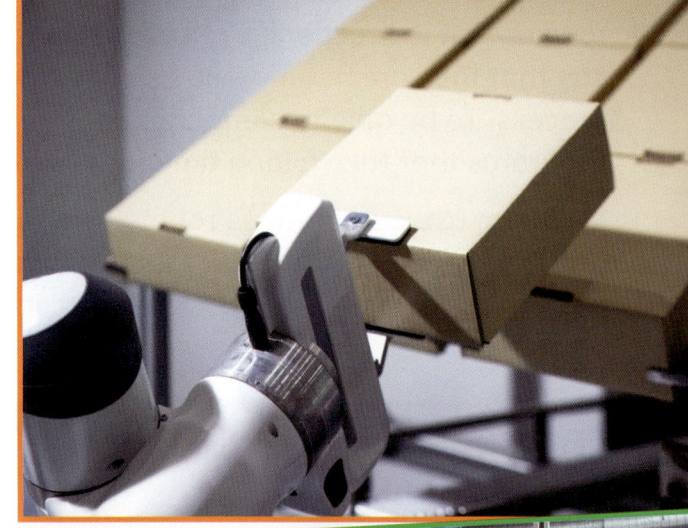

Robotic arms that make cars need to be able to move and twist to connect parts together.

226

## 4.5 Robots in industry

Robots can be very small. The circuits on electronic devices are connected together using tiny robotic arms. These robots are very accurate.

Some robots look like dogs! They can walk on four legs.

## Advantages and disadvantages

Advantages of using robots include:

- They can work without needing to take breaks.
- They can be very accurate in what they do.
- They do not need to be paid any money to work.
- They can work in places that are dangerous for humans, for example underwater.

Disadvantages of using robots include:

- They can be very expensive to buy.
- They can break down and be difficult or expensive to fix.
- They run complex programs that are difficult to create.
- They can only do the job they are programmed to do.

# 4 Computer systems

Advantages of using humans include:

- They can work well in a team and change jobs easily.
- They can spot things that robots may not be able to.
- They do not need complex programs to work.
- They are able to do many jobs that robots cannot do like creative tasks or looking after people.

Disadvantages of using humans include:

- They make more errors than robots.
- They have to be paid money to work.
- They need to take breaks and have time off.
- They work more slowly than robots.

## Unplugged activity 1

Have a short discussion with a partner about the advantages and disadvantages of using robots and humans in industry.

Copy the table below to show all the advantages and disadvantages of using humans and robots. Try to think of extra advantages and disadvantages and include them in your table.

|  | Advantages | Disadvantages |
|---|---|---|
| Human |  | Needs to take breaks |
| Robot | Can work for a long time without a break |  |

Share your ideas with another pair in your class.

### How am I doing?

How many advantages and disadvantages did you think of?
Do you have more advantage for humans or robots?

How confident do you feel about identifying the advantages and disadvantages of using robots in industry? Give yourself a score out of 5, where 1 is not very confident and 5 is very confident.

## 4.5 Robots in industry

Large companies that sell products online have huge warehouses of items that need to be sent to customers. Robots drive themselves around these warehouses and collect the items. The robots then put the products in a place where they can be packed up and sent to the customer.

## Robots in car manufacturing

Building cars can be dangerous because engines, doors and other parts of the car are very heavy. Also, cars need to be built carefully, for example robots weld and build things very accurately. This helps to make the car safer for the person driving it. To produce as many cars as possible, building needs to happen all through the day and sometimes all through the night as well!

Robots are very useful when manufacturing cars. They can lift heavy items that humans cannot lift. They are also very accurate when measuring and fixing parts together. Robots can work through the whole day and night, allowing more cars to be built in the same period of time.

# 4 Computer systems

There are some things that robots cannot do, however. For example, they cannot put the electrical circuits in the car. This task is too difficult for a robot because of all the wires that need plugging in. This is something a human needs to do. A human will do this as the circuits and wires are very small. Human hands are better at pushing wires through small holes, or connecting small plugs to each other.

## Robots in food manufacturing

How much food do you think people eat in the world each day? Imagine how much food your school uses per day. Now think how long a single person would prepare to grow all of the food, package it and send it to the shops.

Robots in food manufacturing can do lots of these tasks quickly. Because robots can measure very accurately, they can fill hundreds of containers per minute with exactly the same amount of food.

Robots can even do things like harvesting crops automatically.

4.5 Robots in industry

## Activity 2

> You will need: a desktop computer, laptop or tablet with access to the internet, a pen and paper

You are going to carry out a news interview for 'Cambridge International News'.

The interview has the title: 'How robots are helping us in industry'.

Work in a pair.

- One of you will be the reporter.
- One of you will be a factory owner.

Together, pick one industry you are interested in. Write a short interview about how robots are helping in the industry you have chosen.

You may use this book and the internet to help you research ideas.

The reporter needs to ask the factory owner questions about how they use robots.

The factory owner needs to say how robots have helped their factory.

Your interview should be about two minutes long.

Act out the interview in front of your class.

### How are we doing?

Watch another pair's news interview. Write down:

- three good things about it
- one area you think they could improve on, or one thing they have not mentioned.

## Look what I can do!

- [ ] I can give examples of how robots are used in industry.
- [ ] I can describe how robots can work on their own.
- [ ] I can discuss the benefits of using robots in industry.

## 4 Computer systems

### Project

**Designing computers and robots**

Imagine you own a robotics and computer company.

**Task 1**

You need to design and advertise a new computer. You will create a marketing presentation to send to people to encourage them to buy your new computer.

1. Identify the purpose of your new computer. For example, it could be used in medicine, it could be used by vets, in farming or to design new cars.
2. Design a computer that will be fit for purpose. You will need to think about the:
   a   processor
   b   RAM
   c   hard disk
   d   graphics card.
3. Research the prices for these items.
4. Create the marketing presentation to show:
   a   what your computer will look like
   b   the different parts you are using
   c   the total cost of the computer (remember that you'll want to make a profit so it should cost more for people to buy than it cost you to build).
5. Research some software that you think will be useful for your computer, and add this to your presentation.
   a   Is it free or paid-for?
   b   Why will this be useful?
6. Write a few sentences to describe why this computer will be the best computer for the purpose you have designed it for.
7. Add anything else you think may help sell this computer. Think about things like:
   a   the way the computer looks
   b   the longevity of the computer.
8. Think of five advantages that this computer will give the person who buys it.

4.5 Robots in industry

### Continued

**Task 2**

Your company is also going to design a new robot to sell to customers.

Think of an industry that interests you. How could a new robot help?

1. Think about what the robot will look like, and what it will do.
2. Draw your robot on a large piece of paper.
3. Think of five advantages that this robot will give the person who buys it. Add these to your drawing.

## Check your progress

1. State three pieces of hardware that a computer needs.
2. Write a definition for the word 'functionality'.
3. State two examples of software that you might find on a computer.
4. If you buy higher-quality components for a computer, what might increase?
5. What are text-based programming languages good at creating?
6. You can drag and drop code in a block-based programming language. Is this statement true or false?
7. Which of these might a new programmer find easier to use: a block-based programming language or a text-based programming language?
8. What does a programming environment allow you to do?
9. Why do we change analogue data into digital data?
10. State one thing you could do with digital data.
11. State the smallest and the largest units of storage.
12. What is the purpose of a computer processor?
13. Give two advantages of using robots in industry.

# Glossary

| | | |
|---|---|---|
| **aesthetics** | how things look or appear to people<br>*Zara likes the aesthetics of the car. Marcus does not.* | 190 |
| **analogue** | not digital, a type of signal that uses waves such as light or sound, that humans and animals can create and understand<br>*The sound coming from the speakers was analogue data.* | 210 |
| **antivirus software** | software that identifies, removes and prevents malware<br>*My antivirus software scanned a file I downloaded and identified a virus.* | 172 |
| **arithmetic operator** | a symbol that instructs a computer about what type of calculation to perform on values, for example division or multiplication<br>*The + symbol is an arithmetic operator for addition, and the − symbol is an arithmetic operator for subtraction.* | 23 |
| **attribute** | the data found in one field of a record in a database<br>*In the record, the attribute for the 'Colour' field was 'red'.* | 137 |
| **authentication** | the process of checking that the user is who they say they are, for example by seeing if their password is correct<br>*My laptop uses user authentication to keep my data safe.* | 177 |
| **autonomous** | able to act without human input<br>*The autonomous robot vacuum cleaner plugs itself in when its battery is low.* | 225 |
| **AVERAGE** | a spreadsheet function, written =AVERAGE(), that finds the mean value of the selected cells<br>*I can use the AVERAGE function to work out the mean of my test scores.* | 124 |
| **bandwidth** | the maximum amount of data that can be transmitted between two points in a network in a specific amount of time, measured in bits per second<br>*On a network with a high bandwidth, it takes only a few seconds to download files.* | 168 |

| | | |
|---|---|---|
| **bit** | a single binary digit (number) – the smallest unit of binary counting<br>*A bit can either be 1 or 0.* | 214 |
| **block-based programming language** | a way of writing program code that uses drag-and-drop ready-made lines of code to build working algorithms<br>*Scratch is a block-based programming language.* | 204 |
| **broadcast** | a block in Scratch that can be used to run a sub-routine (to broadcast is to send a message out into the world for people to receive)<br>*In their project, they used a 'broadcast' block to call the sub-routine.* | 41 |
| **byte** | a group of eight bits (binary digits)<br>*The file was only one byte in size.* | 214 |
| **call** | to use a sub-routine or function in an algorithm<br>*Sofia can call the helper sub-routine from her main code, which will sort the list into alphabetical order.* | 36 |
| **cell reference** | a little code for the location of each cell, made up of the cell's column letter and row number<br>*We use cell references to give spreadsheet software instructions about certain cells.* | 121 |
| **character** | the data type for any individual symbol, letter or number found on a computer keyboard<br>*I struggled to find this character on my keyboard, but then I saw it.* | 24 |
| **chatbot** | an algorithm designed to have a conversation with a user in a human way<br>*I spoke to a chatbot on the website when I needed support.* | 26 |
| **clock speed** | the number of calculations a computer can perform every second<br>*The clock speed of the computer was two gigahertz.* | 220 |
| **collaborate** | to work jointly with others on a project or task<br>*Marcus and Sofia will collaborate to make a presentation about computing careers.* | 111 |

| | | |
|---|---|---|
| **comparison operator** | a symbol that compares two numbers in an algorithm, for example, to see if one number is greater than, less than or equal to the other | 28 |
| | *A comparison operator is used to check when the score goes above 5.* | |
| **component** | an individual part of something | 186 |
| | *A computer is made up of many connected components.* | |
| **condition** | a situation that must be true for something else to be possible | 21 |
| | *The condition has been met: 'score > 5' is true, so the 'say score' line will run.* | |
| **conditional statement** | a section of code that tells a program to either run one set of instructions or another set of instructions, depending on whether a certain situation is true or false. | 21 |
| | *An 'if then else' block is one way to include a conditional statement in your program.* | |
| **continuous** | uninterrupted, unbroken | 210 |
| | *The sound of the fire alarm was continuous.* | |
| **continuous data** | numerical data that can have any value in a certain range, for example data about time, weight or length | 97 |
| | *A datalogger collects continuous data.* | |
| **cost** | how much money you have to pay to buy something | 192 |
| | *The cost of a computer depends on the cost of the parts it contains.* | |
| **criteria** | requirements or conditions that need to be met, for example, search criteria are words or conditions we search for in a spreadsheet, database or on the internet, to find data that matches | 105 |
| | *There are six records that meet my search criteria.* | |
| **data type** | the form of data, for example, text or numbers | 138 |
| | *Each field in the database has a suitable data type.* | |
| **database** | a set of organised data | 136 |
| | *We store data in a database.* | |

| | | |
|---|---|---|
| **decision** | a choice you make after thinking about the options, or a flowchart symbol that tells the program to decide which path to follow next | 12 |
| | *When they got to the decision in the flowchart, they had to decide whether to follow the 'Yes' arrow or the 'No' arrow.* | |
| **decomposition** | breaking a large problem into smaller parts that are easier to understand and simpler to solve | 53 |
| | *Programmers use decomposition to help them find repeating patterns so they can create more efficient programs.* | |
| **define** | to give a sub-routine a name and then create the sequence of commands that it will follow | 35 |
| | *First define your sub-routine, then call it from the main code.* | |
| **digital** | stored electronically on a device using binary digits (0s and 1s) | 210 |
| | *A digital signal has square waves when its values are shown on a graph.* | |
| **digitise** | to convert analogue data into digital data | 212 |
| | *We must digitise the sound wave so that the computer can process it.* | |
| **encryption** | means to scramble a message | 167 |
| | *In such a way that only the people who are meant to read it can* | |
| **evaluation** | a judgement of the quality of a program and how well it solves a problem | 68 |
| | *Our evaluation showed that the program met its success criteria.* | |
| **facial recognition** | a system that takes an image of a face and compares this to a stored image to identify a person | 180 |
| | *My phone uses facial recognition in order to log in.* | |
| **field** | a set of data items about something you are collecting data on – a category of data within a record | 137 |
| | *If you collect data about flowers, a field could be 'Flower Colour'.* | |
| **filter** | a tool that selects specific data based on search criteria and hides all other data | 146 |
| | *I used a filter to show only people with birthdays in January.* | |

| | | |
|---|---|---|
| **fit for purpose** | suitable for the job we want to use it for<br>*A hockey ball is fit for purpose.* | 198 |
| **flowchart** | a diagram that shows the steps of an algorithm<br>*The flowchart helped people see how the algorithm worked.* | 10 |
| **formula** | a sequence of operators, numbers and/or cell references written in a spreadsheet cell, which tells the software to do a calculation<br>*This column calculates the total for each row using a formula.* | 122 |
| **freeware** | software that is free of charge (you do not have to pay to use it)<br>*The cooking app on my smartphone is freeware.* | 192 |
| **function (programming)** | a type of sub-routine – a separate section of code that runs when it is called from the main code and may be called several times in one program<br>*I called the 'AtoZ' function to put the items into alphabetical order.* | 87 |
| **function (spreadsheets)** | a code we can use in a spreadsheet program to save us having to write very long formulas<br>*The SUM function adds together all the values in a row or column.* | 124 |
| **functionality** | the range of tasks that an item or piece of software can do<br>*The software has high functionality.* | 190 |
| **gigabyte** | a unit of data storage equal to 1000 megabytes<br>*The hard drive has 1 gigabyte of storage.* | 214 |
| **gigahertz** | a unit of speed equal to 1000 hertz (cycles/calculations per second), used to measure computer processor speed<br>*The CPU operates at 4 gigahertz.* | 220 |
| **GPS (Global Positioning System)** | a navigation system that uses satellites in space to show the location of devices on the earth<br>*According to the GPS on my phone, I am at my local library.* | 166 |
| **hack** | to gain unauthorised access to a digital system<br>*My bank account has been hacked and they have taken my savings.* | 177 |

| | | |
|---|---|---|
| **hardware** | **the physical parts of a computer or digital device – the parts you can touch** <br> *A computer's hardware includes the motherboard and graphics card.* | 186 |
| **healthcare** | **an organised way of looking after the medical needs of individuals or a community** <br> *Sets of organised data are very useful for solving problems in healthcare.* | 151 |
| **hertz** | **cycle per second, the unit used to measure computer processor speed** <br> *Calculations were made at a speed of 50 hertz.* | 220 |
| **initialisation** | **getting everything ready for the start of the game, making sure any changes made to the stage or sprites when a Scratch program is run are reset** <br> *I added the 'clear pen' block to my program: this initialisation block makes sure the stage is clear each time the program is run again.* | 42 |
| **input** | **to provide data to a computer** <br> *A mouse click is a type of input.* | 79 |
| **input variable** | **a piece of data that a user puts into a program for the program to store, such as the response to a question** <br> *An input variable was used to remember the user's password.* | 23 |
| **input-process-output (IPO) model** | **a way of describing how a program or system operates: it takes in data, works on it then gives out data** <br> *A smart speaker follows the input-process-output (IPO) model – it listens to speech through the microphone, searches for the song online then plays it.* | 80 |
| **integer** | **the data type for a whole number** <br> *7 is an integer but 7.5 is not.* | 24 |
| **interaction** | **two or more things meeting and having an effect on each other** <br> *The interaction between the sprites is fun: they change colour whenever they touch.* | 24 |

| | | |
|---|---|---|
| **interface** | the part of a program that the user sees, and that tells them what they need to do | 54 |
| | *The program's coding was very clever but the interface needed more work.* | |
| **interrelate** | to be connected in such a way that each object has an effect on or depends on the other | 49 |
| | *The two sprites interrelate by calling each other's sub-routines.* | |
| **intranet** | a private network in an organisation that is only available to its members | 163 |
| | *My school files are stored on our school intranet.* | |
| **iteration** | another name for a loop, where code or instructions are being repeated | 22 |
| | *A count-controlled loop is one type of iteration.* | |
| **kilobyte** | a unit of data storage equal to 1000 bytes | 214 |
| | *The text document was 10 kilobytes in size.* | |
| **longevity** | how long something lasts for, or its ability to last | 191 |
| | *A plastic fork has low longevity.* | |
| **malware** | software designed to disrupt or harm a computer system | 172 |
| | *A virus is a type of malware.* | |
| **manufacturing** | making large numbers of goods in factories using machines | 225 |
| | *Robots are widely used in car manufacturing.* | |
| **megabyte** | a unit of data storage equal to 1000 kilobytes | 214 |
| | *My collection of songs is 750 megabytes in size.* | |
| **network overload** | the extreme slowing of data transfer speeds across a network due to too many requests for data at the same time | 170 |
| | *Trying to stream three different films at the same time caused network overload.* | |
| **nibble** | a unit of data storage equal to 4 bits | 214 |
| | *Half a byte is called a nibble.* | |
| **operator** | a symbol used in calculations and logic statements to do a particular action, like adding or comparing | 23 |
| | *The multiplication operator we use with computers is *.* | |

| | | |
|---|---|---|
| **output** | **information that you get out of a computer system after data has been processed** | 79 |
| | *After the play button was pressed, a song was output through the speakers.* | |
| **packet** | **a small parcel of data – part of a sent file that travels through a network** | 167 |
| | *Sofia's email was split into many hundreds of packets when she sent it.* | |
| **password** | **a secret combination of letters, numbers and other characters entered with a username to log into a system** | 177 |
| | *My account is protected with a password.* | |
| **persistent storage** | **data storage that keeps its data when the power is turned off** | 221 |
| | *A hard disk is a persistent storage device.* | |
| **phishing** | **stealing valuable information by tricking users into giving it away, for example by emailing a link to a fake bank website and asking them to log into it** | 176 |
| | *A phishing email was sent to my parents asking them for their bank details.* | |
| **phrase searching** | **searching for data that matches a series of words** | 146 |
| | *I used phrase searching to find the phrase 'Omani rial' in the database.* | |
| **physical programming device** | **a small computing device that you can program and hold in your hands** | 81 |
| | *Arun downloaded his program onto the physical programming device and then took it to show his friends.* | |
| **portable game console** | **a small, handheld computer that is used to play games** | 81 |
| | *Zara received a portable game console for her birthday and now she can play games on the way to school.* | |
| **primary storage** | **short term data storage that loses the data when the power is turned off** | 221 |
| | *RAM is a kind of primary storage.* | |
| **prioritising** | **deciding how important something is and what should be worked on first** | 58 |
| | *You should prioritise finishing the introduction before working on the ending.* | |

| | | |
|---|---|---|
| **procedure** | a type of sub-routine, a small section of code that can be reused multiple times in a program<br>*She made her code clearer and more organised by using procedures.* | 24 |
| **process** | to carry out calculations and instructions<br>*A computer will process the input data to produce an output.* | 79 |
| **processor** | the device that carries out calculations in a computer<br>*The processor is very fast.* | 220 |
| **programming constructs** | programming ideas about code structure, such as sequence, selection and iteration<br>*Selection is an important programming construct that programmers use regularly.* | 21 |
| **programming environment** | software that allows you to write and test programs<br>*The Scratch 'Create' screen is an example of a programming environment.* | 202 |
| **programming language** | a way of writing commands to create a program a computer can understand<br>*I wrote my game in a text-based programming language.* | 202 |
| **prompt** | a message on the screen that shows a program is waiting for input<br>*A prompt appeared on the screen asking for my date of birth.* | 55 |
| **prototype** | a basic version of something that users can test and evaluate<br>*She built two prototypes of the bridge before the construction began.* | 56 |
| **question type** | the way in which a question is asked and answered, for example multiple choice (provides a set of answer options to choose from) or open question (the user types their answer freely)<br>*I can choose from different question types when I create my form.* | 111 |
| **questionnaire** | a series of questions, usually presented as a form, that is used to collect information from people<br>*I completed the questionnaire about which computer games I like to play.* | 106 |

| | | |
|---|---|---|
| **radio waves** | a type of energy used for long-distance communication that is generated by a transmitter and detected by a receiver | 165 |
| | *The radio in my garage uses radio waves to receive the music I listen to.* | |
| **random** | in an order that does not have a clear pattern and cannot be predicted | 58 |
| | *Sofia couldn't decide which book to read so she shut her eyes and picked one at random.* | |
| **record** | provides all the data about one thing in a database – usually a row of data, which connects all the fields that are linked | 137 |
| | *Each record contained the fields 'Name', 'Age' and 'Height'.* | |
| **retail** | industry related to shopping and the sale of items to people, for example clothes, cars, food or games | 151 |
| | *My favourite toy shop is just a small part of the retail industry.* | |
| **robot** | a machine that we can program to carry out instructions by itself | 225 |
| | *Each car is built by a robot.* | |
| **secondary storage** | long term data storage | 221 |
| | *A CD drive and hard disk are both secondary storage devices.* | |
| **secure** | safe and protected from unauthorised access | 175 |
| | *The data has been kept secure from other users.* | |
| **selection** | choosing which commands to run from among the options when the code carried out depends on the answer to a condition | 21 |
| | *A selection statement was used to check if it was raining before deciding to take an umbrella.* | |
| **sequence** | a set of instructions or commands carried out in order, or the order itself | 21 |
| | *The sequence of instructions for the dance routine has to be carried on in the right order for the dance to look good.* | |
| **server** | a computer that provides services such as programs and storage to other computers in a network | 160 |
| | *I saved my work to the school server.* | |

| | | |
|---|---|---|
| **server farm** | a collection of computer servers that are connected together in a network. | 160 |
| | *Our school has eight servers that are connected together in the server farm.* | |
| **software** | programs that enable us to use computers to complete tasks | 185 |
| | *Word processing software is very useful for writing up investigations.* | |
| **sound waves** | analogue data in the form of air vibrations that we hear as sounds | 211 |
| | *My ears can detect sound waves.* | |
| **spam** | junk emails that an account holder has not asked for | 176 |
| | *My email account receives 12 spam emails a day.* | |
| **spreadsheet** | a document full of cells arranged in rows and columns, into which you can type data | 120 |
| | *Spreadsheets are a useful way to organise and analyse data.* | |
| **statistical investigation** | the collecting of data to answer questions | 96 |
| | *We carried out a statistical investigation to find out what the most popular computer game was in our school.* | |
| **streaming** | playing a video or sound file over an internet connection instead of downloading it | 161 |
| | *Zara has been streaming a film on Netflix on her tablet.* | |
| **string** | the data type for two or more characters in a row, that can include spaces | 25 |
| | *The 'say' block in Scratch requires us to enter a string.* | |
| **sub-routine** | a separate set of instructions in an algorithm that performs a specific task | 35 |
| | *A single sub-routine can be used again and again in an algorithm.* | |
| **success criteria** | the things a program or solution should do in order to be successful | 69 |
| | *The success criteria for the program are: there should be a friendly greeting at the start, then ten spelling test questions and a score displayed at the end.* | |

| | | |
|---|---|---|
| **SUM** | a spreadsheet function, written =SUM(), that finds the total value of the selected cells | 124 |
| | *I can use the SUM function to add all of my costs together.* | |
| **systematic** | thoughtful and logical, according to a method that makes sense | 74 |
| | *He created the seating plan in a systematic way, starting with the children.* | |
| **terabyte** | a unit of data storage equal to 1000 gigabytes | 214 |
| | *My hard disk has a storage capacity of 1 terabyte.* | |
| **text-based programming language** | a way of writing program code that uses words and text to create working algorithms | 206 |
| | *Python is an example of a text-based programming language.* | |
| **transistor** | a tiny device that controls the flow of electricity in a computer processor | 220 |
| | *The computer has millions of transistors in it.* | |
| **transmission** | the action or process of sending files, usually digital, between devices | 175 |
| | *Zara received a digital transmission of photos from Marcus.* | |
| **trends** | patterns in data | 150 |
| | *This bar chart shows that there is a trend for taking a holiday in March.* | |
| **unique** | one of a kind, different from everything else | 120 |
| | *Marcus has a unique fingerprint.* | |
| **upgrade** | to improve something or replace it with a better version | 192 |
| | *I made my computer faster with an upgrade to the processor.* | |
| **user experience** | what it feels like to use a program | 70 |
| | *The game's graphics and music made for an excellent user experience.* | |
| **username** | a unique name that identifies who a user is when they try to log into a network | 177 |
| | *I have to type my username into my laptop in order to log in.* | |

| | | |
|---|---|---|
| **validation rules** | restrictions that only allow certain types or formats of data to be entered into a spreadsheet or form | 112 |
| | *I used validation rules in my spreadsheet to make sure dates were in the right format.* | |
| **variable** | a named container (like a box) in a program, that temporarily stores a value that can change | 23 |
| | *We stored points won in the game in a variable called Score.* | |
| **volatile storage** | short term data storage that loses the data when the power is turned off | 221 |
| | *RAM is an example of volatile storage.* | |
| **wi-fi** | a way to connect computers using radio waves instead of wires | 166 |
| | *It is important that my laptop has wi-fi.* | |
| **wireless** | without wires or cables, but using radio waves instead – wi-fi and cellular networks use wireless connections | 165 |
| | *I use a wireless connection to access the internet on my tablet.* | |

# Acknowledgements

The authors and publishers acknowledge the following sources of copyright material and are grateful for the permissions granted. While every effort has been made, it has not always been possible to identify the sources of all the material used, or to trace all copyright holders. If any omissions are brought to our notice, we will be happy to include the appropriate acknowledgements on reprinting.

Thanks to the following for permission to reproduce images:

**Unit 1** Enot-poloskun/GI; SrdjanPav/GI; Flashpop/GI; Sarayut Thaneerat/GI; StockPlanets/GI; Catherine Falls Commercial/GI; Wonry/GI; Ariel Skelley/GI; Johnny Johnson/GI; Izabela Habur/GI; Dinodia Photo/GI; Jasmin Merdan/GI; A-Digit/GI; Mayur Kakade/GI; Yamtono/GI; Nora Carol Photography/GI; Jamie Grill/GI; Ariel Skelley/GI; mixetto/GI; Korrawin/GI; Photo_Concepts/GI; Virojt Changyencham/GI; Boris Panov/GI; BongkarnThanyakij/GI; dlewis33/GI; AleksandarNakic/GI; SrdjanPav/GI; ATHVisions/GI; Kirill Smyslov/GI; Erik Von Weber/GI; Jayk7/GI; Olemedia/GI; Maskot/GI; Zeljkosantrac/GI; LumiNola/GI; Roberto Jimenez Mejias/GI; RobinOlimb/GI; Guido Mieth/GI; Yagi Studio/GI; Malerapaso/GI; Bill Polo/The Boston Globe via GI; UniversalImagesGroup/GI; nemke/GI; Hutchings Stock Photography/GI; Dan Kenyon/GI; JGI/GI; Emilija Manevska/GI; Jennifer A Smith/GI; **Unit 2** Sean Gladwell/GI; Steve Greaves/GI; Sandi Rutar/GI; Image Professionals GmbH/GI; Appfind/GI; Karanik Yimpat/GI; Bernard Van Berg/GI; Alubalish/GI; Yellow Dog Productions/GI; Designer29/GI; Jamie Grill Photography/GI; Tetra Images/GI; Peter Dazeley/GI; Martinedoucet/GI; Alex Potemkin/GI; Jasmin Merdan/GI; Thanasis Zovoilis/GI; Zurijeta/GI; Jxfzsy/GI; Ivetavaicule/GI; Manuel Breva Colmeiro/GI; Maryna Terletska/GI; Jude Evans/GI; Dougal Waters/GI; Paul Biris/GI; Edwin Remsberg/GI; Jamie Grill/GI; Ray Kachatorian/GI; Prapass Pulsub/GI; M_a_y_a/GI; MoMo Productions/GI; Maryna Terletska/GI; Tuul & Bruno Morandi/GI; Jasmin Merdan/GI; Ida Marie Odgaard/GI; Isabel Pavia/GI; MirageC/GI; Alexmatamata/GI; Light to enjoy the world/GI; Nitat Termmee/GI; Patcharanan Worrapatchareeroj/GI; Catherine Falls Commercial/GI; Andrew Brookes/GI; TommL/GI; Erik Isakson/GI; Shapecharge/GI; Mint Images/GI; **Unit 3** enjoynz/GI; Zhihao/GI; Pictafolio/GI; MoMo Productions/GI; Witthaya Prasongsin/GI; Bestshortstop/GI; PJjaruwan/GI; Jasmin Merdan/GI; Steven Tritton/GI; Oscar Wong/GI; Stock photo and footage/GI; MerveKarahan/GI; Jamie Grill/GI; JGI/GI; Cuba/GI; Skynesher/GI; Samere Fahim Photography/GI; Cheunghyo/GI; Kohei Hara/GI; Anyaberkut/GI; Peter Dazeley/GI; Tim Robberts/GI; Maskot/GI; Life On White/GI; Peter Dazeley/GI; Ole_CNX/GI; Thomas Barwick/GI; Catherine MacBride/GI; Melinda Podor/GI; **Unit 4** SasinT Gallery/GI; Phynart Studio/GI; Marko Geber/GI; Vadim Krupnov/GI; Witthaya Prasongsin/GI; Maciej Frolow/GI; Nitat Termmee/GI; Tim Grist Photography/GI; Javier Zayas Photography/GI; Manifeesto/GI; Creative Crop/GI; Leonello Calvetti/GI; Oleg Begunenco/GI; Lorado/GI; Sam Barnes/GI; VacharapongW/GI; Alistair Berg/GI; Lya_Cattel/GI; Jose Luis Pelaez Inc/GI; Marko Geber/GI; Norman Posselt/GI; Traffic_analyzer/GI; Luis Alvarez/GI; Victor Habbick Visions/GI; Songsak Rohprasit/GI; Juanmonino/GI; Fotograzia/GI; Jamie Grill/GI; selimaksan/GI; Boonchai Wedmakawand/GI; Ezra Bailey/GI; Donald Iain Smith/GI; Jonathan Kitchen/GI; Yuichiro Chino/GI (x2); Mikroman6/GI; Mark Garlick/GI; Richard Newstead/GI; Narumon Bowonkitwanchai/GI; Thamrongpat Theerathammakorn/GI; Xia yuan/GI; Monty Rakusen/GI; Comezora/GI; Mikkelwilliam/GI; Humberto Ramirez/GI; Nitat Termmee/GI; Teera Konakan/GI; Monty Rakusen/GI; Photostock-Israel/GI; Imaginima/GI; Dusan Stankovic/GI; Maskot/GI

**Key** GI = Getty Images

Cover image by Pablo Gallego (Beehive Illustration)

Scratch is a project of the Scratch Foundation, in collaboration with the Lifelong Kindergarten Group at the MIT Media Lab. It is available for free at https://scratch.mit.edu

Illustrations and photos showing the BBC Micro:bit are created and used with permission from the Micro:bit Educational Foundation

Screenshots from Microsoft Excel are used with permission from Microsoft